Handshake in Washington
The Beginning of Middle East Peace?

John King

Ithaca Press

First Edition

Hardback ISBN: 0 86372 180 X
Paperback ISBN: 0 86372 184 2
British Library Cataloguing-in-Publication Data.
A catalogue record for this book is available from the British Library.

Cover design by Mark Slader.
Production by Anna Watson.
Typeset by Columns Design & Production Services Limited, Reading.
Printed in the UK by Bell & Bain, Glasgow.

Published by Garnet Publishing Ltd,
8 Southern Court, South Street,
Reading RG1 4QS UK.
Ithaca Press is an imprint of Garnet Publishing Ltd.

CONTENTS

ISRAEL

AND THE

OCCUPIED
TERRITORIES

N

BEIRUT

LEBANON

DAMASCUS

SYRIA

GOLAN HEIGHTS

Haifa   Tiberias

Nazareth

Mediterranean
Sea

Jenin ×

×
× × × ×
Nablus × × ×
× × × ×/

TEL AVIV
(Jaffa)

× ×
Jericho × ×
JERUSALEM ×

×
× ×

Gaza   × ×

Hebron ×

Beersheba

*Dead
Sea*

AMMAN

JORDAN

ISRAEL

SINAI

EGYPT

Scale

0	10	20	30	40	50 miles
0	20	40	60	80 km

—·—·— International Boundary

Occupied Territory

Annexed Territory

× Settlement

PROLOGUE

As this book went to press, the killing by an armed Israeli settler of 43 Palestinians in the ancient Ibrahimi Mosque in Hebron, while they were at dawn prayer, caused shock waves that have reverberated through Palestine and Israel, and across the Arab world. Violence erupted in the Occupied Territories and in Israel proper in the following days, and within ten days 30 more Palestinians had been killed, and two Israelis died in addition to the original mass killer, who died during the course of his attack. A massive security operation by the Israelis failed to halt this reaction. The massacre has wrought havoc in the already delicately balanced structure of international negotiation. Talks at all levels came, at least temporarily, to an end. The new hope that came into being on 13 September 1993 in Washington, when the Declaration of Principles was signed, seemed for the moment to have been dashed. Israel and the Palestinians had appeared to be poised on the brink of a new era of peace. That prospect is now more distant, but it still exists. Indeed, it can be argued that Hebron showed only that the need for peace is more urgent than it had already seemed. The vision of peace has not yet been shown to be a mirage. The reason is not that either side in the conflict has moderated its distrust, dislike, or even hatred of the other. It is simply that peace is the only way of avoiding more bloodshed, further as yet unimaginable incidents and atrocities, piled one upon the other.

The massacre was carried out on the morning of 25 February 1994 by a Jewish settler, an embittered man who believed his government and his country had betrayed him by entering into peace talks with the Arabs. The views of Dr Baruch Goldstein, an immigrant from Brooklyn in the American city of New York, are representative of a small community of religious settlers. Many of these are connected with the extremist anti-Arab Kach movement, and others are linked with the wider movement known as Gush Emunim. The religious settlers are determined to stop the peace settlement and to hold on to the Occupied Territories, which they assert are intended by God to be inhabited by the Jews. But they are a minority within a minority, and do not speak for Israel. The religious settler movement accounts for only a few thousand of the 120,000 settlers in the West Bank, who in turn are a small minority within Israel's Jewish population of four million.

The question must be, can this act by one man, a sole representative of a minority movement, halt the momentum of Middle East peace? Will the Palestinian leadership draw back from the prize they had aimed to seize: a political foothold in the historical territory of Palestine and the ultimate prospect of a Palestinian state? Will Israel's Labour government be deterred from pursuing the goal it has set itself: to secure the peaceful future of the Jewish people within the frontiers of Israel, free from the permanent fear of war, and the underlying terror of annihilation which haunts the Jews? Must pessimism colour the future prospects for the Middle East?

At first sight, the answers to these questions seem to be pessimistic. There was a current of opinion in Israel which instinctively backed the horrific acts of Baruch Goldstein, and insisted on seeing what were in reality no more than cold-blooded and senseless murders as a defence of Israel and of the Jews. Opinion polls showed that such views were frighteningly prevalent among Israel's young people. The despair of Jewish liberals and the way in which Israel's politicians distanced themselves from the murders was apparently not representative. That seemed to augur badly for the survival of the newly germinated peace process. On the Palestinian side the people erupted with a frenzy against any and every Jewish target, and again it was especially the young people who have thrown themselves into a new outburst of the intifada. For the first time that has involved Israeli Arabs as well as Palestinians in the Occupied Territories, and violence has engulfed Jaffa and Haifa as well as Gaza and Hebron. This too has seemed to cut the ground away from under the feet of Yasser Arafat and the PLO leadership in their hope of finalising an agreement based on the Oslo text.

But in the end, violence can only triumph if the two peoples turn their backs on their own best interests. When the rage has abated, peace will still ultimately be understood to be the only solution to the problems of the Middle East, by the responsible politicians of the region, and by the vast majority of people on both sides who envisage a future free of fear. It has been widely said that the handshake of 13

September 1993, and what has followed from it, is the last chance for peace. That might seem to imply that if the opportunity is lost, then the Middle East will progress down some other path. But what lies at the end of that alternative route is unthinkable. There still seemed to be a chance, in March 1994, that the politicians on both sides would ride out and master the wave of violence, and return to the more prosaic process of steadily elaborating the Declaration of Principles embodied in the Oslo text into the workable shape of a practicable peace agreement.

Let's stand aside for a moment and try to imagine the unthinkable alternative to peace. Perhaps it would be like the future Greater Israel envisaged by the Likud government of Yitzhak Shamir, which held power until 1992, where Israeli power in what was called Judaea and Samaria would grow, while the Arabs of the Occupied Territories would become an increasingly marginalised underclass. That would have brought about a situation in which Israel's security would have been founded on the permanent exercise of force. Some extremists imagined that the Arab population would go away, could be driven out, or "transferred", would take over Jordan and make that the Palestinian state. All these seemed like solutions which it was almost impossible to believe could be held by the Jewish people, which itself has suffered expulsion and persecution, and whose identity is founded on a passionate belief in the right to be free of oppression.

Meanwhile, on the Palestinian side, what would be the alternative to peace? It would be the permanent struggle, the ultimate sacrifice of the lives of young men to the fruitless battle to establish a utopia, a paradisaical return to the integral territory of Palestine, fantasised by frequently cynical leaders. The power of the leaders of the radical Palestinian factions of the old guard, on the one hand, and of the Islamic religious movements on the other hand, depends on the continuing battle. Israel's undoubted capacity to continue to dominate by force the Occupied Territories would be matched by an increasingly irreconcilable and violent evolution of the intifada, in which the whole Palestinian people would come to accept permanent upheaval as a way of life, abandoning the ordinary ambitions felt by so many Palestinians today: to enjoy a time of peace and a little normality in their home country during their lifetime.

But if peace will still, in the long run, be the objective of both sides, what has happened in the shorter run is that the massacre and the reactions it has provoked have changed the focus. They have brought into the centre of the political stage the crucial question of the future of the Israeli settlements in the Occupied Territories. That is an issue of great complexity and emotional depth that the negotiators, in Oslo and after, hoped could be put on one side: to be settled when the two sides have come to understand and trust each other more. But the very reason why the settlement issue was sidelined by the negotiators is also the reason why it must now be seen to stand at the centre of the Israeli–Palestinian confrontation. It was set aside because it was hard to solve. Now it seems clear it must be tackled urgently, because true peace will always remain elusive without its resolution. The Palestinians will feel they do not control their territory if the settlements among them mean the continuing presence of Israeli forces, widely dispersed through the West Bank. Meanwhile the Israelis will feel a permanent and detrimental gap in their security if they cannot protect the Jews who live in the settlements. The settlement issue has come home to roost. Labour permitted the earliest settlements soon after the territories were conquered in 1967. Likud began its own more sweeping settlement policy with a vengeance as soon as it took power in 1977. The settlements have now become, as Israeli politicians have often said, "facts on the ground". Prime Minister Yitzhak Rabin's government is continuing to settle Jews around Jerusalem, but he must wish that some of the settlements elsewhere posed a less intractable problem.

Rabin may have hoped that the settlement problem could at least partially resolve itself. He has indicated that he believes permanent settlement in Gaza is not necessary to Israel. Government policy seems to be founded partially on the tacit hope that many settlers in the West Bank may move out as Palestinian authority there develops, especially those who have gone there for economic reasons rather than ideological ones. But the ideological settlers, who present the real problem, will not move out. They have not gone to live in Judaea and Samaria, as they call the West Bank, in order to have an easy life, and they see no reason why others should be spared. They believe they are obeying the will of God, and that makes them uncompromising and alarming. They are an irritant, a source of stress, an obstacle, and a barrier to peace: precisely as they intend to be.

The Israeli government groped for a solution in the early days after the massacre. Prime Minister Rabin condemned the Kach movement, to which the most militant settlers belong. Kach is especially the guiding spirit of the settlers in Hebron, where they have existed amid an environment of Arab hostility, sustained only by their own gun-wielding bravado. Armed Jewish settlers in Hebron have terrorised the Arab population. The mosque where the massacre took place is also the site of an ancient synagogue, where the Jews also claim the right to worship. Rabin has said he will break the power of Kach, founded by the late Meir Kahane. He also drew attention to the American origins of many of the settlers at Kiryat Arba, on the outskirts of Hebron, and to what he said was their lack of genuine identification with the needs and aims of the state of Israel. Commentators inside and outside Israel have drawn attention to the link between the most militant Jewish settlers in Israel and the Jews of Brooklyn, where many of them originated. Some of these New York Jews have been raised in the context of an intolerant racist rhetoric that many of them have found easy to transfer to a hatred of the Arabs.

In the early days after the massacre, it seemed as if the Palestinian leadership was drawing back from the process of negotiation, while the Israelis were pressing for talks to be resumed. The Palestine Liberation Organization said it could not continue with negotiations while "the guns of the settlers are pointed at the heads of the people". The PLO demanded the disarmament of the settlers, which Israel has refused: only the extremists identified by the government as specifically dangerous will be disarmed or controlled by the Israeli army. The Palestinians have also asked for international intervention in the Occupied Territories: for United Nations troops to be interposed between the settlers and the Palestinian population during the transitional period. The Palestinian position is the result of three factors. First the PLO leaders were genuinely outraged at the Palestinian deaths in Hebron. In addition, they realised that the Palestinian anger which erupted throughout the Occupied Territories and inside Israel itself must be allowed time to work itself out. And thirdly, they believed that the moral edge they derived from the outrage will help in the longer run to earn more concessions from Israel.

On the other hand, while the Israeli leadership went into paroxysms of apology and recrimination over the massacre, and expressed anxiety and concern that the negotiations towards the interim peace agreement should continue, it did not offer anything approaching what the Palestinians wanted. The paradox of the mismatch between Palestinian and Israeli intentions and practices has continued. Under the former Likud government, it was often said that the Israelis and the Palestinians were interested in different aspects of the peace process: the Palestinians were interested in peace, while Israel was concerned more with the process. Under Labour, it has seemed that the Israeli government genuinely wants peace, at least if it can have peace on its own terms, but as if it is at the same time unwilling to do what the process actually requires, namely to make real concessions that will address Palestinian fears.

In the short term, what would emerge after the massacre could not be easily predicted. In the early days following the events in Hebron some observers speculated that, paradoxically, the very horror of the incident could itself assist the peace process, by driving Israel to bite the bullet, and to make the real concessions that the Palestinians need. It could also make Israel see that the presence of the settlements, and the ever-present armed Jewish encampments, planted on the Judaean hillsides, are a drawback rather than an enhancement of Israel's real long-term plan to achieve security based on peace and freedom. That may well prove to be what happens. Much depends on whether the Israeli and Palestinian people grasp the truth that in the end they have more to gain from peace than from the satisfaction of their anger against each other. The respective leaderships may be able to keep this in view: it is more difficult for individuals, closer to the ground, seeing only from their own more immediate points of view, and unable in the heat of the moment to achieve the detachment to make a longer range assessment.

But if the perspectives of March 1994 are sombre ones, the possibility of peace, and the struggle to achieve it, still dominate the progress of discussions in the region and elsewhere where the problems of the Middle East are discussed. In the rest of this book we analyse where the peace process stands today, after the historic beginning made in Washington last year, the pathways which have led to the present situation, and the vistas which the future presents.

I

The White House Lawn

CHAPTER 1

HOW PEACE BEGAN

The Handshake

For a moment, on 13 September 1993, the world held its breath. On the lawn in front of the White House, watched by President Clinton, the seed of peace between Israel and the Palestinians was about to be planted. Seated at a table, the Foreign Minister of Israel, Shimon Peres, and the representative of the Palestine Liberation Organization, Mahmoud Abbas, put their signatures to the document inaugurating the peace accord between Israel and the Palestinians which was to begin with Palestinian autonomy in the Gaza Strip and Jericho. Flanking President Clinton, on a dais in front of the seated ranks of the 3000 invited guests, stood Israel's Prime Minister, Yitzhak Rabin, and the Chairman of the PLO, Yasser Arafat. The audience included many who had played a part in trying to forward the Middle East peace process over the years: among others Henry Kissinger, Jimmy Carter and James Baker. In the bright late summer Washington sunshine, Rabin was sombre in a dark suit, and those who had been close to him say he was nervous and on edge; Arafat, in military uniform but without his customary gun, smiled determinedly, and seemed jubilant but tense, a breeze gently stirring the fringes of his habitual kefiyyeh.

As the ceremony drew to an end there was a single question in the minds of the spectators at the White House, as well as for a television audience of many millions round the world: would the old antagonists seal the bargain by shaking hands? The question was soon answered. To the accompaniment of an intake of breath that was not quite a gasp from the onlookers, the unthinkable was thought, and the handshake took place. Cued by a gesture from President Clinton, Arafat reached across to Rabin. Then after what seemed like a moment's hesitation on Rabin's part, the two men took each other's hand. The world's cameras avidly recorded the resulting handclasp: a real handshake, as it seemed, and not just a diplomatic gesture.[1]

What the two men had agreed to was a Declaration of Principles, in effect an accord between the Israeli government and the PLO which would result in limited autonomy for the Palestinians in the Gaza Strip and in the area of Jericho. This would be the first stage in a process which was planned to spread to the rest of the Occupied Territories, and would cover all the 750,000 Palestinians of the Gaza Strip and the million Palestinian inhabitants of the West Bank. Complex arrangements were due to ensure Israel's security and frontiers, and the safety of the settlers who might remain in the former Israeli-occupied zones, but in principle the administration was set to come into Palestinian hands, accompanied by consultation with Israel over matters of mutual concern. Israeli troops were to be withdrawn from Gaza and Jericho in a first gesture of confidence, and a Palestinian authority would be set up to oversee the transition to an elected Palestinian administration. Not all this was to run according to plan, but the principles were laid down, and they were reason enough for optimism after all the years of hostility and hatred.[2]

Only a matter of weeks before, Yitzhak Rabin, asked by a journalist when he would like to meet Yasser Arafat, had replied, "Never." If proof were needed that the handshake in Washington had altered things for ever, a clear sign of change was that on 6 October, only a few weeks after their first meeting in Washington, Rabin and Arafat held a first summit in Cairo, to discuss the implementation of the agreement they had signed. This time there were no handshakes: the two leaders were photographed sitting stiffly one on each side of President Mubarak of Egypt. But the point was that they had met. The pace of change in the Middle East, in the autumn of 1993, irrevocably and irreversibly quickened, relations between Israelis and Palestinians underwent a qualitative change, and both sides soon found themselves committed to forms of cooperation whose outcome could only be an evolution of the interaction between Israel and the Palestinians from confrontation into something new.

The effect of the peace process has now been to turn the ratchet of negotiation and of relations between Israel, the Palestinians, and the other Arabs, beyond the point where either party could contemplate a

1. The ceremony was shown live on CNN television on 13 September 1993.
2. See the text of the agreement in the appendix.

return to the violence and unthinking antagonism which characterised the Palestine conflict for 45 years. This was the key achievement of the negotiation carried out in secret in the Norwegian capital Oslo during 1993 by Israeli and Palestinian representatives, where the agreement to begin the move to self-determination for the Palestinians within the limited framework of Gaza and Jericho was concluded. Having agreed to work together, even within a restricted framework, it would take a definite decision, an act of will, for either side to return to its erstwhile hostile stance, and such a decision would be hard to justify. A step towards peace may have been hard to take, but a backward step, under the full glare of world publicity, would now be even harder. Though there have been setbacks, delays and confrontations between the two sides as they have sought to negotiate the details of putting their pact into effect, it has not been derailed.

Meanwhile, it would have been impossible for the Oslo negotiations themselves to have taken place without the public forum of the formal Middle East peace talks, begun in Madrid at the end of October 1991. Here again, the main achievement may have been that Israeli and Palestinian negotiators sat down at the same table to talk, but that in itself was a step forward, and once taken, under international auspices, it was impossible to reverse. Even though relatively little of substance was achieved within the framework of the formal peace negotiations, they did succeed towards the end in creating a situation where the Israelis became willing to take a major step forward. That was their acquiescence in the de facto involvement of the PLO in the talks, when PLO advisers began to consult with the Palestinian negotiators from within the Occupied Territories. That step which was soon followed on 19 January 1993 by the lifting by the Israeli parliament of the ban on Israeli citizens talking directly to members of the PLO, which led to the inclusion of Feisal Husseini in the Palestinian negotiating team on 9 April.

Another and fundamental factor, at the root of why the Middle East peace process got under way in earnest when it did, has been the commitment to peace displayed by the United States since the Gulf War. At the outset American policy was guided by the determination of the US administration of President Bush, President Clinton's predecessor. George Bush wished to see changes in the Middle East to correspond to the realignment of power in the region following the victory of the US-led alliance over Iraq in the Gulf War, and the subsequent end of the Cold War between the United States and the

Soviet Union. The United States had in the course of the Gulf War cemented its ties with Saudi Arabia and the Gulf States, and had confirmed its link with Egypt. Even Syria was drawn into the alliance. A solution to the Palestinian problem would be something to offer America's Arab friends, and would enable them to make their own peace with Israel. At the same time Israel itself, though it would always be the friend and protégé of the United States, was no longer part of any American policy of Cold War containment of Soviet-backed Arab states.

New Friends?

Of course, though much progress has been made, it must not be supposed that Israel and the Palestinians have suddenly become friends, even though they have ceased to be enemies. Much difference will continue to exist between the two sides over such fundamental issues as the validity of their final aims. The Palestinians want, and will not cease to want, sovereignty in a state of their own. The Israelis will continue to wish, in the interests of their own security, to reject the Palestinian goal. These differences have been made clear by the chief protagonists themselves in statements they have made since the agreement was made in September. Mr Rabin, for example, said this to a *Jerusalem Post* reporter in October: "I stick to my position: no Palestinian state, Jerusalem must remain united under Israeli sovereignty, and be our capital forever."[3] Arafat, on the other hand, told reporters in Cairo in October after his first meeting with Rabin that he had appointed Faisal Husseini to negotiate issues relating to Jerusalem.[4] Jerusalem and statehood are sure to be the issues which will divide Israel and the Palestinians for the longest time, and they are the key questions which will eventually have to be faced.

It might be asked, why did Israel and the PLO decide now to attempt to negotiate an end to their conflict, a conflict which has been going on since the foundation of Israel in 1948, or even longer: since the first Palestinian uprising in 1936, since the Balfour

3. Yitzhak Rabin, interviewed by David Makovsky, *Jerusalem Post*, International Edition, 16 October 1993.
4. *The Guardian*, 7 October 1993.

Declaration of 1917, or since the arrival in Palestine of the earliest Jewish immigrants in the closing years of the nineteenth century? The reason is that a tide of opinion has begun to run in Israel, under pressure from the United States, to normalise its relations with its neighbours, and that prompted Israel's new Labour government to favour the idea of ending the strain of the ceaseless antagonism with the Arabs inside and outside its frontiers. In addition, Yitzhak Rabin, aged 72 and serving as Prime Minister of Israel for the second time, came to office seeing himself as a peacemaker, and wants to be so remembered.

It should also be seen that the problem of peacemaking is firmly rooted in the demography of Israel and the Occupied Territories. The population of Israel proper is almost five million, of whom some 900,000 are Arabs. A million Palestinians live in the West Bank, and three-quarters of a million in the Gaza Strip. The total number of Arabs in Israel and the Occupied Territories is therefore 2.65 million, almost half the overall population of 6.65 million. The higher birth rate among the Arabs would soon bring them to outnumber the Jews. In spite of the hundreds of thousands of Jews Israel still hopes to bring from the Soviet Union, a Greater Israel would soon become demographically a state with an Arab majority. If the Occupied Territories were ever to have been annexed, either the Arabs would have soon outvoted the Jews, or two classes of citizen would have had to be instituted, one without the vote. That situation would have been seen to be an abomination and could never have been contemplated in Israel. At the same time, 100,000 settlers live in the West Bank, as the result of a quarter of a century of Israeli policy, as well as a few thousand in Gaza. In addition, at least 120,000 settlers live in the neighbourhood of Jerusalem, in formerly Arab land which the Israelis claim as sovereign territory. The right-wing believes the presence of the settlers substantiates Israel's claim to the Territories. The intifada has brought clearer sighted Israelis to understand that this can never be the case. On the far right, the extremists of the Moledet and Tehiya parties, have defied reality with their view that the problem can be solved by moving the Arabs across the frontiers into neighbouring Arab states. On the left and in the liberal centre, Israelis have for some time seen clearly that only some fashion of disengagement can solve the problem. The current policies of Yitzhak Rabin's Labour government are the result of the intellectual apprehension, by a politician who though a Labour leader is a Zionist and an instinctive

hawk, that a separate political future for the Palestinians is Israel's
only option.

Meanwhile on the Palestinian side, Yasser Arafat, now 64 and head
of the PLO for a quarter of a century, came to the conclusion, though
he was once Israel's most vehement opponent, that there was never
likely to be more on offer. The seasoned Middle East observer Edward
Mortimer, writing in the *Financial Times*, draws a powerful parallel
from the myths of antiquity. He likens the situation of the Palestinians
to a story told about the last King of Rome, King Tarquin II. Tarquin
was offered the priceless gift of her nine books of prophecy by the
Cumaean Sibyl. Edward Mortimer tells the story: "When he refused
them, she burned three and offered him the remaining six at the
same price. Again he refused, so she burned three more and offered
him the remaining three, still at the same price. This time he bought
them." Tarquin bought the three books on the last occasion of
offering because he knew that if he refused again there would be no
more books to be bought. Thus Yasser Arafat has accepted the offer of
some form of limited autonomy from Israel because it is all that is
realistically on offer, even though, as Edward Mortimer says, "many
Palestinians think he is a fool or a traitor to accept so little after
struggling so long."[5]

The implication of the parable is, of course, that it is Israel which
has dictated the terms of the agreement, and that the Palestinians are
obliged to make the best of what Israel chooses to offer. Put in those
terms, it is not surprising that Yasser Arafat has his opponents among
the Palestinians. These range from mild critics to fanatical adversaries.
At one end of the scale are those who question Arafat's apparently
impetuous decision to talk to Israel, such as those inside the currently
Occupied Territories who question the wisdom of accepting such a
limited offer while at the same time welcoming any form of autonomy.
At the other end of the spectrum stand Arafat's bitter enemies from
the militant Muslim Hamas movement and the radical Palestinian
factions. Outside the historic land of Palestine there are also critics
among the Palestinian diaspora, and of these the most extreme are
the group of ten Palestinian rejectionist movements based in Damascus,
of whom Ahmed Jibril, the most virulent against Arafat's leadership of
the Palestinians, has threatened the PLO Chairman with death.

5. Edward Mortimer, "It's better late...", *Financial Times*, 15 September
1993.

Weeks of Tension

Though the Palestinians have waited at least 45 years for the settlement of their grievances, the prize of the interim autonomy agreement almost slipped from their grasp at the last moment. In the last few weeks which elapsed between the announcement that the negotiators had made a breakthrough in Oslo on 19 August and the signing ceremony in Washington on 13 September, both sides continued to have grave doubts about whether to go through with the accord, outweighed in the event by their greater determination to push the agreement through. News about the proposed agreement began to leak out at the end of August. On 27 August, Israel's Foreign Minister, Shimon Peres, announced what he called a historic breakthrough. Then the text of the proposed agreement appeared in Hebrew in the Israeli newspaper *Yediot Aharonot* on 31 August, and was published round the world.[6] But a key issue was the need for the PLO and Israel mutually to recognise each other. That was achieved on Friday 10 September when Yitzhak Rabin accepted the text of a letter he had received from Yasser Arafat and signed his own letter recognising the PLO.

The difficulty had been for Yasser Arafat to write a letter couched in terms acceptable to the Israeli Prime Minister. Both Arafat and Rabin had faced difficulties since the agreement became public. Rabin had faced vehement criticism at home, not least from the settlers in the Occupied Territories who saw their livelihoods or their homes at risk. Fifty thousand demonstrators had stood outside the Prime Minister's office in Jerusalem until the police brought water cannons to drive them away. Unless he received an acceptable text from Arafat he would not be in a position to persuade the Israeli public and the Knesset to accept it. Meanwhile Arafat had travelled round the Arab world looking for backing from the leaders of the Arab states, getting much support but also facing some rebuffs, while in Tunis many senior officials of the PLO were known to be unhappy about the course of events.

A breakthrough came only when Israeli foreign ministry officials went to Paris for a meeting on 8 September with Abu Ala, the Palestinian negotiator who had clinched the Oslo deal. But the key was for Arafat to agree to control the Palestinian uprising, the intifada,

6. The full text can be seen in *Middle East Mirror*, 1 September 1993.

inside the Occupied Territories, which he eventually found a form of words to enable him to do, adding in a separate letter addressed to the late Norwegian Foreign Minister, Johan Joergen Holst, his assurance that the PLO would commit itself to promoting peace in the Occupied Territories, and implicitly would bring the intifada under control. When Arafat had signed his letter on 9 September, Rabin was at last prepared to sign his own letter on the morning of the following day, 10 September. As he did so, he is reported to have said that he hoped that the peace deal the two sides were approaching would "bring about an end to the hundred years of bloodshed and misery between the Palestinians and Jews, the Palestinians and Israel".[7]

The Oslo Connection

The months of patient negotiation in Oslo which preceded the handshake, and produced the key documents that the PLO and the Israeli government were eventually able to subscribe to, will be one of the subjects of a later chapter of this book in which we shall look at the history of peace negotiation in the Middle East. But a brief account here will set the scene.[8] The initiative is widely credited to the Norwegian academic, Terje Larsen, who discussed with Israel's Deputy Foreign Minister Yossi Beilin in late 1992 the viability of establishing what he called a "back channel" for negotiating between Israel and the Palestinians, away from the glare of publicity associated with the official peace talks in Washington. In fact, by Larsen's own testimony, much of the credit must be taken by Yossi Beilin, a young, ambitious and open-minded member of the Israeli Labour Party who became Deputy Foreign Minister when Labour came to power in July 1992. That these talks got under way at all is certainly to do with the personal negotiating skills of Terje Larsen, but it was Yossi Beilin who sought out Larsen and asked him to try to initiate contacts between the two sides.

---

7. Marie Colvin, "New Friends", *Sunday Times*, 12 September 1993.
8. The negotations in Oslo were the subject of a revealing edition of Panorama, shown by BBC television on BBC1 on 13 September 1993. The quotations from Abu Ala and Uriel Savir in this section are taken from the programme.

The choice of Norway for the clandestine channel of negotiation between Israel and the PLO may have been a historical accident, but the talks seem also to have benefited directly from a particularly Norwegian input. Norway is a Scandinavian country with a good international image of non-aggression and a perceived orientation towards peace-making. It is regarded as friendly by both sides, and shares the Scandinavian tradition of benevolent neutrality, and a magisterial detachment from the conflicts and partiality of world politics, a position likely to give it the necessary impartiality to adjudicate between Israel and the Arabs. This was certainly the impression gained by the Palestinian negotiator in Oslo, Ahmed Qurei, known as Abu Ala, who said: "Of course I know Norway, it's a small country and it's an important country: it is a friend to the Palestinians, and friends to the Israelis, and therefore we are convinced they may play the role as a facilitator." The Israeli negotiator Uriel Savir, who became involved in the talks later, also paid tribute to the Norwegians' skill in calming a difficult situation: "A certain harmony in Norway and among Norwegians did in a way have an impact on all of us. We became a little bit Norwegian in the process, something we called the Oslo spirit, and the Oslo spirit carried off a little bit of the Middle East spirit."[9]

What was in effect to be the first meeting of the new negotiations took place in London in 1982 when Larsen engineered a meeting at a London hotel between an Israeli representative chosen by Beilin, namely Professor Yair Hirschfeld, a professor of politics at Haifa University, and Abu Ala, the PLO's financial chief. That initial encounter turned into a series of meetings in Norway, held in a relaxed atmosphere at a country house which belongs to a Norwegian industrialist. There, talk turned into negotiation, working documents were prepared, and gradually the process became more official. On the Israeli side, Yossi Beilin took the initiative to bring Foreign Minister Peres into his confidence. At the PLO headquarters in Tunis, Yasser Arafat and a few advisers close to him were the only ones to know about the existence of the talks. The late Norwegian Foreign Minister Johan Joergen Holst was told at this stage what was going on, and the talks were upgraded in May 1993 when Israel sent its diplomatic envoy Uriel Savir to put its case and listen to the Palestinians' demands.

9. Panorama, BBC1, 13 September 1993.

The talks in this alternative channel of negotiation went on through June and July, while the official talks in Washington were resulting only in a sterile confrontation, but though Norway was ultimately to yield the breakthrough, the way seemed at the time anything but smooth. The Norwegian social scientist Terje Larsen who was so closely involved in the process described the atmosphere: "I think I'd describe the process within the channel as a roller-coaster. There were the highest peaks of optimism, but we were also pretty deep down in the valleys of depression all the time. It was really a roller-coaster and there were tough negotiations up to the very moment of the initialling of the Declaration of Principles document."[10]

The Oslo process came to an end when Mr Shimon Peres, the Israeli Foreign Minister, arrived in Norway for an arranged official visit on 19 August 1993. The Palestinian and Israeli delegations were locked in negotiation over the final details of the agreement until the last moment, but they succeeded in coming to an agreement in time to initial the document in Shimon Peres's presence. As the Norwegian mediators stressed, secrecy was essential right up to the last moment, to prevent the negotiators coming under pressure from factions within Israel and at the PLO headquarters in Tunis who might have been able to bring pressure to bear on Yitzhak Rabin and Yasser Arafat to stop the agreement going ahead.

Around the Table in Madrid and Washington

The role played by the official Middle East peace talks in Madrid will also be part of a later chapter, but as with the Oslo talks we should in this prologue describe the part they have played in the creation of the dialogue between Israel and the Palestinians that in turn has brought about the agreement today being put into practice. The official talks were of great significance because they were the first occasion on which an official Israeli delegation had met any representatives of the Palestinians. The talks were convened in the aftermath of the Gulf War at the insistence of President Bush of the United States, and the

10. Ibid.

government of Israel, under the leadership of Likud and led by Yitzhak Shamir was pressured by the Americans to take part. They began in an atmosphere of great hope in Madrid in October 1991, but were always a disappointment. For the first eight months their lack of success was indubitably the fault of the intransigent attitude of the Likud government's Israeli delegation. In retrospect, it seems as if the right-wing Israelis came not so much to negotiate a compromise with the Palestinians, but rather to prove that they were willing to take part in talks. Nevertheless, their participation at least got the peace process under way.

The Israelis had always been very resistant to the idea of any kind of an international peace conference at which the issues of Middle East peace would be discussed in open session, or where outside powers would take part in any effective capacity, or in which the United Nations would claim to play any determining or organising role. The reason for this reluctance appears to have been the fear that if the issues of Middle East peace were to be debated in public, the joint voices of the Arab states might overwhelm Israel's single voice, and a solution not in Israel's interests might be dictated by outside parties. Israel was also very wary of any kind of talks with Palestinians, which might imply that they had extended any kind of recognition to any Palestinian body.

Instead, Israel had begun to indicate in a tentative way that it would be willing to discuss the issues of peace with the individual Arab states surrounding it in a series of separate conferences, each held on a bilateral basis, though it would not be willing to talk directly to the Palestinians at all.

The Madrid conference was therefore a concession on the part of the Israelis, under the terms of which an open conference would be held, under international rather than United Nations auspices, at which issues of substance would not be discussed. This would then be succeeded by bilateral talks with each of Israel's neighbours, and a group of Palestinians drawn strictly from the Occupied Territories would take part only in association with the Jordanian delegation. The PLO was excluded, as were Palestinians whose place of residence was Jerusalem, which Israel regarded as its own sovereign territory. But that the conference was held at all, however limited its make-up, was already an achievement. The opening session was held on 30 October 1991, and world television showed the Israeli and Arab negotiators from Jordan, Syria and Lebanon sitting together, with President Bush and President Gorbachev at the top table representing the United States and the former Soviet Union, the joint sponsors, and a European Community delegation also in the room.

Optimism was untempered at the time by the sense of frustration and lack of progress which would later characterise the talks, and there were high hopes around the world that the talks would bring real change. After the opening conference the bilateral talks wanted by Israel opened on 3 November in Madrid, after which the venue shifted to Washington. By January the Palestinians had achieved their own independent delegation at the talks, which was in effect the first major negotiating breakthrough. But over the following 20 months, and the eleven sessions of talks which followed, little of substance was achieved, and perhaps the biggest disappointment was that even after Labour came to power in Israel and the government changed, there still seemed to be little will to move forward at the talks.

It had begun by the summer of 1993 to appear to outside observers, who were unaware of the highly secret Oslo talks that were going on throughout that year, that there was little hope of progress, and that the official Middle East peace talks might either wither away, or might become an empty ritual, stretching on into the future, at which Israeli and Palestinian negotiators, probably increasingly disempowered by their parent bodies, would appear regularly to hold nugatory discussions. There were precedents for such travesties of international negotiation, for example the standing conference of North and South Korean representatives on reunification set up in 1972. But the existence of these talks, though fruitless in themselves, was a necessary condition for the more productive Oslo talks to be held.

When the Oslo breakthrough was revealed, the Israeli and Palestinian negotiating teams were as taken aback as other observers, and must at first have been angry that they had been allowed to continue to struggle with their frustrating task while the real work was going on elsewhere. But the official peace talks still exist, though much of the work of negotiation was transferred to Taba, on the Egyptian–Israeli border, where the details of the limited autonomy agreement covering Jericho and the Gaza Strip began to be worked out in October 1993. Of course, the bilateral talks between Israel and the three of its Arab neighbours with whom it did not have peace treaties, Syria, Jordan and Lebanon, would still carry on as before through the vehicle of the bilateral Middle East peace talks.

What Lies Ahead?

There are still fundamental differences between Palestinians and Israelis about the future. For the Palestinians, the process now begun seems to lead inexorably to the creation of a Palestinian state. It is the view of members of the negotiating team and their advisers that statehood is now inevitably at the end of the road on which they have set foot, though Israel may still refuse to recognise the fact. An American lawyer of Palestinian origin, Judge Eugene Cotran, says the international recognition already given to Palestine as a state, together with the establishment of the new Palestinian governing body means that a state has in effect already come into existence, and he offers words of encouragement to the Palestinians: "The Oslo accords give them the chance to build a new nation. I hope and pray they will take it."[11]

In Israel, on the other hand, the fact or the potentiality of Palestinian statehood will continue to be denied. Israel believes that it can deal with a Palestinian entity, which will be somehow drawn into a political and economic framework which will probably include both Israel and Jordan, but that the entity thus created will still not be a state. It may be that though Israeli politicians are aware that the denial of Palestinian statehood cannot be maintained indefinitely, it is necessary for them to hold to this position for the moment, to continue to get backing for the deal from an electorate some of which at least is nervous about the future.

The timetable set out in the document signed by Israel and the Palestinians was clear. In the short term, elections for a Council to run the Palestine Interim Self-Government Authority are to be held no later than nine months from the date the agreement comes into force, in other words by June 1994. The military withdrawal from Gaza, under the terms agreed at Taba in mid-December 1993, was set to be completed before the election date. In the longer term, a permanent settlement, which the agreement says specifically should be based on Security Council resolutions 242 and 338 is due to come into effect no more than five years after the setting up of the Palestinian Council. Prime Minister Rabin has also set himself a more distant but still definite goal, when he said in November 1993 that he expected all

11. Eugene Cotran, "Why there is now a state of Palestine", *Middle East International*, 22 October 1993.

Israel's outstanding disagreements with its Arab neighbours to be settled by the end of the period of the current Israeli legislature, in other words by June 1996.[12]

We shall look later in detail at the economic and political challenges which will face the new Palestinian entity. But we should be aware now while reading the history of the Israeli–Palestinian dispute that the present stage is one only of transition, and that there are many difficulties ahead. Palestinian representatives since 13 September in Washington have not ceased to stress that central to these are the issues of security and economics. Without mutual trust between the new Palestinian authority and Israel, peace cannot be guaranteed. Unless the Palestinians are in firm control of their own country, they will not be able to create and guarantee stability. On the other hand, unless Israel knows it can count on the security of its own people, both in Israel proper and in the settlements which will, for the moment at least, continue to exist in the Occupied Territories, Israel will not be able to stay out of Palestinian affairs. Security is therefore essential, and that means that both Israel and the Palestinian entity must have authority and the means of enforcing their will, as well as a clear division of responsibilities.

In the field of economics, of course the Palestinian entity cannot survive unless its people have work and an income. The international community had already offered by the end of 1993 to provide over two billion dollars for the construction of an infrastructure for Gaza and Jericho, where the Palestinian governing body's writ will initially run, and the Palestinians say more will be needed. The aim of Palestinian economists is to reduce the disparity between the standard of living in Palestine and that in Israel proper, where Israelis already earn over ten thousand dollars per head each year, ten times more than in Gaza and seven times more than in the West Bank. Jordan, on the other hand, has a GDP per head less than that of the Occupied Territories, and Jordan's fears about the economic relationship between itself and the new Palestinian entity will also need to be addressed.

There will also be political problems in the new Palestinian region. No system of government has been specified for the new entity, but the assumption is that democratic elections will lead to a democratically governed state. That has certainly always been the assumption of

12. AFP despatch, 5 November 1993.

the Palestinians of the interior, those resident in the Occupied Territories and Jerusalem. Questioned on that subject the day after signing the peace accord in Washington, Yasser Arafat said the new entity would be based on "democracy, and more democracy, and more democracy".[13] Other Palestinians fear for the future of democracy, especially as the Palestinian people of the Occupied Territories come face to face with the PLO leadership, which has behind it three decades of experience of an autocratic structure, answerable only to the biddable and seldom summoned Palestine National Council. Only practice will tell whether Palestinian democracy will take root and flourish after the new entity comes into being.

And finally it should not be forgotten that the Palestinian state will not exist in a vacuum. It will form part of a pattern of international relations, and will itself be the object of international concern and interest. Factions in the Arab world and in the wider Middle East will attempt to draw it into their orbit. Israel, Jordan and Egypt will hope that the Palestinians will remain in close relationships with their immediate neighbours and form part of a local political system whose relations will draw closer. But there are other centres of influence. President Saddam Hussein of Iraq, whose relations with Yasser Arafat during the Gulf War were close, will certainly make his overtures and will attempt to appeal to radical Palestinian opinion. Syria also regards itself as the patron of what it sees as the purest radical stream of Palestinian thought. Saudi Arabia and the Gulf States have had substantial Palestinian populations in the past, and may try to build links with the new Palestinian entity. Finally, Iran will also hold out its hand to the radical Muslim militants of the Hamas movement and Islamic Jihad, in an attempt to create an Islamic society in Palestine.

All these problems lie ahead for the new Palestinian entity. But the miracle is that after so many decades of struggle and misunderstanding between the Palestinians and Israel, which has led to mutual hatred and fear, Israelis and Palestinians have nevertheless been able to take the initial steps on the road which may lead to peace. That would not have been achieved if it had not appeared to both sides to be in their mutual interest to do so. Perhaps the reason may be that the Middle East conflict between Israel and the Palestinians no longer has any relation to the wider world conflict of the Cold War, which is

13. Quoted by David Hoffman in "Model Palestinian political system", *International Herald Tribune*, 16/17 October 1993.

now at an end. It may be that economic struggle between Western nations which need the oil resources of the Middle East on the one hand, and on the other hand other states which control or seek to control those oil resources, may yet give rise to a further scene of conflict within the Middle East. The Gulf War may only have been the first episode in that struggle. But in the present window of calm, the Palestinians and Israel have a chance for reconciliation and reconstruction.

II

The Road to Peace

CHAPTER 2

MIDDLE EAST REALITIES: THE POWER OF HISTORY

The Twice-Promised Land

What was achieved at the White House in September 1993 was not just the resolution of an incidental quarrel between neighbours. It was the decision by two parties to turn their backs on a history of deep-seated antagonism so profound that the determination of the two sides to communicate with each other was in itself already of great significance. The clash between Arabs and Jews in Palestine goes back to the First World War and beyond, and the ideological commitments of the protagonists are strongly held and passionately entrenched. To understand why the Middle East conflict has been so hard to end, the obsessions of its participants demand comprehension. As we shall see below, the basic issue by the time of the Second World War was the incompatibility between the Zionist ambition to have a Jewish state in Palestine, and the Arab nationalist determination to see Arab states in Arab lands.

Britain has been blamed for much that has happened in the Middle East, and it is undeniable that there is much to criticise in British policy in Palestine. At first it was an attempt to help the Jews without offending too greatly the Arabs, a dichotomy which reflected a cleavage between some British politicians and administrators and others. Britain was determined during the First World War to take on the responsibility for Palestine's future, but thirty years later, after the Second World War, had become only too anxious to extricate itself from an apparently insoluble dilemma. The first agreement made by the Allies about the future disposition of Palestine was embodied in the Sykes–Picot agreement of 1916, in which Britain and France agreed that the British should control part of the country and the historic heartland should be subject to international supervision. That was eventually abandoned at the peace conference of 1919. But Britain's Middle East policy up to 1918 was in reality already based on the assumption that Britain would take charge of postwar Palestine.

In November 1917, the famous Balfour Declaration was made by the British Foreign Secretary, Arthur Balfour: in a letter to Lord Rothschild, agreed by the cabinet and read out in the House of Commons, Balfour confirmed that Britain favoured what was called a "national home for the Jews" in Palestine.

On the other hand, Britain had also in October 1915 made a promise to Sharif Hussein of Mecca, the Arab leader with whom the British had concerted the so-called Arab revolt in the Middle East. That promise was made in a letter from Sir Henry McMahon, then British High Commissioner in Cairo, and its substance was that the British government would regard the liberated Arab lands of the Ottoman Empire as Arab territory, where "Great Britain is prepared to recognise and support the independence of the Arabs". This was an undertaking whose validity was much disputed in the years after the First World War, when it was argued by Winston Churchill as Colonial Secretary, among others, that territorial exceptions to the British pledge were meant to include Palestine. Other documentary evidence argues against this view.[1] Britain was confirmed as the Mandatory power in charge of Palestine by the League of Nations in July 1922, and the British government found itself saddled with the problem of resolving the future of what had long been known in the Christian West as the Promised Land, but was now, in a postwar witticism, sometimes referred to in British circles in Cairo and London as the "Twice-Promised Land".[2]

The conclusion must be drawn, that there were many causes for the violence in Palestine which followed the end of the Second World War and the upheaval which preceded and surrounded Israel's independence, but one cause was the inconsistency and uncertainty of purpose of British policy from 1918 to 1948. That failure indubitably arose from the incompatibility of Britain's two undertakings, to the Arabs and to the Zionists. Neither the Arabs nor the Jews were satisfied with the administration of the country under the British Mandate. But given the determination of the Zionist leadership of the Jewish faction to create the conditions for statehood in Palestine and then to seize it, and the growing desire of the Arabs to prevent that

1. *The Times*, 17 April 1964.
2. Arthur Goldschmidt Jr, *A Concise History of the Middle East*, 2nd edition, AUC Press, Cairo 1983, p. 227.

seizure taking place, it would have been hard for British administrators, no matter how beneficent or impartial, to have brought about a better solution. The head-on opposition of Arabs and Jews was transformed into an ideological clash, between two philosophies, Zionism and Arab nationalism. These are ideas which grew and evolved into the respective driving forces of the apparently irreconcilable antagonism between Arabs and Jews in modern Israel and Palestine.

Two Ideologies in Competition for a Nation

What therefore had to be settled, in principle at least, by Israel and the Palestinians before the question of peace could be discussed was the question of how to resolve this long-standing and entrenched ideological hostility between Zionism and Arab nationalism. The answer has been that by the Palestinian leadership at least, and by the government of Israel, the philosophical ideas have not been rethought: they have simply, for the moment at least, been set aside. The participants in the Oslo discussions said that they realised from the beginning that the only way progress would be made was by refusing to think about the past, or to recriminate about grievances, but rather to look only to the future. The old hostilities were simply set on one side, and with them the ideas of the established ideologies.

Their abandonment was in practice achieved by an act of will on the part of the two leaders, Yitzhak Rabin and Yasser Arafat. The two simply decided to allow the urgency of reaching a peaceful settlement of the Palestine issue to override their commitment to their respective ideologies. They were thus able to effectively dam the contradictory streams of history which had seemed likely to make the conflict between Israel and the Palestinians virtually impossible to resolve. That was why the exchange of letters between the leaders, on 9 and 10 September 1993, in which each side recognised the legitimacy of the other's existence, was so vital a stage of the preliminaries to peace. The determination of the two was expressed in the commitments to each other and to the world which they made at their meeting on the White House lawn. Rabin's words were emotional: "We who have fought against you, the Palestinians, we say to you today in a loud and a clear voice, enough of blood and tears, enough!" Yasser Arafat was more controlled, but equally clear that what had been done implied a profound change: "Let me address the people of Israel and their leaders, with whom we are meeting today for the first time, and let me assure them that the difficult decision that we have reached together was one that required great and exceptional courage."

That is also why the militants, the extremists, and the diehards on each side of the fence were so vehement in their rejection of the peace process. For the stand-fast element of the Likud opposition in Israel, the relinquishment of any morsel of Zionist dogma was tantamount to an admission that Israel's existence was founded on a fallacy. For the Arab nationalists of the radical PLO factions, or the Muslim militants of Hamas, to concede that Israel had any shred of justification for its existence in any part of the historic territory of Palestine was, equally, to undermine a faith whose integrity had alone legitimised the long struggle to which lives have been devoted, and in which lives have been sacrificed.

The Idea of Zionism

The Jews did not capriciously decide to go to Palestine, "to return to their biblical home", as they might put it, nor was the aim of Zionism to antagonise the Arabs, whose numbers and whose attachment to their land many underestimated. They were driven by the two aims of finding a place safe from anti-semitic persecution, and of realising the goal of combining their ancient myth of the possibility of a return to Jerusalem with the modern goal of establishing a nation state. Anti-semitism and the persecution of the Jews became an alarming reality in Russia in the 1890s, and in Germany in the 1930s it took on an even more frightening aspect, culminating in Nazi attempts during the war to exterminate the Jews. Zionism was not a luxury for the Jews, it was a necessity.

For the Jews inside and outside Israel, Zionism, as a way to restore both the dignity and the safety of the Jewish people, has in the hundred years since its conception been an ideology which has played a crucial role in the formation of minds. It is not a religious idea, but a historical and a social one, and a programme for action which is seen by its zealots as vital for the salvation of the Jews. Its essence is that the Jews not merely can but must return to their historic homeland in Palestine: to Eretz Israel, the lands of the Jews in biblical times. At their greatest extent, these were the lands held by King David, which comprised not only modern-day Israel but also land east of the River Jordan which today belongs to the Hashemite Kingdom of Jordan, an Arab state, ruled by King Hussein, which is a key participant in the Middle East peace process.

That return to the lands of the Bible, and the foundation of a Jewish state there, according to the movement's activists, has not been merely desirable but also became essential for the survival of the Jewish people, faced by persecution.

Zionism has been an idea of compelling power. Though an intellectual construct, and an invention of the last century, Zionism as an idea became a force in the minds of the Jewish people as strong in its own way as the religion of Judaism itself. Zionism is in a sense a form of nationalism, and derives its strength and its persuasive force in much the same way as do the ideas of nationalism. Though it has old roots, it was newly minted at the end of the nineteenth century; but it has come in the minds of many Jews to appear as obvious, as inevitable and as basic as do nationalist ideas to many in the nation states of Europe and elsewhere who are unaware of the relatively recent origin of nationalism and the intellectual artificiality of the concept. To be a Jew, according to the Zionists, is to enjoy the consciousness of belonging to a community with the backing of history behind it, and the bonds of common purpose within.

Zionism as History

"Shall we choose Palestine, or Argentina?"[3] That was the question posed by the father of Zionism, Theodor Herzl, in his book *Der Judenstaat*, published in Vienna on 14 February 1896. Though a few thousand Jews had fled persecution in Russia and elsewhere to settle in Argentina by the time Herzl wrote *Der Judenstaat*, and 40,000 were eventually to go there, the question was for him a rhetorical one. Herzl goes on to argue passionately in favour of the choice of

3. Theodor Herzl, *The Jewish State: an attempt at a modern solution of the Jewish question*, translated by Sylvie d'Avigdor, revised with a foreword by Israel Cohen (fourth edition), Rita Searl, London 1946, p. 30. (*The Jewish State* was originally published as *Der Judenstaat* in February 1896.)

Palestine: "Palestine is our ever-memorable historic home. The very name of Palestine would attract our people with a marvellous potency." And he makes a statement that would appeal to Europe: "We should there form a rampart of Europe as against Asia, an outpost of civilisation as opposed to barbarism. We should as a neutral state remain in contact with all Europe, which would have to guarantee our existence." After the Second World War the United States of America took on Europe's prior world role as the leader of the Western world, and Herzl's words ring out as the justification for American policy towards Israel from 1948 to 1994.

That justification was not however very convincing in Arab ears. From a moral point of view, the Palestinians and other Arabs saw it as fundamentally flawed, in ways that were fatal for the moral basis of Zionism, and America's support of Israel. Not unnaturally, those characterised by Herzl as barbarians, the Palestinian Arabs, were enraged by such assertions. That outrage would grow as awareness of the Zionists' philosophy and intentions became more available to the Arabs. However much the Zionists were impelled to search for a new home because of the injustices they faced in Europe, parallel injustices committed in Palestine were not justified. The Zionists themselves were blind to what was happening. Levy Eshkol, later Israel's Prime Minister during the 1967 war, moved to Palestine from the Ukraine in 1913 at the age of 18. In his maturity he asked: "What are Palestinians? When I came here it was desert — more than underdeveloped: nothing."[4] The mutual lack of understanding between the Jews and the Arabs was the root of Palestine's tragedy, but it must be said that in their urgency to find a new home it was the Jews who turned their backs on the reality of the Palestinian people and the existence of an established society in the land they had chosen to colonise, or, as they saw it, re-colonise. The Palestinians always had the better case because they simply wished to remain on their own land, in their own country. In 1994 the state of Israel has become a fact, and the best the Palestinians can hope for is compromise. At an earlier stage, the reality was the absolute injustice of the pre-emption by Israel of what had been Palestine. Even at the year of Israeli independence, 1948, Jews owned only ten per cent of the land of Palestine and yet were offered half of it in the UN partition proposal.

4. Quoted by Donald Neff, "The Long Struggle for Recognition", *Middle East International*, 459, 24 September 1993.

In the hundred years and more since Jews first began to settle in the Middle East their numbers have dramatically increased. At the beginning of the nineteenth century there had been very few Jews in Palestine. Out of a total population of less than 300,000 there were fewer than 7000 Jews, according to Yosef Gorny, an Israeli historian of Zionism.[5] In the second half of the nineteenth century a trickle of Jews began to emigrate from Europe to what some of them argued was their rightful home in the Middle East. By 1880 there were 24,000 Jews out of a total population of 525,000 or 4.5 per cent of the total population. At this time, estimates another Israeli scholar, David Vital, half of the small population of Jerusalem was Jewish: 17,000 out of a total of 30,000.[6]

But it was the events of 1881 and the succeeding years in Russia which prompted what became the modern phenomenon of Zionism. Repressive laws and pogroms against Jews prompted them to think of leaving Russia, which was at the time the home of half the world's Jewish population. The preferred destination of most of them was – as it still is more than a century later – the United States of America. In these early days even Jewish leaders themselves did not see Palestine as an attractive destination for Jewish emigrants from Russian persecution. Here is a contemporary Jewish view of one scheme to settle in the Middle East: ". . . Palestine is a poor country, where there is no commerce, no industry, and where there are no roads nor [other] means of communication; that the Jews who inhabit it now are destitute and for the most part live on charity which is sent to them from elsewhere. The arrival of new immigrants can only add to the misery."[7]

Nevertheless there were Jewish idealists in both Russia and Romania at a very early stage who believed that their future lay in Palestine, and enough chose Palestine as their goal to swell the Jewish population there to some 90,000 out of a population of almost 600,000 by 1915.[8] The ideology of Zionism was elaborated by a number of the movement's leaders, but the father of the Zionist movement was

5. Yosef Gorny, *Zionism and the Arabs, 1882–1948: a study of ideology*, Oxford University Press, Oxford 1987, p. 5.

6. David Vital, *The Origins of Zionism*, Oxford University Press, Oxford 1975, p. 16.

7. Alliance Israélienne Universelle, *Bulletin Mensuel*, August–September 1881, quoted in Vital, op. cit., p. 62.

8. Gorny, loc. cit.

indubitably Theodor Herzl himself. In 1897, a year after the appearance of *Der Judenstaat* he convened the World Zionist Congress in Basel in Switzerland, which gave shape to the modern Zionist movement and initiated the twentieth-century process of immigration into Palestine, the economic consolidation and the political pressure that led inexorably to the foundation of the modern state of Israel. The Congress itself fought shy of calling for a Jewish state, though some participants argued for precisely that, but its resolution said: "Zionism aims at the creation of a home for the Jewish people in Palestine to be secured by public law."[9]

The Balfour Declaration

Zionism might have succeeded in any event in promoting Jewish immigration into Palestine, but its likelihood of success was enhanced in the event by historical concurrence. The First World War enabled Britain to take a guiding role in Palestine, and allowed the Zionist leaders to exploit to the full the credit they had built up in Britain by sympathetic contacts with British statesmen. The war, in which all the European powers as well as the United States became embroiled, led to the collapse of the old Turkish state, the Ottoman Empire, and gave the victorious Allies the opportunity to redistribute the Empire's lands. The Middle East was divided up into Arab states, under French and British Mandates, confirmed and given a backing in international law: a system under which France and Britain would administer the territories and bring them to the point of readiness for independence.

In anticipation of the award of the Mandate over Palestine to Britain, the Zionist leaders induced British statesmen to support their case. Arthur Balfour, the British Foreign Secretary, put on paper on 2 November 1917, in a letter to the British Zionist champion Lord Rothschild, the following well-known words, now known as the Balfour Declaration:

> His Majesty's Government view with favour the establishment in Palestine of a national home for the Jewish people, and will use their best

9. Vital, op. cit., p. 368. The declaration was drafted in German and the word rendered here as "home" was "Heimstätte".

endeavours to facilitate the achievement of this object, it being clearly understood that nothing shall be done which may prejudice the civil and religious rights of the existing non-Jewish communities in Palestine, or the rights and political status enjoyed by Jews in any other country.[10]

The Balfour Declaration reflected the views of the British cabinet, and had, in the Prime Minister David Lloyd George's own words, his "zealous assent".[11] Lloyd George was strongly inclined towards the Zionist cause, and a principal influence on him was Chaim Weizmann, a distinguished industrial chemist, originally from Russia, whose ingenuity in his research laboratory in Manchester had contributed greatly to the British war effort. Weizmann was later to become the first President of Israel. Weizmann had met Balfour and other British political figures, and earned Lloyd George's gratitude in the war by inventing, in response to an urgent plea from the government, a completely novel way of making much needed acetone for the production of explosives, using a biological technique based on fermentation.[12]

Zionism Between Two Wars

After the war, Jews began to immigrate into Israel in larger numbers, and the Jewish population increased to almost one-sixth of the total of over a million in 1931, and a third of the total of almost two million in 1947.[13] From the start of the inter-war period, the Zionist leadership pressed for as much official recognition as possible of the special status they wanted in Palestine, not least through demanding the official use of the Hebrew language. David Ben Gurion, who became in due course Chairman of the Jewish Agency and then the first Prime Minister of Israel, had himself come to Palestine in 1906, but lived through these years of Jewish immigration. Ben Gurion was a man of passion and determination who gave his life

10. See for example Ritchie Ovendale, *The Origins of the Arab–Israeli Wars*, Longman, London 1984, p. 33.
11. David Lloyd George, *The Truth about the Peace Treaties*, Gollancz, London 1938, Volume 2, p. 1117.
12. Chaim Weizmann, *Trial and Error*, Hamish Hamilton, London 1949, pp. 220–2.
13. Gorny, loc. cit.

to the Zionist cause and had the unique satisfaction of signing Israel's declaration of independence. He gives in his autobiography a graphic account of those early post-war years: "For myself I laboured in grove and vineyard and wine press, later joining the farming settlement of Sejera in Galilee. There I followed the plough, and as the black clods of earth turned and crumbled, and the oxen trod with the slow and heedless dignity of their kind, I saw visions and dreamed dreams. We were still hardly more than a handful; but young pioneers ... continued to land at Jaffa and to spread throughout the land."

Though the Jewish presence in Palestine increased, not all went according to the Zionists' wishes, not least because Britain, as the Mandatory power, began to take a more pragmatic view. Britain's first civilian High Commissioner, Sir Herbert Samuel, appointed in 1920, was a Jew and a Zionist, but hoped to be able to reconcile the antithetical ambitions of the two parts of the population of Palestine by reconciling the Palestinian Arabs to the idea of accepting the aims of the Zionists. Meanwhile, British administrators in day-to-day contact with the realities saw that the Arab population also had its rights, and persuaded the British government to begin to think seriously about them. There was one moment when the Zionist leadership may have thought that it had obtained Arab acquiescence in its projects. That was in 1919, when the Emir Feisal indicated during the Paris Conference that he was not opposed to the Zionist programme.[14] Weizmann signed an agreement with Feisal, while the latter was still in Damascus, but this was never taken seriously by the Arabs of Palestine.

There were Arab riots directed against the Jews in Palestine in 1920 and again in the following year, in which lives were lost on both sides. That made clear both to the Zionists and to the British administration the extent of Arab alarm over the growth of the Jewish presence in Palestine and the reality of Arab fears that the Jews were set to take over the country. The Jewish reaction was to begin to organize the defence of their settlements, in a step which led ultimately to the setting up of Jewish defence forces. At the same time, the Zionists felt that the British were trying to control the numbers in which the Jews were able to immigrate and to keep a curb on their activities. The Zionist leaders feared that the British government wanted to go back on the spirit of the Balfour Declaration. The events of the next two

14. Emir Feisal, letter to Felix Frankfurter, 3 March 1919, quoted by Walter Laqueur, *The Israel Arab Reader*, Pelican Books, London 1970, p. 38.

decades were certainly marked by a continuing ambiguity on the part of the British which led each side in the Palestine conflict, both Arabs and Jews, to believe that the Mandatory power favoured the other party.

There were more attacks on Jews in 1929, and fuel was given to Jewish suspicions by reports compiled by the British administration critical of Zionist activities, culminating in the White Paper of 1930, which refused an Arab request for self-government but agreed to curb Jewish immigration. The truth seems to have been that Britain's apparent indecision signalled a very real inability of successive British governments to decide what they wished to achieve in Palestine. In the short term, a letter from Prime Minister Ramsay MacDonald to Chaim Weizmann in 1931 marked a swing back to a pro-Zionist position by Britain. MacDonald reassured Weizmann that Jewish immigration would be limited only by Palestine's economic ability to absorb the newcomers.[15]

The Zionist leadership became ever more sophisticated in its organisation of work, land ownership, society and self-defence among the Jewish community in Palestine, the "Yishuv". Jews bought Arab land, often from absentee landlords, and Palestinian Arabs, including tenant farmers and farm-hands, found themselves dislodged from lands they had for centuries regarded as their own. The Arabs began to surmise that the intention of the Jews was to make good the establishment of their National Home. The anti-Jewish riots of 1936, were more deliberate and concerted than the relatively spontaneous riots of 1920, and grew into a more sustained anti-Jewish campaign. It was clear that on the one hand the Arabs had seen that if the Zionism phenomenon was not to be firmly opposed, Arab land would be lost. On the other hand, the Zionist leadership had concluded that the moment had come for the final push towards statehood.

The British were prompted to set up a Royal Commission, the Peel Commission, to enquire into the causes of the rebellion and to propose a solution to what was becoming an increasingly unmanageable situation in Palestine for the British administration. In 1937 the Peel Commission proposed a partition of the country, under which the Jews would have received a relatively small slice of territory, which the Arabs nevertheless furiously rejected. Ben Gurion, on the other

15. Weizmann, op. cit., p. 415: see Hansard of 13 February 1931 for the text of the letter.

hand, supported by most of the Jews, welcomed the idea of partition: "This is the beginning of the redemption for which we have waited two thousand years. We have established a great new political fact . . . A Jewish state in part of Palestine will help in the realisation of Zionism more than a British state in the whole of Palestine".[16] Ben Gurion saw in the Peel Commission's proposals the chance for which the Zionists had been waiting and the opportunity to create a Jewish state. The Arabs, determined to prevent the Zionists from achieving their goal, returned to their campaign of violence.

The British government, in the White Paper it eventually produced in May 1939, after yet another commission of enquiry had visited the country, disappointed and angered the Jews, who had been so elated by the Peel Commission. This they achieved without really appeasing the Arabs, by attempting to achieve an impossible compromise. The British proposal was a bi-national solution, in which an unpartitioned Palestine with an Arab majority would also contain a Jewish National Home. On the other hand, the Arabs were promised that no more than 75,000 further Jewish immigrants would be permitted over the coming five years, after which immigration would end. Under the plan envisaged in the White Paper, both Jews and Arabs would participate in political institutions whose role would be to prepare the country for autonomy, which would ideally come within ten years, in a state in which the Jewish population would have been one-third of a population of some two million.

Both Jews and Arabs rejected the content of the 1939 White Paper, though the Arabs recognised it as a small advance towards what they saw as the proper recognition of their rights. Nevertheless, the scene seemed set for a renewal of their increasingly bitter conflict. However, the onset of the Second World War in September 1939 brought about a temporary end to active hostility between the two communities, and initiated what was in effect an uneasy truce. The Arabs were hostile to the British, but not actively so. David Ben Gurion, by this time head of the Jewish National Agency, said that the Jews must behave as if they expected to become the government of Palestine. In an effective truce which lasted until the war was over many of the Jews cooperated with the British, and some of Israel's future leaders even served in the British forces. Ben Gurion was later to write: "We must help the British in their war as though there were no White Paper, and we must

16. Barnett Litvinoff, *Ben Gurion of Israel*, Praeger, New York 1954, pp. 127–8.

oppose the White Paper as though there were no war."[17] The Zionist conference at the Biltmore Hotel in New York City in 1942 reaffirmed Jewish opposition to the White Paper, and called for the establishment of what was described as a Jewish Commonwealth in Palestine. After the war, Zionist hostility to Britain was to be resumed with increased ruthlessness.

The Idea of Arab Nationalism

Arab nationalism became a factor in the Palestine equation later than did Zionism, to which the form it took in Palestine was to some extent a reaction. The classic text of Arab nationalism, which is still a valid document for our time, is *The Arab Awakening* by George Antonius, first published in 1938.[18] It was written in haste by George Antonius as the situation in Palestine became ever more grave. The book was meant to be not only a commentary on the origins of Arab nationalism, but also a contribution to the nationalist struggle.

> . . . the Arab claims rest on two distinct foundations: the natural right of a settled population, in great majority agricultural, to remain in possession of the land of its birthright; and the acquired political rights which followed from the disappearance of Turkish sovereignty and from the Arab share in its overthrow, and which Great Britain is under a contractual obligation to recognise and uphold.[19]

George Antonius had already realised in the years before the war that the battle for Palestine between Arabs and Jews was coming to its final phase when, as we have seen, the Arabs were struggling for their freedom in Palestine while the Zionists moved seemingly inexorably towards the establishment of their Jewish state. George Antonius himself was of Lebanese Christian origin, but was born in Alexandria and educated in the British system at Alexandria's Victoria College and at Cambridge University. He knew Palestine and the Palestinian situation well, as he served in the British administration from 1921 to

17. David Ben Gurion, *Ba-Ma'arakhak* [In the Struggle], vol. 4, Am Oved, Tel Aviv 1964, pp. 22–3, cited by Avraham Avi-Hai, *Ben Gurion, State Builder*, Israel Universities Press, Jerusalem 1974, p. 31.

18. George Antonius, *The Arab Awakening*, Hamish Hamilton, London 1938.

19. Ibid., p. 391.

1930, but when he wrote his study of Arab nationalism he was employed by an American research institution. He played an active part in Arab diplomacy, but died during the Second World War, in 1942, while the outcome in Palestine was still in the balance.[20]

The Arab Awakening places the earliest stirrings of effective Arab nationalist thought in the first decade of the twentieth century. The Arabs began to be conscious of their own cause after the Young Turks, an officers' movement within the Ottoman Empire, forced reform on Sultan Abdul Hamid in 1908. The result of the internal upheaval within the Ottoman Empire and the perception by others of its moment of apparent weakness was the onset of action against it by its enemies within and without. Austria annexed Bosnia and Herzegovina, Bulgaria declared its independence, and Crete announced its union with Greece.[21] This was only the beginning of a campaign of attrition which would erode away Ottoman possessions until the end of the First World War, when the division of the spoils by the victorious Allies resulted in the loss by the Empire of all the territory not actually populated by ethnic Turks, except that inhabited by the hapless Kurds. As the other non-Turkish subjects of the Ottoman Empire began to liberate themselves or to be liberated from Turkish rule, the Arabs too began to have their own ambitions to achieve self-rule.

At this early stage, the potential menace of Zionism was nothing more than a distant martial drum, unheard by the Arabs who were more preoccupied with problems which at the time seemed closer to home. A problem was to define an Arab nation, its bounds and its confines, as well as what drew together the Arab nation, with its Christian minorities among its Muslim masses, and its geographical diversity. That has remained an issue until the present day, when attempts at union between Arab states still remains an ambition of some Arabs. Meanwhile the defining role of Islam was always discussed, and is still a bone of contention between secular and religious nationalists.

Of course there had been earlier stirrings of Arab separatism during the nineteenth century, but it was in 1908, after the Young Turks

20. These details are provided by Albert Hourani in his essay "The Arab Awakening Forty Years Later", in *The Emergence of the Modern Middle East*, Macmillan, London 1981.

21. Bernard Lewis, *The Emergence of Modern Turkey*, Oxford University Press, London 1961, p. 210.

made their move and the Ottoman Empire faltered, that the Arabs first began consciously to organize. Arab intellectual and political societies came into being, involving Arab writers, teachers, soldiers, and political figures. The earliest agitation for Arab independence from the Ottoman Empire was the work of these groups, some of which worked in the open, while others were clandestine. By the time that the Hashemites, Feisal and Abdullah, the sons of Hussein, the Sharif of Mecca, came to Damascus with the British, there were many Arabs ready and waiting to make nationalist capital out of the British-aided triumph of the Hashemites.

The fact that Arab nationalism in the form it took in Palestine was a reaction to the Zionist thrust does not diminish its independent validity. Just as much as Zionism was a response to a threat, Arab nationalism was also in its own way the response to the challenge of imminent domination by the ethnic Turks. The Turks themselves were becoming more nationalistic, with the result that the Arabs feared the possibility of a regime perhaps even more unsympathetic than that of the old Ottoman Empire, where at least oppression was distributed impartially. Arab nationalism was also the embodiment of an idea that seemed increasingly to express the spirit of the times, and was certainly viewed favourably by the victorious powers at the conferences which followed the end of the war. Elsewhere than in Palestine the new Arab states which came under British and French protection were prepared, albeit with varying degrees of speed and commitment, for their full independence under Arab self-rule. Only in Palestine was there an ominous lack of movement, as the British administration tried and failed to extricate itself from the trap it had itself created with the ambiguous promises made to the Arabs and the Jews.

Arab Nationalism in Palestine Between the Wars

The apparently spontaneous riots of 1920 and 1921 were an early manifestation of Arab discontent. The promulgation of the Balfour Declaration in Palestine in May 1919 and the ambitious aims of the Zionists seem to have been the underlying reasons for the riots. As an observer of the scene recorded, the trouble was waiting to flare up, and seemed almost to have been seeking a spark to ignite it:

That was provided on the occasion of the Nabi Musa festivities on 4 April 1920, when a procession acclaiming Feisal passed through the Jaffa Gate . . . How it actually started has not been discovered. It was alleged that someone addressed the crowd, already excited, blaming the Jews for all the troubles in Palestine . . . In any case the Arabs attacked the Jews, with whatever weapons were at hand, sticks, stones and occasionally a knife . . . The crowds dispersed and in small groups attacked the Jews. Five Jews and four Arabs were killed and 211 Jews and 21 Arabs were wounded. The military forces took the situation in hand and order was restored after three days.[22]

Sir Ronald Storrs, the military governor of Jerusalem, made this comment: ". . . for the time, all the carefully built relations of understanding between British, Arabs and Jews seemed to flare away in an agony of fear and hatred."[23]

A person widely believed to have taken a hand in rousing the Arab crowds to violence in the riots was Hajj Amin al-Husseini, the brother of the Mufti of Jerusalem, the leading Muslim dignitary, and a kinsman of the modern Palestinian leader Feisal Husseini, the leader of the Palestinian delegation at the Washington peace talks in 1993. Hajj Amin was soon himself to be appointed by Sir Herbert Samuel to the office of Mufti, after his brother's death, but was at this stage seen as an agitator. In 1919, after the announcement in Palestine of the terms of the Balfour Declaration, Hajj Amin set up the Arab Club, one of a number of such organizations that came into being in Palestine as the Arabs grasped the importance of organisation and self-defence. On 12 April, the British tried to arrest Hajj Amin and succeeded only in causing offence to his brother the then Mufti and to the Arab Muslim community at large. Hajj Amin fled to Damascus, where the British writ did not run, where, with a few like-minded spirits he formed the Palestine Youth Society. The aim of all these groups was an independent Palestine, under Arab rule. At this early stage, Hajj Amin went further, and wanted Palestine to merge with Syria under the rule of Feisal.[24]

Samuel believed it was in the interest of the British administration to bring Arab nationalist figures into official circles, rather than to

22. M. E. Abcarius, *Palestine*, Hutchinson, London 1946.

23. Sir Ronald Storrs, *Orientations*, Ivor Nicholson and Watson Ltd., London 1939, p. 342.

24. Taysir Jbara, *Palestinian leader: Hajj Amin al-Husayni, Mufti of Jerusalem*, Kingston, Princeton 1985, pp. 32–4.

shut them out and allow them to become a focus for discontent, and this applied particularly to the influential Hajj Amin al-Husseini. In the event, Hajj Amin was appointed Mufti of Jerusalem in 1921, in succession to his brother, and also became the president of the Supreme Muslim Council set up by Sir Herbert Samuel to take independent charge of the religious affairs of the Muslim community of Palestine.

With the other old-established Palestinian families of Palestine, such as the Nashashibis and the Khalidis, the Husseini family roused and rallied the Arab population against the changes which were taking place in Palestine. Hajj Amin had his enemies among the British, some of whom believed that the Mufti's entrenched opposition to British policy and to Zionism was nothing but a millstone to British policy. Others simply believed him to be duplicitous and dishonest. His eventual defection to Berlin during the Second World War and his willingness to help the Germans to make propaganda was particularly galling to his later British critics, who saw it as a vindication of their earlier distrust.

In the event, Hajj Amin was a key figure during the Palestinian revolt of 1936, which led to the appointment of the Peel Commission of 1937, and perhaps would have been the head of some kind of Palestinian entity if the Second World War and his disastrous flirtation with Nazi Germany had not intervened. In April 1936, Arab leaders called a strike in Palestine, and Hajj Amin became president of the newly convened so-called Arab Higher Committee, which would determine Arab policy. The ordinary people suffered as the result of the withdrawal of Arab labour; the Arab leadership called off the strike, hoping for action in their favour from the Peel Commission to limit the increasing Jewish immigration and to control the activities of the Zionists. But the proposal for partition made in 1937 as the result of the Peel Commission, outraged the Arabs even though, as we have seen, it gave the Jews a relatively small area in the north of Palestine, and a strip of coastline.

A meeting of Arab delegates in Syria rejected partition totally, and the scene was set for the Arab uprising to begin again. The British dismissed Hajj Amin from his posts, and he fled the country. The Arab insurrection recommenced, this time in more deadly earnest. In 1938 69 British citizens, 292 Jews, and at least 1600 Arabs died in the fighting, while the world's press reported the growing unrest. In the words of the *New York Times* on 26 January 1938, "The hangman's black flag was hoisted three times today over Acre fortress as a grim token of Britain's determination to stamp out terror in Palestine."[25] Britain hoped to close this chapter in 1939, with the White Paper and the proposal for a bi-national Palestine and the limitation of Jewish immigration.

The Postwar World

After the war, the banner of Arab nationalism was taken up by a more moderate and secular leader, Musa al-Alami. A member of another of Palestine's old families, Musa al-Alami was able to use his legal training and his knowledge of British attitudes, which he had acquired while studying law at Cambridge University, to present himself in a way the British found more sympathetic. Speaking to the leader of Saudi Arabia, Musa al-Alami put the Arab position with the utmost succinctness: "We stand on the White Paper."[26] This was not to be, as we know. The Jews continued to organise and to lobby, while the Arabs failed to organise. After the war, the history of Jewish success was also the history of Arab failure, and the steady progress of the Jews towards the realisation of their state marked also the decline and frustration of remaining Arab hopes in Palestine.

It was not surprising, meanwhile, that the emerging truth of the extent and horror of the Holocaust, the programme for the extermination of Europe's Jewish population carried out by the Nazis, aroused a sympathy around the world for the Jews which virtually ensured the success of their endeavour to create a Jewish state in Palestine. In particular the sympathies of the United States of America were massively engaged. The British administration vainly tried to stick to a policy of limiting Jewish immigration ahead of a political settlement, but found themselves opposed not only to the Jewish population of Palestine and to the Zionist leadership but also to world opinion. Jewish guerrilla activity was now directed against the British, and culminated in what was perhaps the most spectacular incident, the blowing up on 22 July 1946 of the King David Hotel in Jerusalem, used by the British administration, which caused 91 deaths and embittered the British against the Jews.

25. Nicholas Bethell, *The Palestine Triangle*, André Deutsch, London 1979, p. 36.
26. Ibid., p. 195.

A conference was held in London in September 1946, which was boycotted by both Arabs and Jews. The Arabs stayed away because the British were unwilling to accept Hajj Amin al-Husseini as a delegate; the Jews because they were unwilling to accept the current plan put forward by Britain and the United States, which had since the end of the war become a key participant in the process of deciding the future of Palestine. This plan spoke of autonomous provinces for Arabs and Jews, but the Zionist leadership had now definitely opted for partition. The United States began to move in the direction of advocating partition, and partition was what was proposed in the end by the United Nations. A General Assembly resolution was passed on 29 November 1947 embodying a partition plan which gave the Jews 56 per cent of Palestine's land area, and Britain prepared to relinquish its Mandate over Palestine, which it did as midnight ushered in 15 May 1948 in London, the day it had said it would end its responsibility.

The United States considered plans for setting up some kind of United Nations Trusteeship over Palestine, which would have taken the place of the old League of Nations Mandate, but the Zionists successfully lobbied against their plan. The existence of the state of Israel was formally proclaimed on 14 May 1948, by David Ben Gurion in a ceremony in Jerusalem, and the new state was recognised the same day by President Truman of the United States. The war between the neighbouring Arab states and the Israelis in Palestine which followed that declaration will be discussed more fully later. In terms of the unfolding of Arab nationalism in its modern form in Palestine, the most significant feature of the conflict, and the disturbances which preceded and followed it, was the displacement of large parts of Palestine's Arab population. This is a subject on which much that is misleading has been written.

Historians who have looked at the events of the time from a Zionist point of view have tried to show that Arabs left their homes in Palestine at the instigation of their own leaders, who believed that they would shortly be able to return, after the end of a short conflict which the Arab armies would win. There is some truth in this position, though it does not serve in any sense as an excuse for Israeli aggression. On the other hand, some Arab historians have exaggerated the ruthlessness of the campaign to expel the Arabs, especially by some of the irregular Jewish formations, though it was undoubtedly brutal and certainly deliberate. Modern scholarship puts the matter into perspective, and perhaps if peace between the two sides in the conflict is achieved a historical consensus on the truth of the events of 1947 and 1948 may eventually be reached. From the Arab side, the book *Blaming the Victims*, edited by Edward Said and Christopher Hitchens[27] debunks some of the less plausible myths about how the Arabs came to leave their land, while from the standpoint of a revisionist Israeli historian, Benny Morris gives an impeccably sourced and reasonable account.[28]

The exodus meant that many young Palestinians were left to be brought up in refugee camps, in the Gaza Strip under Egyptian administration, or in the West Bank, soon to come under Jordanian sovereignty, as well as in the neighbouring countries. These were the seed beds of Palestinian nationalism, as the young men of the camps came to understand how they had been cut off from their homes and their land. In the camps, the mythology of the return to Palestine came to occupy a central role in the lives of a generation of displaced Palestinians, and the ideology of Palestinian nationalism spread throughout the whole Palestinian diaspora. It came eventually to permeate the entire Palestinian community abroad, involving Palestinians displaced from their homes who were able to make new lives for themselves and had travelled farther afield to other Arab states, to the Gulf, to Europe, or to the United States.

Palestinian nationalism also came to occupy a central role in the thinking of other Arab states. The Arab armies of Jordan, Iraq, Syria and Egypt had been involved in the fruitless war against Israel in 1948, and that left behind a legacy of resentment and humiliation at the defeat. The ease with which the Zionist leadership had transformed the Jewish community in Palestine into a state and had appropriated Arab land was a slur on the collective honour of the Arabs and seemed to present an ever-present danger to the international Arab community which no Arab government could ignore. The advent of a new generation of Arab leaders which began with the successful revolution in Egypt in 1952 led to growing international support for the Palestinians' own nationalist ideals, and ultimately to the formation of the Palestine Liberation Organization in 1964.

27. Edward Said and Christopher Hitchens, eds, *Blaming the Victims*, Verso, London and New York 1988.
28. Benny Morris, *The Birth of the Palestinian Refugee Problem, 1947–1948*, Cambridge University Press, Cambridge 1987.

Immovable Object; Irresistible Force

These, then, are the entrenched positions and their genesis; the sources of the bitter confrontation from which Israel and the Palestinians need now to extricate themselves. The history of the conflict goes back to the foundation of Israel, and in a sense its very existence is predicated on hostility to the Arabs. There is much anti-Arab feeling in Israel, on an instinctive rather than a thought-out level, which springs both from the long saga of confrontation and from the mythologies about the Arabs which took root in Jewish thinking as the need to expropriate and expel their Arab adversaries gave rise to the need for self-justification. At the same time, an anti-Jewish sentiment has sprung up among some Arabs which was scarcely a feature of Arab thought in Ottoman days or in the earlier times of the Arab empires. That is not an unnatural development, when it is the presence of the state of Israel, embodying the Zionist idea, which has seemed to flourish at the expense of Palestinian rights.

These instinctive antipathies will need to be examined and rejected by the parties to the dispute over Palestine's future, if they are to reach some accommodation. Zionism and Arab nationalism will need to identify for themselves separate arenas in which their ambitions can be independently realised without rancour or envy. If Israelis can forgo the ideal of occupying Eretz Israel, and the more extreme will abandon the belief that they have been allocated rights by God, there will be some hope of success. The Arabs must likewise limit their erstwhile political ambition to recover the whole territory of Palestine, while those who believe they have a religious mission must also relinquish their contention that Palestine cannot be other than a Muslim state. Then, when each side allows politics and realism to govern its aspirations, and realism to govern its politics, a new Palestine in which the state of Israel can exist alongside an Arab political entity will be able to emerge. In the process of negotiation in Oslo, the delegates soon discovered that the only way of making progress was to resolve always to look forward, and never back.

CHAPTER 3

NEGOTIATIONS, PRESENT AND PAST

A New Kind of Talking

What has been happening in the talks between Israel and the Palestinians is really new in two ways. One of these novel elements is that the Israelis have met the Palestinians face to face. The other is that there has been a new atmosphere of optimism, to contrast with the weary cynicism of former contacts. The two new features of the situation are both traceable to changes in the attitude of the chief protagonists, Yitzhak Rabin and Yasser Arafat. Rabin has always been in favour of a "peace of the brave", even when he was minister of defence in 1989 in the government led by the then Likud chief Yitzhak Shamir as Prime Minister. Rabin worked out the details of the so-called Shamir plan of May 1989. Now at the head of his own government, Rabin has been willing to seize the chance for real peace. He would like, say those who know him, to be remembered as a peace-maker.

Meanwhile Yasser Arafat has undergone an evolution towards what can be described as realism. Many of his aides and associates deplore his willingness to accept Palestinian autonomy in a very limited field, and some have left him as a result. But Arafat knows this is all he is going to get. During the 1968 student disturbances in Paris, a popular slogan was: "Be realistic: ask for the impossible." That might have its relevance to a student revolt which had no concrete aims and little hope of success, but it is not adequate for the needs of a mature statesman, and Arafat was 64 in 1993, who wants to achieve change in his lifetime.

Both the new elements are also in contrast with the *mélange* of futile clandestine meetings and vacuous public wrangling that have characterised earlier negotiations between Israel and the Arabs. In particular, it was refreshing in 1993 for diplomats from many countries who have tried to help resolve the Middle East problem to find that the Israeli government accepted, under American pressure, that it would need to talk to the Palestinians themselves rather than carry on trying to achieve the desired result through the intervention of a mediator. That was certainly the feeling in Cairo, where President Mubarak has for years tried to bring the Israelis and the Palestinians together. It was also the feeling in Brussels, where European Union leaders have long known that direct talks, abandoning the diplomatic reservations, the evasions, and the refusals to talk face to face which have characterised earlier attempts, were the only way to move forward. It was also the case in the Scandinavian capitals, where both the Swedish and the Norwegian governments, with their long history of involvement in international peacemaking, have hoped to use their relatively informal approach to produce a meeting of Arab and Israeli minds. Of course, in Oslo in particular the diplomats who fostered the 1993 breakthrough are basking in the knowledge that their efforts have borne fruit.

The problem in the past has been that Israel has always wanted to resolve the Palestinian problem, in the sense of seeing it disappear, but hoped it would be able to do that without the necessity of talking directly to the Palestinians. That was the aim of the Likud government in the late 1970s, after President Sadat's visit to Israel, when it seemed as if the Palestinian issue could after a fashion be resolved, at Camp David, perhaps by getting a major Arab state in effect to acquiesce in the status quo, in exchange for vague promises concerning the status of the Arab inhabitants of the Occupied Territories. To devise a policy to solve the Palestinian problem with the help of the intervention of an Arab state was also at the same period the policy of the Israeli Labour Party, then in opposition.

Abba Eban, at that time the Labour foreign affairs spokesman, was energetically lobbying in the late 1970s for what was known as the Jordanian option. This was the hope that Jordan would take back partial responsibility for the administration of the occupied West Bank and allow Israel to rid itself of the burden of administration while assuring its security needs. More extreme right-wingers were meanwhile already toying with a more extreme version of what might still be called the Jordanian option, envisaging a scenario in which Jordan would actually become a Palestinian state, to which Palestinians could if they wished move from the Occupied Territories. The so-called "transfer" of population became an issue for public discussion in Israel later in the 1980s.

The reason why Israel was so keen not to talk directly to the

Palestinians, either to the PLO which it regularly condemned as a terror organization which would for ever be excluded from any conceivable dialogue, or with any other Palestinian group, was connected intimately with the issue of recognition. It was precisely that hitherto unpalatable medicine which Israel swallowed in September 1993, when the letters of recognition were exchanged between Yitzhak Rabin and Yasser Arafat. Recognition of the Palestinians, in any form, had hitherto been seen by Israel as potentially implying the diminution of its own sovereignty. It was this line of thought which, famously, prompted Mrs Golda Meir, the Israeli Prime Minister of the early 1970s, not merely to refuse to recognise the Palestinians but to deny that they existed. In the past, therefore, the denial of recognition to the Palestinians has been a reflection of the centrality in Israeli thinking of the importance of its own recognition by others. To quote Henry Kissinger: "Of all Israel's nightmares, none was more elemental than the Palestine Liberation Organization, founded in 1964. The possibility that a group claiming all of Palestine for itself might gain any legitimacy whatever was considered a basic threat to Israel's survival. On the other hand the imminence of negotiations [in 1973] increased the PLO's ambitions for a role."[1]

In the early days of the existence of Israel as a state, the leadership was aware of the potentially precarious nature of its position, and of the extent to which its self-declaration depended on international acceptance. The recognition given to Israel by the United States on the first day of its independence was crucial to its ability to sustain its own justification of its right to exist. As a young statesman, Abba Eban recalls how thrilling was the vital moment when a sign saying "Israel", was placed in front of him for the first time at a United Nations negotiating table.[2] That thirst for recognition was not soon to depart. In 1956, when Israel played a part in the Anglo-French attack on Egypt over Suez, Ben Gurion was anxious, as well as to ensure Israel's security by undermining President Nasser of Egypt, for Israel to take part in an internationally organised operation on an equal footing with Britain and France, which would underline its status as a state and a power in the Middle East.[3]

1. Henry Kissinger, *Years of Upheaval*, Little Brown, Boston 1982, p. 624.

2. Abba Eban, *An Autobiography*, Weidenfeld and Nicolson, London 1978, p. 127.

3. Mordechai Bar-On, "David Ben-Gurion and the Sèvres Collusion", *Suez 1956*, ed. Roger Owen and Wm Roger Louis, OUP, Oxford 1989, p. 149.

We shall look in this chapter at phases of negotiation in the past between Israel and the Arabs, which have been in the main contacts between Israel and the neighbouring Arab states. The contrast between what has taken place in the past on the one hand, and what seems to be the nature of the present negotiations, underlines the differences that characterise the present phase of Israeli–Palestinian contacts. Even with the setbacks that have beset the new talks since they began, there has been a genuinely different spirit. Though there have been many difficulties, the degree of progress that has been made since the first meeting between Yitzhak Rabin and Yasser Arafat in September is a new departure in Middle East peace talks. Never before have Israelis and Palestinians sat down to talk about the details of a Palestinian autonomy which is envisaged as coming into being in the near future. The very fact of the ongoing meetings between Israelis and Palestinians from the PLO were in themselves a major breakthrough, and the relative amity with which they have been conducted has been impressive.

Though the first deadline was missed, when the hoped-for date of 13 December when the withdrawal of Israeli troops from positions in Gaza and Jericho was not met, optimism continued into 1994. The end of 1993 saw a period of relative disappointment. An attempt to recover the open spirit of the original Oslo talks failed, when renewed talks in Norway in December did not bear fruit, and a further round of talks in Paris was also unsuccessful. However, the negotiating process was eventually restarted in January 1994 after meetings between Arafat and Rabin, and much anxious negotiation behind the scenes, so that talks began again in January 1994. The upshot is that it does now seem hopeful that the optimism of some Palestinians that the ultimate outcome may be a state of their own is not misplaced. What caused the slow progress of the talks was the inability of the negotiators to agree on specific points, mainly concerning security and boundaries, but there have also been detractors of the peace process on both sides who have tried to hamper its progress. Those obstacles in the way of the negotiations which have led from the handshake in September need an assessment.

Internal Opposition

It is an understatement to say all has not run smoothly in the current negotiations which have followed the unveiling of the Oslo agreement.

Naturally, Yasser Arafat's radical opponents, from groups such as the Popular Front for the Liberation of Palestine, PFLP, and the Democratic Front for the Liberation of Palestine, DFLP, utterly reject the peace deal. The PFLP leader, George Habash, exercises an influence in the Occupied Territories which extends beyond the ranks of the extremists, and his frosty disapproval of the agreement may yet be a factor Chairman Arafat will need to worry about, just as he will also have to cope with the rejectionism of Hamas. More worryingly for Yasser Arafat, there have also been hostile comments from eminent and more mainstream Palestinian spokesmen, who in September began by showing a willingness to believe an end to the Israeli–Palestinian confrontation could be at hand, but who have since become deeply pessimistic.

For example, the eminent American Palestinian spokesman Professor Edward Said, who resigned some time ago from his seat as a member of the Palestine National Council, had this to say: "Let us call the agreement by its real name: an instrument of surrender, a Palestinian Versailles. What makes it worse is that for at least the past fifteen years the PLO could have negotiated a better arrangement than this . . ."[4] Undoubtedly, Edward Said is not alone in these views, and he certainly represents the points of view of some within the Palestinian diaspora. Intellectuals like Edward Said may have been unable to accept the willingness to compromise shown by the Palestinian participants in the talks, and their agreement to settle for small gains. For an old guard, this may have been too hard to reconcile with the aim of Palestinian nationalism: the recovery at least of the land lost in 1967 and a recognition at least of Palestinian moral rights in the whole historical territory of Palestine.

More alarming yet for the Palestinian leadership, some prominent Palestinians closer to the negotiation process began to lose heart. Even some of those who have been intimately associated with peace moves in recent years have implicitly expressed their pessimism by dissociating themselves from further talks. For example, the resignation in December of Hanan Ashrawi from her position as spokeswoman for the Washington negotiating team, robbed the Palestinians of an accomplished advocate of their cause, and of a television personality able to put over the Palestinian case to a Western audience in a convincing and sympathetic way. Hanan Ashrawi has expressed

4. Edward Said, "The Morning After", *London Review of Books*, 21 October 1993.

her intention of setting up institutions to monitor the democratic credentials of any new Palestinian administration that might come into being, as well as respect for human rights in the former Occupied Territories as they come under Palestinian control. The announced departure to an academic sabbatical in the United States of Sari Nusseibeh, another Palestinian intellectual from Bir Zeit University, was also a tacit vote of no confidence.

Palestinian discontent has also shown itself closer still to Yasser Arafat's power base, at the PLO headquarters itself in Tunis. By the time of the Washington handshake, only 11 members of the 18-member PLO Executive Committee were still attending meetings, because of their concern with what they saw as an increasing tendency on the part of the PLO to make what seemed to be excessive compromises with Israel. In December 1993, three more members of the PLO's executive committee temporarily distanced themselves from the organisation's decision-making procedures, including notably Mahmoud Abbas, who signed the document of agreement for the PLO on the White House lawn. The concern here seemed to be mainly a disagreement with Yasser Arafat's style of leadership, and the aim of the dissenters was to get a more open and democratic mode of operation into the PLO's decision-making procedure, especially where it concerned crucial and delicate negotiations with Israel.

Nevertheless, the balance of opinion remains on the side of optimism. The simple reason is that those at the heart of the decision-making process, on both the Israeli and the Palestinian sides of the fence, have come to the conclusion that the talks must be made to work. In the view of these pragmatists, there is no longer an alternative. In the balance against the pessimism of Edward Said, we may weigh the views of younger Palestinians who have taken a part in the Washington talks as advisers, such as Yezid Sayigh and Ahmed Khalidi. These technical specialists who have supported the Washington negotiating team throughout, and who are largely from a younger generation than the leadership, show a strong commitment to making the interim agreement between Israel and the PLO succeed.

It has been difficult to see what has distinguished those Palestinians within the PLO or close to it who have lost some of their faith in the peace process, from those who have doggedly continued to place their faith in the possibility of success. If anything, it is by the more seasoned nationalists that pessimism is evinced, people who may have been more influenced by ideological considerations. On the other hand, optimism is consistently coming from the side of the more pragmatic technocrats, many of them younger than their more political colleagues, or at least more open-minded. The conflict however seems not to be in principle one between generations, but rather a clash between representatives of different attitudes. Some at least of those for whom the struggle for Palestine has become an axiomatic part of their existence seem almost to want to go on struggling, rather than to aim at a settlement. They are perhaps reluctant to relinquish a part of their identity by settling for less than everything. Others on the other hand, the more pragmatic, are in favour of seizing the moment, and grasping what territory and political status they can.

Misgivings in Israel

Meanwhile there was also concern on the Israeli side as 1993 wore on that the negotiations did not go as well as had been hoped at the outset. By December, the question was beginning to be asked in Jerusalem and Tel Aviv: why has the peace process got bogged down. The secretary-general of the Israeli Labour Party Nissim Zwili said that the talks failed because the Palestinian negotiators were not sufficiently flexible. The problems which were proving at that time the most difficult to overcome, Zwili said, were always the same in successive negotiating sessions, namely the extent of the proposed Jericho autonomous zone, the security of frontiers and who would check the identity of those who come and go across them, and the security of the Jewish settlers who will remain. Of those points, the thorniest was the control over frontiers and crossing points.[5]

The Israeli government's view seemed to be that in demanding control over the frontiers, Yasser Arafat was in effect demanding sovereignty, which Israel was not prepared to concede. But if the problems were those of Arafat's negotiating stand, Nissim Zwili added that he was nevertheless without doubt that the PLO Chairman was the only possible negotiator with whom the Israeli government could deal. Another charge which the Israelis made at this stage in the talks

5. Nissim Zwili, interviewed in *Libération*, 21 December 1993.

was that the Palestinians had come unprepared. They had tended to make excessive demands, and hope that a compromise would be reached through bargaining. On the other hand, claimed the Israelis, the Palestinians did not seem to have thought their negotiating positions through in detail. Rightly or wrongly, the Israeli negotiators said that most of the detailed proposals had come from their side.

Inside Israel, it began to seem as if the antagonism shown to the peace agreement by some groups mirrored that within the Palestinian camp. Just as the anticipated opposition to the plans of Yasser Arafat shown by his determined enemies in Hamas, and by the Palestinian radicals, began to be reinforced by misgivings in his own camp, from long-time associates at the PLO headquarters in Tunis, so there was hostility from various quarters in Israel. The Likud opposition was passionately against what was happening, mirroring at the other end of the political spectrum the virulence of the opposition of the radical Palestinians. Likud's leader, Binyamin Netanyahu, promised strikes and obstruction, but did not succeed in rousing enough popular feeling to discourage Prime Minister Rabin and the other Labour advocates of the peace deal.

Further still to the right, an element in Israel whose importance, especially in their own eyes, is disproportionate to their numbers, is the settlers, who have gone to live in the Occupied Territories over which the Palestinians now hope steadily to regain their sovereignty. Their detestation of the settlement has a strong religious motivation, and it parallels that of Hamas, which claims an Islamic religious justification for the ownership of the land of Palestine in the same way as the religious settler movements, such as Gush Emunim, claim their own God-given right to the territory of Eretz Israel. They have staged violent demonstrations, directly against the Prime Minister and other members of the government, and have announced their unwillingness to comply with the changes which the agreement would bring about. In particular they scorn and reject the proposal of a Palestinian police authority.

On the other hand the Israeli government's policy is to insist on the right of settlers to stay in the Territories as areas are progressively handed over to Palestinian administration, but with the unspoken hope that they will gradually move out. A Labour Knesset member Yossi Katz said in December that up to 40,000 of the 100,000 Jewish settlers living in the West Bank and Gaza had already indicated they were willing to leave if the government was willing to provide them with sufficient compensation.[6] Enquiries by settlers seeking compensation were coming from the so-called commuter settlements, where most of the inhabitants work in Israel proper and live in the Territories because of the relative cheapness of property there. But residents also wanted to quit the settlement of Ariel, one of the biggest, and home to 13,000 people. Jewish settlers were paid compensation in 1982 when Sinai was handed back to Egypt, and the present generation hope the precedent will be applied to them. In the last resort, the major problem may come from the religious settlers, whose extremism is as virulent and unreasonable as that shown by some Hamas supporters on the Palestinian side.

Meanwhile, within Israeli government circles, not all were as sure in the months after the agreement was made that it would succeed as the team who oversaw the Oslo talks. Paradoxically, the doubters here were in the Prime Minister's own office. Yitzhak Rabin himself is said to have felt from the outset that the scheme left too many questions unanswered, and would lead to difficulties in the detailed negotiations needed to implement it. Those fears were justified by the snags hit by the negotiators in Taba, el-Arish and Cairo, as well as back in Oslo and Paris, in the closing months of 1993 and at the start of 1994. The peace deal's warmest supporter was Deputy Foreign Minister Yossi Beilin, who of course had been its instigator and had anxiously overseen the process which brought it into being. But Yossi Beilin has irritated parts of his own Labour Party by his radical views and his commitment to making the agreement work.

Other ministers believe he has gone too far and some of Labour's more hawkish cabinet members have even called for his resignation.[7] In early December, there were reports in Israel that the government had a secret plan to give full compliance to UN resolutions and return to the pre-1967 frontiers, which caused public alarm and anger. A Labour commentator said a complete withdrawal, retaining no foothold in the Occupied Territories for security purposes, was certainly not Labour's policy, though Labour does believe Israel should in due course withdraw from most of the Territories. So where had the reports originated? The possibility appeared to be that dissident Labour "hawks" had themselves begun the rumour in order

6. Reuters, 23 December 1993.

7. Leslie Susser, "Leading Rabin by the Nose", *The Jerusalem Report*, 30 December 1993.

to discredit the government's peace plan.[8] All these considerations must be set against the history of Arab–Israeli contacts and attempts at peacemaking, which go back as far as the existence of the state of Israel itself.

Early Contacts with Jordan

Though the progress made in the latest negotiations between Israel and the Palestinians may be something new, the idea of talks between Israelis and Arabs is not a new one. The two sides have a long history of public aloofness and private contact. However, what differentiates the current talks from earlier efforts may be Israel's attitude and its goals. From the inception of the state of Israel, Israeli politicians have hoped that a solution to the Palestinian problem would be presented to them by the neighbouring Arab states. The first occasion on which Israel hoped that, with the aid of its hostile but self-interested Arab neighbours, it would be able to rid itself of the incubus of the Palestinians was in 1948, after the war against the Arab states which followed the end of the Mandate and Israel's unilateral declaration of independence.

It was Transjordan, as Jordan was then known, on which Israel on this occasion placed its hopes for a solution of the Palestinian issue, and hoped would become a vehicle for the settlement of the potentially hostile Arab population of the part of Palestine which Israel did not occupy. While the Gaza Strip, with its now dense population of refugees, fell under Egyptian administration, the West Bank was annexed in due course by Jordan, a move which would put an end, so Israel hoped, to the Palestinian problem by making Jordan the Palestinians' home. "Jordan is Palestine": this was a slogan which it was hoped would by repetition become true. The Palestinians would come to regard Jordan as their home, and Amman would be the Palestinians' capital. This was a delusion which continued throughout the years to obsess Israelis of various political persuasions, from the so-called Jordanian solution favoured by Abba Eban in the 1970s to Ariel Sharon's plans to get rid of King Hussein and make Jordan a Palestinian state in the 1980s.

8. Susan Hattis Rollef, *Jerusalem Post, International Edition*, 25 December 1993.

In 1948, Israel was no longer interested in seeing the partition of the historic territory of Palestine between itself and a Palestinian state. Partition would, as we have seen, have been accepted by the Zionist leadership in 1937, and a vote for partition was the diplomatic outcome earnestly striven for and achieved by Israel's statesmen at the United Nations in 1947. But having fought for its new state in 1948 against the Palestinians and against the neighbouring Arab states, the Israeli government, as the Zionist leadership had now become, found itself by the force of arms in possession of much more of the territory of Palestine than it had expected. The conference at Lausanne between Israel and the neighbouring Arab states petered out in failure. Israel's reaction was that it was reluctant to see an independent Palestinian entity take control of any of the neighbouring territory, especially as it would have no control over the political direction of a Palestinian enclave, which seemed likely in practice to fall once more under the sway of the former Mufti, Hajj Amin al-Husseini.

For that reason, the first approach to Jordan was made. As early as 1947, Israeli representatives were in contact with King Abdullah. One of these was Golda Meir, later to be Prime Minister of Israel but who was at the time head of the political department of the Jewish Agency, met King Abdullah at Naharayim, on the River Jordan. According to Golda Meir, Abdullah undertook not to attack the Jews when the inevitable conflict came.[9] "He soon made the heart of the matter clear: he would not join in any Arab attack on us. He would always remain our friend, he said, and like us he wanted peace more than anything else." King Abdullah was not able to keep that promise, when the time came, because of his commitment to the Arab League, but the conflict between his troops and the Jewish forces was restrained.[10] Later, after the end of the war, there were prolonged negotiations with King Abdullah, which are the subject of a major study by the Oxford-based Israeli historian Avi Shlaim.[11] Exchanges between Israel and Jordan began to touch on a peace treaty, which was never signed.

There was a public and a private side to the Israeli talks with Jordan.

9. Golda Meir, *My Life*, Weidenfeld and Nicolson, London 1975, p. 176.

10. Benny Morris, *1948 and After*, Oxford University Press, London 1990, pp. 11–12.

11. Avi Shlaim, *The Politics of Partition*, Oxford University Press, Oxford 1990; abridged and revised from the same author's *Collusion Across the Jordan*, Oxford University Press, Oxford 1988.

Just as for two years from 1991 to 1993 the peace talks which were initiated in Madrid were carried on in the full glare of publicity in Washington, while behind the scenes contacts culminated in the breakthrough talks in Oslo, there was a public forum and a private one for the contacts between the Israelis and the Hashemite monarch. The official armistice talks began in the Greek island of Rhodes in March 1949, while the real negotiations took place in King Abdullah's winter palace at Shuneh in Jordan. This time the negotiators were Moshe Dayan, Walter Eytan, Yigael Yadin and Yehoshafat Harkabi, and the result was an agreement with Jordan effectively establishing the border line between Israel's territory and a West Bank which Jordan would occupy and in due course annex with Israel's tacit blessing, though without its explicit sanction.

Those talks were the first of many meetings in 1949 and 1950 where details and revisions of the proposed agreement were thrashed out, and culminated in Jordan's annexation of the West Bank. Israel would have liked a formal treaty with Jordan, in exchange for which it would have given its own recognition to the annexation. This did not happen, and relations with Jordan lapsed once more into sporadic hostility, but nonetheless, the lines of Israeli policy were clear. Israel hoped that it had expunged once and for all the possibility of the establishment of a Palestinian state, by conniving to put the Palestinians under Jordan's political authority, and to erase the remnants of sovereignty which the Palestinians might claim to have devolved to them after the end of the Mandate in areas neither assigned to them under the United Nations partition plan nor taken by force of arms.

Israeli links with Jordan were dealt a blow when King Abdullah was assassinated in 1951, on the steps of the Aqsa Mosque in Jerusalem, with the young Prince Hussein, now King Hussein of Jordan, at his elbow. The possibility of a peaceful settlement seemed to be at an end, and Israeli Prime Minister David Ben Gurion called for contingency plans for annexing the territory up to the Jordan River which he had hoped could have become Israel's in the 1948 war, and even for the annexation of Sinai. The seeds of Israel's participation in the 1956 Suez conflict were clearly already growing in Ben Gurion's mind. Relations across the frontier between Israel and Jordan became hostile, and as guerrilla infiltrators crossed the border into Israel the possibility of renewed military action intermittently loomed. Top-level contacts with Jordan were not to be renewed until the late 1960s, after the war of 1967 had effectively ended Arab hopes of beating Israel on the field of battle.

Later Overtures to Jordan

It is a commonplace that King Hussein of Jordan has developed clandestine contacts with successive Israeli governments over the quarter of a century which has elapsed since the end of the Arab–Israeli war of 1967, and especially since the last Arab–Israeli war in 1973, when Jordan stayed on the sidelines. He has met representatives of Israel while on trips abroad, in Britain and in the United States, and has maintained other discreet channels of communication. Stories abound of his meetings with Israelis in unusual circumstances, and there is even a recurrent tale that Israeli agents spirited him into the country and showed him, incognito, the sights of Tel Aviv and the nightlife of Dizengoff Street.

Jordanian contacts with Israel began to take on an almost official character in 1987 after the meeting in London between King Hussein and Shimon Peres, then as now Israel's Foreign Minister, though he was at the time acting as part of a Likud-led government. On 11 April 1987 Hussein and Peres agreed a document suggesting that an international conference on the Middle East should be held under the auspices of the United Nations, with the Security Council resolutions 242 and 338 as its guidelines, and that the Palestinian issue could be discussed in a meeting where Palestinian delegates would form part of a Jordanian delegation.[12] These ground rules foreshadowed the talks which actually opened in Madrid in October 1991, after the Gulf War was over.

Though the contacts were continued for the sake of keeping quasi-diplomatic channels open, they really lost their purpose when King Hussein renounced Jordan's administrative connection with the West Bank in his speech to the nation made on 31 July 1988. Until then, Jordan had continued in many ways to act as if the Occupied West Bank was still a part of the Kingdom of Jordan, paying its civil servants,

---

12. The text of the agreement is given by Madiha Madfai, *Jordan, the United States, and the Middle East Peace Process, 1974–1991*, Cambridge University Press, Cambridge 1993, p. 235.

looking after the educational system, and maintaining the fiction that the River Jordan was not an international frontier. King Hussein's announcement effectively closed off the so-called Jordanian option, and meant that Israel could no longer hope to look to Jordan to help it solve the Palestinian problem by taking the West Bank off its hands.

From then until 1991, relations between Israel and Jordan actually deteriorated, hitting a low point when King Hussein spoke out in favour of Iraq's President Saddam Hussein during the Gulf War. Today, however, the discourse in Israeli Labour circles once again concentrates on a new version of the Jordanian option, namely the need for a new Palestinian entity to be federated with Jordan. This appears to Israelis to be necessary for two reasons. One is that in their view the new entity will be too small to be wholly self-sufficient, and the second is that it would once again be a way of denying to the Palestinians the full recognition which Israel has always in the past feared would detract from its own sovereignty.

Kissinger: Israel and Egypt

Though peace efforts followed the 1967 war, notably the mediation of Dr Gunnar Jarring for the United Nations, and the so-called Rogers Plan of 1969, named for the then US Secretary of State William Rogers, these were mainly to do with settling the dispute between states. The earliest Israeli plan for the Occupied Territories following 1967 was the Allon Plan, which envisaged returning the West Bank to Jordan, while keeping a strategic line along the Jordan river. Though this never became official Labour policy, it coloured the thinking of Labour governments about the Occupied Territories until the Likud takeover in 1977. Under the Allon Plan settlements were held within the putative limits of Israeli control covering some 30 per cent of the area of the Territories. This was never really the basis for a possible arrangement between Israel and the Palestinians, who would have had to be represented by Jordan. But it was in the period that followed the war of 1973, while Jordan maintained its wary contacts with Israel, that other areas of contact between Israel and the Arabs were opened up, which were to lead ultimately to the Camp David peace talks. The war of 1973 brought about a major change. Though the Arabs in the end had not inflicted a defeat on Israel in 1973, they had shaken its own assumption of its invincibility. "Superman woke up one morning, and discovered he was just an ordinary guy," as the Israeli journalist Amnon Kapeliouk put it.[13] This also inclined Israel to be more aware than before of the need to take seriously the role of negotiation. The then United States Secretary of State Henry Kissinger points out that Israel won the battle in 1973, after some dangerous moments, but that the casualties it sustained were unacceptable and the confidence of both the country and the government were shaken. As Kissinger wrote in his memoirs: "Israel was exhausted no matter what the military maps showed. Its people were yearning for peace as can only those who have never known it."[14]

Even then, Israel combined a feeling of special vulnerability with the extraordinary conviction that the issue of the Palestinians and their rights had been kept alive by the world community in a quite unusual and unjustifiable way. The American Jewish author Saul Bellow reports the views of Israeli historian Jacob Talmon, expressed in conversation in 1976: "The 1973 war badly damaged [Israel's] confidence. The Egyptians crossed the Suez Canal. Suddenly the abyss opened up again. The United Nations bloc vote revived the feeling that she 'shall not be reckoned among the nations'. While Israel fought for life, debaters weighed her sins and especially the problem of the Palestinians. In this disorderly century refugees have fled from many countries. In India, in Africa, in Europe, millions of human beings have been put to flight, transported, enslaved, stampeded over the borders, left to starve, but only the case of the Palestinians is held permanently open."[15]

After the 1973 war an energetic diplomatic stance was taken by the United States, and the period of shuttle diplomacy began, when Henry Kissinger was mainly responsible for implementing American diplomacy. The United States was interested in seeing stability return to the region and, in a longer term, reduction of tension between Israel and its neighbours. The Americans were beginning to count the cost of sustaining a belligerent Israel in its wars against its neighbours, and were also coming to realise the significance of the Arab control of oil. For the United States, friendship with the Arabs, it was beginning to be perceived, would be as important in the future as ties with Israel.

---

13. Amnon Kapeliouk, *Israel: la fin des mythes*, Albin Michel, Paris 1975, p. 272.
14. Henry Kissinger, *Years of Upheaval*, Little Brown, Boston 1982, p. 560.
15. Saul Bellow, *To Jerusalem and Back*, Penguin Books, London 1977, p. 135.

An abortive conference was held under joint American and Soviet auspices at Geneva in late December 1973, attended by Israel, Jordan and Egypt, but was immediately adjourned and never reconvened.

Nevertheless, Kissinger succeeded in bringing about disengagement agreements between Israel and the Arab states which diminished the likelihood of further immediate hostilities and, incidentally, also brought the lifting of the Arab embargo on oil exports to the United States. Though it would be a mistake to suppose that the embargo was the sole motive for the American diplomatic effort, it certainly helped to concentrate Washington's attention. In making deals with its Arab neighbours, Israel's hope was that it might be spared the necessity of dealing directly with the Palestinian issue on its doorstep. If there had been no Palestinians, as Golda Meir had insisted, in defiance of the evident truth, Israel's task would have been easier. The Arabs within its frontiers could have had no national aspirations. But even if Israel had to admit that the Palestinians did in reality exist, reasoned the Israeli leadership, a framework of agreements with Arab neighbours could make them easier to deal with. If the Arab states had a vested interest in not disturbing the stability of their agreements with Israel, then they would be less likely to support Palestinian dissidence. This was at least one further motivation for Israel's willingness to go along with the kind of diplomacy in which Kissinger was engaging. Meanwhile, the United Nations upset Israel's hopes of sweeping the Palestinians out of sight by inviting PLO Chairman Yasser Arafat for the first time to address the General Assembly, in October 1974 shortly after the Arab summit in Rabat.

Though the agreements negotiated by Kissinger were a climbdown for Israel, for the Palestinians they were nugatory. All that had been achieved was to bring about the main American objective of reintroducing some stability into the relations between Israel and the neighbouring Arab states, and to offer some guarantees to Egypt and Israel, without addressing what for the Palestinians was the key issue. This was the problem of the territory lost by the Palestinians in successive wars, which had now culminated in the total loss of Palestinian territory in the occupation of the West Bank and Gaza in 1967. Israel had refused since the 1967 war, in the interests of its own security, to recognise the validity of United Nations resolution 242, which called for a return to the pre-1967 frontiers, and did not now seem inclined to be more flexible on that issue, in spite of the exercise of some American persuasion.

PLO guerrilla groups tried to upset the agreement and keep hostilities against Israel alive by attacking targets inside Israeli territory. Syria, then as now, stood out against contacts with Israel, and though it had entered into its own disengagement agreement with Israel it was adamant in its support for the Palestinians. It also backed the PLO, which was at this stage still an organization relatively new to the public arena and had operated effectively only since Yasser Arafat had succeeded to its leadership in 1969.

Nevertheless it was at this stage that the PLO began to be a factor in the international politics of the Middle East. The hijackings of airliners by Palestinian groups which began in 1968 had the effect of focusing the attention of the world on both the organisation and on the grievance of the Palestinians in the Middle East. The massive conflict between the Palestinians and the loyal Jordanian forces of King Hussein in 1970 also brought them very much to the forefront of attention. This was the episode now known as Black September, when the armed Palestinians were driven out of Jordan. From the world point of view, the Palestinians again leapt to the forefront of the stage when an armed group kidnapped and held hostage Israeli athletes at the Munich Olympic games in 1972. Nonetheless it was not until after the 1973 war that the Palestinian organization began to play a part on the political stage.

To quote Kissinger again: "It is difficult to remember now [i.e. in 1982] the relatively marginal role played by the PLO until after the October war . . . Until well into 1974, the common assumption was that Jordan, not the PLO, would negotiate with Israel over the West Bank."[16] Kissinger says that in an unexpected approach to the United States, Yasser Arafat indicated he was willing to negotiate while accepting the principle that Israel had a right to exist, but that he also raised the possibility of installing a Palestinian regime in Amman. This was unacceptable to the Americans, who saw King Hussein as a friend and ally of the United States. Kissinger also describes a secret meeting which took place between an American representative and the PLO in Rabat in November 1973. By 1976, at Syria's insistence, but with American acquiescence, the PLO was allowed to be represented and to put its case at a Security Council meeting. Given this range of contacts, it is not inconceivable that the government of Israel, whose Prime Minister was, then as now, Yitzhak Rabin, who was enjoying his

16. Henry Kissinger, op. cit., p. 503.

first period of office, could have taken the opportunity to sound out Palestinian views through the Americans, though this is of course speculation.

The Flight to Israel: Sadat in 1977

The most spectacular rapprochement between the Israelis and the Arabs at this period was of course President Anwar Sadat's precipitate flight to Israel in 1977 and his address to the Israeli parliament, the Knesset. That seemed at the time like a bolt from the blue. We now know it was preceded by a range of diplomatic contacts, through Morocco and Romania among others. But in general in the 1970s, in contrast to the obdurate Syrian stand, it was Egypt, under the leadership of President Sadat, which at this stage seemed most interested in the diplomatic process initiated by the Americans, and in contacts with Israel. Egypt's reward was ultimately to be the recovery of its territory in Sinai, which it had lost in 1967 and failed to recover in 1973.

Sadat was excoriated by the Arabs as the result of his volte-face towards Israel and the Camp David Accords of 1978, brokered by the leader of the new American administration, President Carter. That agreement led on to the peace treaty between Egypt and Israel, which was signed in 1979, but also brought an ostracisation of Egypt by the Arab world which was not to be revised until 1987, when most of the major Arab states re-established their links with Cairo. With the death of Sadat in 1983, the main obstacle to reconciliation had gone. The late president was killed by the bullets of assassins, who regarded him as a traitor, as he attended the military parade marking the celebration of the crossing of the Suez Canal by Egyptian forces in the 1973 war, and his death was an early indication of the upsurge of Islamic sentiment in Egypt.

Sadat's successor, Hosni Mubarak, was able to rebuild his links with the Arabs, persuading them that Egypt's value as an ally, and its latent power as the leader and coordinator of the Arab nations, was sufficient to outweigh anything to be gained by the Arabs from Egypt's continued isolation. In addition, as the mood in the Arab world has veered towards an increasing interest in solving peacefully the problem presented by Israel's existence, rather than perpetuating hostility, Egypt's peace treaty with Israel has begun to appear an advantage, providing the infrastructure for a channel of communication. That has been evident during the two years of the Madrid talks, and also during the post-Oslo negotiations, where the good auspices of Egypt and President Mubarak have been called on by the various parties.

Nonetheless, in spite of Egypt's return to the centre of the Arab diplomatic scene, it is clear that the Camp David Accords were in practice a betrayal of the Palestinians. On paper, the sections dealing with the resolution of the Palestinian problem do not look unlike the provisions of the interim accord agreed in Oslo. They envisage a self-governing authority, and a withdrawal of Israeli forces to strategic areas, with negotiations over a transitional period to determine the nature of the Palestinians' eventual status. An international body, consisting of representatives of Egypt, Israel, Jordan, and the self-governing Palestinian authority would determine issues connected with the return of refugees and the maintenance of law and order. Palestinian sovereignty is nowhere mentioned, and Israel would strenuously have rejected anything which might imply that Palestinian sovereignty had come into being, but nonetheless the agreements would have been something for the Palestinians of the Occupied Territories to grasp, if they had ever come into force.

In practice, the right-wing Likud government of Menachem Begin, who had been happy to sign the agreements, was determined to evade the handover to the Palestinians of any real autonomy. It was a paradox that the first great breakthrough in relations between Israel and the Arabs should have been put into effect by Israel's first right-wing Prime Minister. Begin had just come to power in the election of 1977, ending the unbroken run of Labour governments which had ruled Israel since its inception. But his new relationship with Sadat did not mean Begin changed his policies. Tentative approaches by Israel to Egypt, followed by cautious responses, had begun before Begin came to power, and he was the beneficiary of a diplomatic rapprochement he had not created. Instead of modifying its approach, Israel pressed on with a policy which was in effect extending its presence in and its control of the Occupied Territories, enhancing the powers of Israel's military government and encouraging settlers to implant themselves in the formerly Jordanian West Bank, and even in the Gaza Strip, administered by Egypt from 1948 to 1967, in apparent disregard of international law.

Begin's handshake with Anwar Sadat at Camp David, presided over by US President Carter, was as much trumpeted as the onset of a new phase as was the Rabin–Arafat meeting in September 1993. In retrospect, however, it was from the point of view of the Palestinians seen as no more than an exercise in hypocrisy. Indeed it was probably the last major manifestation of the process by which Israel hoped to be able to clinch a deal on the Palestinian issue with an Arab state, without involving the Palestinians themselves in any real way. It must also be said that Egypt's priority, once the agreement was in place, appeared to be the recovery of Sinai, and Egypt under President Sadat did not press Israel on the implementation of the part of the deal which concerned Palestinian self-rule. The process of handing Sinai back to Egypt, apart from the tiny Taba enclave, was completed in 1982.

The PLO Spreads its Wings

While Egypt was formally excluded from the field of Arab diplomacy, the PLO failed to make any impact on the headstrong policies of Israel either by military action or through diplomacy. Nevertheless, in terms of its diplomatic status and its international recognition, the PLO prospered. The European Community's Venice declaration of June 1980, as well as the so-called Reagan Plan of September 1982 and the resolution of the Fez Summit, held later that month, all backed Palestinian participation in peace talks. The Palestine National Council, which had been set up as the PLO's ultimate governing body, succeeded in acquiring more of the trappings of sovereignty and more international status. The organization declared itself to be the government of the independent state of Palestine in November 1988, and at the same time the PLO accepted the validity of UN resolution 242, with all that this implied in terms of the potential recognition of Israel, in order, as Arafat put it, to have a basis for negotiation.

The Arab League has always accepted the status of the delegation from the PLO as that of a sovereign body on a par with the other Arab states, but the PLO gradually and by careful diplomatic efforts extended beyond Arab circles the range of states and bodies which accorded it recognition. It was more widely accepted as an independent, sovereign entity, and was recognised by many states including the Soviet Union and China. Efforts were made by the organisation to acquire observer status in international bodies and institutions, and even, where possible, full membership of some international bodies. On 13 December 1988, in a move of great significance, Yasser Arafat addressed the United Nations General Assembly, at a meeting specially convened in Geneva to circumvent the refusal by the United States to give the PLO leader a visa. This was a different kind of occasion from Arafat's first address to the United Nations in 1973, when the PLO leader was riding on a wave of Third World backing. By 1988 he was seeking American approval. Arafat explicitly said in his address that he renounced terrorism as a weapon, and accepted the existence of Israel. He called for an international peace conference on the basis of UN resolution 242.

In the closing days of President Reagan's administration, the United States was at first unwilling to accept the PLO's position at face value. Mediation by Sweden gradually refined the wording of the PLO leader's statement, to a point where the United States could not go on refusing to accept it as a statement of recognition of Israel and renunciation of terrorism. The breakthrough for the PLO came when talks were held between PLO representatives and the American Ambassador in Tunisia in December 1988. Under the incoming US administration of President Bush, the dialogue between the PLO and the United States continued, though it was suspended in 1990 after the PLO leadership refused to condemn a guerrilla attack at an Israeli beach resort.

The outbreak of the intifada, the popular uprising against the Israeli authorities in the Occupied Territories, which began in December 1987, brought a new dimension to Palestinian diplomacy, and gave the Palestinian leadership a new card to play. Under pressure from the new American administration, which took a much more energetic stand towards Middle East peace than did that of President Reagan, there were a number of moves towards negotiation over the Palestinians and the status of the Occupied Territories. The Americans came up with the Baker Plan, devised by James Baker to meet Israeli objections to an earlier peace initiative launched by Egypt's President Mubarak, and from the Israeli side came the Shamir Plan, for elections and limited autonomy for the Palestinians, devised in fact by Yitzhak Rabin. Shimon Peres and Yitzhak Rabin, the veteran Labour politicians who were serving under Yitzhak Shamir in Israel's coalition, decided in March 1990 to break up the coalition government in Israel, where the right-wing Likud party had been cohabiting with Labour ministers, and after Labour failed to form a government, Likud continued to govern with support from Israel's religious political parties. At this stage the prospects for conciliation between Israel and the Palestinians looked weak.

The Gulf War: The Rules are Changed

Yitzhak Shamir's preferred approach to the Palestinian issue was always one of inaction, tempered by obfuscation. He was instinctively sympathetic to the ideas of his own party's extremists, and in his heart found a lot to agree with in the populist approach of Ariel Sharon, the architect of Israel's 1982 invasion of Lebanon and one of the country's military heroes, who made no secret of his desire to annex the Occupied Territories and if necessary expel the Palestinians. Shamir knew that this would step ahead of too great a segment of public opinion to be politically acceptable. But he had no intention of offering the Palestinians any real autonomy. On the other hand Shamir was under pressure from the outside world, and aware of Israel's deteriorating public image, as pictures from the intifada, of Israeli soldiers mistreating unarmed Palestinians, were seen on the world's television screens. It was this which induced Shamir in September 1989 to propose his own peace plan, essentially a resuscitation of the autonomy proposals from the Camp David Accords, devised by Yitzhak Rabin who was then Shamir's Defence Minister within the coalition government. Shamir's reaction was to keep his lines to the Americans open, and to continue to press his peace plan, but without any real intention of compromise with the Palestinians on any issue of substance. Even the American threat to withhold finance from Israel if the government did not cease to support the establishment of new Jewish settlements in the Occupied Territories did not in reality deflect Shamir from his chosen policies.

But with the Gulf crisis of 1990, and Iraq's invasion of Kuwait, the ground rules were irrevocably changed. The scale of the resulting upheaval caused the United States to change its assessment of its priorities in the Middle East, and the realities of regional politics were transformed. Under the leadership of President Bush, Washington put together an alliance of European and Arab states to eject the invading Iraqi forces from Kuwait, but Israel's role in the crisis was marginal. The United States was chiefly concerned to prevent uncontrolled Israeli reactions to Iraqi missile attacks, and wanted to keep Israel firmly out of the military side of the conflict.

In the aftermath of the war, the United States reassessed its strategic priorities in the Middle East, and decided that maintaining the new and stronger links it had constructed with Arab states was of an importance at least equivalent to that which it had previously put on US ties with Israel. That view was in due course strengthened by the collapse of the Soviet Union and the end of the Cold War, which reduced Israel's importance as a counterbalance and bulwark against Soviet penetration of the Middle East. For all these reasons, the Bush administration decided it was time to pull the Israeli government into line, and strong pressure was brought to bear which resulted in the opening of the Madrid peace talks in October 1991. The then Israeli Prime Minister Shamir brought to those talks all the reluctance he had previously shown towards discussing issues of substance concerning the Palestinians, but as we have seen, his replacement by Yitzhak Rabin after the elections of June 1992 brought a change of atmosphere. We shall look in more detail in the next chapter at the talks which grew out of the opening session in Madrid, and at the bilateral talks which accompanied them, as well as at the genesis of the Oslo meetings.

CHAPTER 4

THE MEETING IN MADRID

An Invitation from Washington

On 30 October the first session of the Madrid peace talks took place, at the Palacio Real in Madrid. That the talks took place at all was the result of intense pressure from the United States and, with hindsight, it is possible to see that the Oslo peace talks could never have been held if the Madrid conference had not preceded them, together with the successive rounds of bilateral peace talks which took place in Washington. The structure of the talks would be complex, and at the time when the first Madrid meeting took place was not yet fully crystallised. In the event, what was to happen was that the first plenary session of the conference would be the only occasion on which all the participants would meet to talk about the central issue. Thereafter, bilateral negotiations between Israel and each of the Arab delegations would discuss their separate problems. Later, in spite of the apparent determination of the Israelis at Madrid that this would not happen, the Israelis would begin to talk to the Palestinians separately from Jordan. Meanwhile the multilateral talks which were to discuss five issues of mutual concern, namely arms control, refugees, water, economic development, and the environment, would begin in various venues round the world.

Meanwhile at Madrid itself, the opening session of the conference was impressive. On one side of the table, under the glittering chandeliers, the classical tapestries and the ornate baroque ceiling of the old Royal Palace, sat the delegation from Israel, flanked on one side by Lebanon and on the other by Egypt, which was attending the talks as an observer. On the other side were Syria, the joint Jordanian and Palestinian delegation, and a delegation from the European Community, also in Madrid to observe. At the top table were the sponsors of the conference, President Bush and President Gorbachev, together with the Russian Foreign Minister Boris Pankin and US Secretary of State James Baker. The Spanish Prime Minister Felipe

Gonzalez presided over the meeting, as its formal host. But at bottom this was the Americans' show: United States diplomats were ubiquitous at the conference, and Washington had put in weeks of meticulous preparation for the event, whose entire costs were borne by the American government. The American diplomatic team was headed by Secretary of State James Baker, and the diplomats themselves were led by Dennis Ross, from the State Department's policy department. A Democrat by political background, as many State Department men are, Ross worked easily with the Republican administration's Middle East policy and, though he is himself Jewish, took a tough attitude towards Israel where the administration thought it necessary. Ross's deputy was William Burns, another cool State Department professional, and two Middle East experts Aaron Miller and Daniel Kurtzer hoped to formulate the State Department's even-handed policy. Finally Richard Haass, an academic by background, was President Bush's own adviser.[1] But however devoted and energtic the American diplomats were, they were conscious, nevertheless, that all depended on the attitudes of the principal participants, the Israelis and the Palestinians.

There was a marked difference in mood between the two delegations. The Palestinians were jubilant at their presence at the international negotiating table, and their satisfaction was increased by the diplomatic status granted to them by the Spanish government. At the same time, they were wary, and determined not to be put at a disadvantage. The Israelis on the other hand took their tone from Prime Minister Shamir, and came to the meeting with a sense of foreboding and a dour determination to protect Israel's interests in the most conservative way. Though the Israelis had secretly determined to attend the conference without any real intention of doing any actual negotiating, their presence was already a diplomatic climbdown for them, and a boost for the Palestinians. Not until the Likud government stepped down six months later and Yitzhak Rabin's Labour-led coalition took power in Israel would there be a real prospect of the talks coming up with any result. But just by sitting down at the conference table, the Israelis had already admitted that there was something to negotiate about, and that Middle East peace was an issue where substantive negotiation was needed. The Palestinians, even though, in deference to Israeli sensibilities, they sat in the room at this stage as part of the Jordanian delegation, were

1. "Focus", *Sunday Times*, 3 November 1991.

aware of the moral victory they had won. "We have reached a point from where there is no going back," said one Palestinian spokesman, Faisal Husseini. "Who, after Madrid, will be able to cut us down or sensibly describe us as a minority without rights?"[2] The journalist who reported those words, Shyam Bhatia, also made this comment: "As it so happens, the Palestinians are in an unusually strong position. Their status has been immeasurably enhanced by the opportunity of sitting as equals at the same table as Israeli Prime Minister Yitzhak Shamir. No television pictures have been able to convey the close proximity of the two delegations inside Madrid's seventeenth-century Royal Palace."[3]

All this had come about as the result of months of diplomatic pressure and urgent behind-the-scenes talking by American diplomatic emissaries, who had pressured the delegations to attend. Mr Shamir and the Israeli leadership had finally realised that they had no choice. The Americans had also achieved the difficult feat of bringing in the Syrians, who came to the conference in an aggressive mood, and did not lose the opportunity while there of levelling accusations at the Israelis and working hard to score points off them. Washington had been trying to make progress on Middle East peace since before the Gulf War, when Yitzhak Shamir's stubborn refusal in 1990 to consider peace talks had brought an end to the coalition government with Labour, when the government failed to win a vote of confidence on 15 March: the first time an Israeli government had fallen in this way. That was when Shamir decided to go it alone, with the backing of religious parties to ensure their parliamentary majority in the Knesset, in a period when the government stepped up its policy of backing Jewish settlement in the Occupied Territories in order to create "facts on the ground".

After the Gulf War, however, Israel could no longer shrug off Washington's pressure. As early as 6 March 1991, President Bush said that, as he put it, "the time has come to put an end to the conflict in the Middle East", and US Secretary of State James Baker began a sequence of gruelling negotiating trips to the region. President Bush's determination to get a peace agreement in the Middle East continued undiminished, and his verdict on the Middle East during his visit to Turkey in July 1991 was that "the time for peace is at hand". The

2. Shyam Bhatia, "Grasping the hand of peace", *The Observer*, 3 November 1991.
3. Ibid.

American leader had made clear since the end of the Gulf War his determination to make every effort to settle the Arab–Israeli issue. Later the same month, James Baker visited Israel, bringing with him President Bush's proposal for a Middle East peace conference to begin in October. It was the fifth strenuous Middle East visit for Baker in the space of five months, and at last he had a tangible result from Damascus. The inducement James Baker brought with him to present to Israel's hard-line, right-wing Prime Minister Yitzhak Shamir was an indication from President Assad of Syria that he was ready for talks. Syria's grievance was the loss of the Golan Heights, captured by Israel from Syria in 1967 and declared by Israel in 1981 to have been annexed. Baker had convinced Damascus that it was at least worth talking to Israel about the issue. All the Arab governments which shared frontiers with Israel, were now willing to attend a peace conference.

The Israeli leader told Mr Baker that he would be willing to talk, but he did so in such a way as to avoid making any concessions. Diplomatic observers differed in their interpretation of Israel's acceptance of the talks. Optimists felt that Israel's agreement to enter negotiations was the necessary first step to real peace talks and that once begun the talks might lead on to a useful outcome. Pessimists declined to underestimate Shamir's ability to stonewall, and to go through the motions of negotiating without actually giving anything away. Yitzhak Shamir agreed in principle to go to the negotiating table as President Bush wanted, largely because the Americans made no preconditions about what would come under discussion. Anticipating American attempts to put pressure on Israel, David Levy, Shamir's Foreign Minister, said such efforts would only be counter-productive. Analysts were amazed at Israel's capacity to attempt to dictate United States policy, even though it had lost many of its bargaining cards. On the other hand, it should be said that some prescient observers suggested that in agreeing to go to the talks, Shamir had probably sacrificed his own political future, and as events turned out he fell from power in June 1992, when Labour won the election that followed the collapse of his parliamentary coalition.

The United States had no hesitation in putting pressure on Shamir, because Israel no longer appeared to the United States as a valuable ally for America to counterbalance the Communist-supported Arab countries: on the contrary, it had become an expensive diversion. According to Seymour Hersh, in his book *The Samson Option*, Israel had readied its nuclear weapons during the Gulf War for a pre-emptive strike against Iraq in the event of further Iraqi missile attacks on Tel Aviv.[4] That alone was enough to impress on Washington the urgency of bringing Israel's right-wing government to heel. But, as it was in due course to appear, what Shamir and his ministers were planning was to meet with delegations from the Arab states, including if necessary, a Jordanian delegation comprising some Palestinians among its membership, without actually ever proceeding to negotiations in substance. In exchange for what would therefore be only an apparent increase in its flexibility, rather than a real one, Israel hoped to be able to continue to derive the benefits from the United States to which it had become accustomed.

The Loan Guarantees: Washington's Lever

In the summer of 1991, the central and most important of those benefits which Israel was anxious to secure was the guarantee to back loans totalling ten billion dollars which the leadership had asked for from the United States, to help settle incoming migrants from the Soviet Union. Israel had already received 300,000 Soviet and Ethiopian Jews since the beginning of 1990, and was looking forward to the arrival of a further half million by the end of 1993. The loans Israel wanted would build houses for the new migrants and help to ease their transition into Israeli society. The principle was that Israel would borrow the money from commercial and international sources, but would be able to get easier credit and better terms of repayment because the United States would guarantee that money lent to Israel would unfailingly be reimbursed. Sceptics suggested that in practice, in the likely absence of enough willing creditors, the United States would itself almost certainly be the source of at least a substantial part of the money. However, having agreed in principle to attend peace talks, Israel anticipated little trouble in getting the money.

The United States turned out to be tougher than Israel had anticipated. In addition to asking for Israel's presence at the peace

4. Seymour Hersh, *The Samson Option*, Faber and Faber, London 1991, paperback edition 1993, p. 318.

talks, Washington also demanded in private that Israel should put a stop to building new settlements in the Occupied Territories, at least until talks had taken place. The reason was to forestall what had become virtually an explicit Israeli policy: to change the situation on the ground by putting Israeli settlers into the West Bank, and even into the Gaza Strip, in order to make it more unlikely that Israel would be pressed to yield territory to the Palestinians in which some Israelis had already established themselves. President Bush had been firm in his opposition to Israel's settlement policy throughout the two and a half years of his presidency, and decided that he would use all the power at his disposal to end the settlements. The loan guarantees, in President Bush's view, should not be looked at until after peace talks had begun. The sudden tightening of American pressure on Israel was to come in September.

On 8 September Prime Minister Shamir told Israel Radio that he believed it would be a mistake for the United States to make its financial assistance to Israel for the first time conditional on political concessions from Israel. He said: "The moment the Arabs get a gift like this they will dance on the roofs, the level of their demands will go up, and this will not permit a peace process."[5] The Israeli leadership was already scheming to subvert President Bush's stubbornness over the loan guarantees by launching a political manoeuvre in Washington involving US senators and congressmen favourable to Israel. In spite of Shamir's warnings, President Bush made it clear to Shamir on 12 September 1991 that he would block any attempt planned by the Israeli leader to persuade Congress to vote through the loan guarantees which the administration did not want to give.

Shamir's plan was to attempt to call in the debt owed to him by American legislators who had received help or funds from AIPAC, the American Israel Public Affairs Committee, by asking Congress to vote the money for Israel in defiance of the US President's wishes. His hope was that the US administration would bow to a vote in Congress. But President Bush indicated that he was prepared to use all his political muscle to prevent Congress from overriding his wish to defer consideration of the loan guarantees until after an Arab–Israeli peace conference had taken place. Officials in Israel called Bush's promise to use his veto "a bombshell" and "a declaration of war", and the

5. Ian Black, "Shamir tells US not to link aid to peace", *The Guardian*, 9 September 1991.

popular newspaper *Yediot Aharonot* said the President's stand was anti-semitic.[6]

A week later, on 18 September, James Baker dropped a further bombshell on the Israelis when he announced that the American administration would actually withhold the ten billion dollars in loan guarantees for Israel unless the Shamir government stopped building new settlements in the Occupied Territories. This was the first time the United States had made economic aid to Israel conditional on the adoption of specific policies by Israel, and marked a major turning-point. This was a break with the past, in which Washington had been content simply to pay the bills and to allow Israeli governments a free hand in making their own policy. Baker is reported to have said: "It is a case, frankly, of not being able to justify in our own minds, or the other parties in the peace process, an unconditional ten billion dollar infusion that doesn't have restrictions . . . on the question of settlements."[7]

The upshot of the confrontation was that President Bush won the day. His threat to use his power of veto to stop the loan guarantees going through was enough to deter the pro-Israel lobby from trying to force the issue. A two-thirds vote of the US Congress is enough to override the Presidential veto which can overturn a simple Congressional majority. But by 25 September the President's opponents had to concede they could not achieve a two-thirds majority, and the issue was never put to the test. On 2 October the US Senate formally accepted President Bush's plan to delay consideration of the loan guarantees. One effect of this which has subsequently pervaded the relationship between the United States and Israel is that it transformed the attitude of the American administration to the pro-Israel lobby in America in general and to AIPAC in particular. Polls taken at the end of September indicated that 69 per cent of the American people backed President Bush's stand on the loan guarantees, while as many as 44 per cent were unsure that Israel should be receiving the three billion dollars of American aid it gets each year. With this popular backing, Bush decided to defy the Jewish lobbyists. Ironically, by November 1991, after the Madrid talks had taken place, a survey of influential American Jews indicated that by now they were backing

6. Ian Black, "Bush upsets the Israelis", *The Guardian*, 14 September, 1993.

7. John Lichfield, "Washington turns up the heat on Shamir", *The Independent*, 19 September 1991.

Bush and favoured the idea of a territorial compromise in Palestine.[8]
All this meant that Israel would come to the peace conference, and
come on the Americans' terms rather than on their own.

On 20 October 1991, after a long and cliff-hanging internal debate
in Israel, the Israeli cabinet finally voted to go to the talks in Madrid.
Shamir spoke of his "heavy heart" at having to agree to go to the
conference.[9] The decision was a tough one, and infuriated erstwhile
right-wing supporters of Yitzhak Shamir. Only after a cabinet meeting
seven hours long did Shamir succeed in persuading his ministers to
back the deal, and in the end he lost the support of Yuval Ne'eman
and his far-right Tehiya party. That still left the Likud-led alliance with
a Knesset majority, and Shamir went ahead with his plan to go to
Spain for the talks. Shamir got his cabinet's agreement by stressing
that Israel would take up the toughest posture at the talks and would
not agree to exchange land in the Occupied Territories for peace. On
the other hand, the Prime Minister also in the end probably made a
tactical error by limiting the scope of his delegation to right-wingers of
his own persuasion. He excluded Israel's then Foreign Minister David
Levy, an oriental Jew of Moroccan origin who would have represented
Israel's important Sephardic community, and he also totally excluded
the Labour Party, even his old coalition partners Yitzhak Rabin and
Shimon Peres, experienced statesmen with more history of contact
with the Arabs than Shamir himself.

Israel also planned to restrict the Palestinians' freedom to choose
the membership of its delegation by insisting on vetting the
Palestinian members. Only Palestinians from the Occupied Territories
would meet Israel's criteria, residents of East Jerusalem would be
excluded, since that was regarded by the Israelis as their own
sovereign territory, and no one with close links with the PLO would be
permitted. In addition, the delegation would have to refrain from any
explicit declaration that it represented the PLO. In spite of these
restrictions, hardliners like the Housing Minister Ariel Sharon, a
former Israeli military hero and the architect of Israel's invasion of
Lebanon in 1982, said he would continue to oppose Israel's
participation. Meanwhile the Defence Minister Moshe Arens summed

8. Michael Sheridan, "American Jews press Israel over peace", *The Independent*,
22 November 1993.

9. Michael Sheridan, "Israel agrees to attend the peace conference", *The
Independent*, 21 October 1991.

up the Likud attitude when he came out of the cabinet meeting and told reporters that the Israeli government would "stand firm" against superpower pressure and would surrender nothing.

Palestinian Participation

On the other side of the fence, the Palestinians had also been agonising over their attitude to the talks. The invitation to Middle East peace talks was one which the Palestinian leadership was unlikely to refuse, but nonetheless Arafat faced the task of selling the idea of peace talks both to his friends and to his enemies within the Palestinian movement. There was resistance even from his own supporters, members of the PLO, and even of his own group Fatah, the largest faction within the PLO, as well as from other Palestinian activists both inside and outside the Occupied Territories. For many Palestinians it has been hard to follow Arafat's own political evolution, from the moment he decided first to make the speech recognising Israel in December 1988 up to the Washington agreement of September 1993. They began in 1991 to suspect Arafat's motives, and some accuse him of making excessive concessions to Israel while receiving little or nothing in return, with power for himself as his main objective. Meanwhile for Palestinians who have spent their lives dreaming of the recovery of their lost land, Arafat's chosen course of action seems to have given away all hope of achieving the traditional objective. For Palestinians within the Occupied Territories, on the other hand, especially the young who by 1991 had devoted themselves for almost four years to the intifada, Arafat seemed to be in the process of robbing their struggle of meaning.

These concerns were also expressed on a political level within the Palestinian movement. A summons from Washington to come to the negotiating table, in the radical view, was no more than an opportunity for the Palestinians publicly to give away their rights to Israel, in a fashion and in a context which would make it very hard for a future Palestinian leadership to reverse. There were and are radical movements within the broad umbrella of the PLO which were bound to oppose Arafat's position. The stand of the radical factions of the PLO was that the talks constituted an invitation to the Palestinians to sell out their hopes of a just settlement. The Popular Front for the Liberation of Palestine (PFLP) led by George Habash, and the Democratic Front for the Liberation of Palestine, DFLP, led by Nayef Hawatmeh, were the two principal groups that looked askance at the American invitation, and they are still the most significant of the group of some ten small radical factions based in Damascus which oppose the pro-peace posture of Fatah. These two groups oppose Arafat from within the PLO. Other factions stand outside the PLO, and these are numerically smaller but more violent and potentially a threat to peace. Of these the most serious are the splinter group led by Ahmed Jibril, known as the PFLP General Command, and the Abu Nidal faction, which Abu Nidal calls the Fatah Revolutionary Council.

Arafat has always had his opponents within the Palestinian movement, but the anguish felt by even some of his supporters at his willingness to engage in what they saw as a futile peace process was acute. Palestinians pointed out that Israel had announced in advance that it would refuse to talk face to face with the PLO, or indeed with any Palestinian delegation that was not under the Jordanian umbrella, and would yield no territory. The opposition to Arafat was an about-face, after the surge in his popularity among the Palestinians during the Gulf War, especially those in the Occupied Territories. From the Iraqi invasion of Kuwait in August 1990 up to the end of the war in March 1991, Arafat expressed his defiance of the Americans and his support for Iraq's President Saddam Hussein. That appealed to the Palestinians, who saw Iraq as the only Arab state successfully to have defied American power, while they also identified the United States as Israel's principal backer, and therefore also as their opponent. During the Gulf conflict, the Palestinians of the Occupied Territories, who had felt themselves oppressed by the Israelis since 1967, could not forbear to cheer as they saw the Iraqi Scud missiles strike targets in Israel, and they felt that they and Arafat were striking a blow against Israel in defying the United States.

As Kuwait was finally liberated, American diplomats in the Middle East made it clear that they did not now regard Arafat as qualified to take part in any Middle East peace negotiations. Because of that hostility, expressed by the Americans only a few months before, many Palestinians suspected that the aim of the talks was only to give a veneer of respectability to a "solution" whose real aim was to strengthen Israel's position. But in fact, that suspicion of the American aim, though it might have had some justification at the start, seemed to become less applicable as the summer of 1991 wore on. American policy-makers appeared to make the decision to rehabilitate Arafat and the PLO, on the grounds that if meaningful talks were to be held, the Israeli side must be faced by a credible interlocutor, and most importantly one whose mandate to speak would be accepted by the Palestinians. They therefore decided to connive at the restoration of Yasser Arafat's credibility.

Of course, at this stage, it was probably too early to have attempted to challenge Israel's refusal to talk face to face with the PLO, so the Palestinians' representatives at the opening conference in Madrid were from the Occupied Territories, as Israel insisted, and were free of formal connection with the PLO. But the presence of the PLO behind the scenes was tacitly accepted from the first, and while Dr Haidar Abdel-Shafi spoke for the Palestinians inside the conference chamber, the real organising power behind the Palestinian delegation was Faisal Husseini, an associate of Yasser Arafat and in effect the PLO's principal spokesman in the Occupied Territories. Faisal Husseini's father, Abdelkader, was a nephew of Hajj Amin al-Husseini, the mufti of Jerusalem who played such an important role in the days of the Mandate. To underline Husseini's primacy, it was to him that the official letter inviting the Palestinian delegation to the conference was delivered by the American Consul-General in Jerusalem on 19 October.

The PLO Gives its Approval

The Palestinian decision to go to the talks was not, of course, Arafat's personal decision. It had to be squared with the PLO and the Palestinian movement. Approval had to be given by a meeting of the Palestine National Council, the PLO's ultimate decision-making body. By the time that meeting was called, at the end of September 1991, the Americans had moved from the dismissive stance towards the PLO they had shown just six months earlier to a very real anxiety to see formal PLO approval given to the Palestinian delegation. The United States was now very aware of the importance of the Palestine National Council's decision, and wanted to give Arafat all the help it could to obtain the Council's approval.

By this stage the Americans had realised that even if the Israelis continued with the charade of refusing to recognise, acknowledge or talk to the PLO, it would be only if the Palestinian delegation had the PLO's full blessing that the talks would be accepted by the majority of Palestinians as a valid dialogue between Israel and a truly representative Palestinian body. By mid-September it had begun to seem as if the Palestinians would be doing the United States a favour by coming to the talks, rather than the other way round. The Americans were at this point pressurising Faisal Husseini and his colleague Hanan Ashrawi to agree that a Palestinian delegation must attend the conference. Hanan Ashrawi, a senior academic in the field of English literature and a specialist in Chaucer at the University of Bir Zeit, was soon to achieve media prominence as the Palestinian spokeswoman at Madrid and through the eleven rounds of subsequent negotiations begun by the Madrid conference. It appeared at the time that at a meeting on 20 September, James Baker had given the Palestinians assurances on three points which were to prove virtually impossible to realise as the negotiations wore on in practice. These were, that Israel would recognise Palestinian sovereignty in some area of territory to be defined, that East Jerusalem would be negotiable, and that Jewish settlement in the Occupied Territories would cease. Only the third of these had actually been reached by 1994, and that only according to a particular definition of the Occupied Territories. Baker's assurances were nevertheless enough to help Arafat swing the Palestine National Council meeting round to his point of view.

The Palestine National Council convened at its usual venue in Algiers three day later, on 23 September 1991. Yasser Arafat's opening speech in his capacity as Chairman of the PLO, probably the most critical in his life, was an earnest plea for support, and he spoke of what he called a "precious opportunity" for peace.[10] Arafat spoke calmly and firmly for 45 minutes, in a speech which was businesslike but determined. The meeting and the debate were to last five days, but Arafat carried the day in the end. On 27 September the Palestine National Council backed Arafat's stand by 256 votes in favour and 68 against, with 12 abstentions. In the end, the PFLP leader George Habash made a threat during the deliberations to take his faction out of the PLO entirely if the meeting voted to endorse the presence of Palestinian delegates in Madrid, but though he and his supporters voted against Madrid he decided to stay inside the organisation. Only

---

10. David Hirst, "Arafat backs precious opportunity", *The Guardian*, 24 September 1991.

Abul Abbas, the leader of the small Palestine Liberation Front, stepped down from the PLO's day-to-day decision-making body, the Executive Committee, after the vote. The contribution of the PLF to a peaceful dialogue would in any case have been small: it was Abul Abbas's men who were responsible for the abortive raid on an Israeli beach in 1990 which had ended the dialogue between the United States and the PLO in Tunis when Arafat refused to apologise for it. In spite of the apparent forbearance of Habash and Hawatmeh at Algiers, however, they were within weeks to form the nucleus of a group of ten "rejectionist" Palestinian groups which would base itself in Damascus, paradoxically receiving the moral backing of the Syrian regime in spite of Syria's own participation in the talks.

In retrospect, it seems that the vital compliance of the Palestine National Council was probably bought by allowing a list of qualifications to be added to the motion it passed welcoming the call for a conference. There were six main conditions. Firstly, the meeting demanded that the conference should be based on what was described as "international legality", in other words UN resolutions 242 and 338. It should also be made conditional on the recognition that East Jerusalem forms part of the Occupied Territories; and on the halting of Jewish Settlements in the West Bank and Gaza. The PLO must have a free hand in picking the delegation. There must be linkage between the stages of negotiation leading to a final resolution: a condition aimed to ensure that the Palestinians do not become bogged down at the point of achieving some form of autonomy, stopping short of the desired goal of independence. And finally the Palestinians and the Arab states should coordinate their bargaining positions, with the aim of achieving the maximum effect, and also to avoid separate solutions emerging for any of the Arab states which would ignore the needs of the Palestinians. This last condition sprang from the lingering resentment felt by the Palestinians at the lack of outcome for them from Camp David, which nevertheless got Sinai back for Egypt.

Virtually the only one of these conditions which was actually complied with by the PLO leadership and the Palestinian delegation before the conference actually met was the call for coordination with the Arab states. This actually took place, and had the useful effect of boosting Arafat's status before the Madrid conference began. The rift between Syria and Yasser Arafat was deep, since Syria had lent its support to the American-led coalition in the Gulf War while Arafat had sympathised with the Iraqi leader Saddam Hussein. The meeting which took place in Damascus on 23 October, when the Syrian and Egyptian foreign ministers sat with Farouk Kaddoumi, the PLO's foreign affairs spokesman, served a double purpose. It brought the PLO back into amicable consultation with Arab nations with which it had just six months earlier been on the worst of terms, and it also helped to strengthen the impression desired by the PLO that it already enjoyed the international status which it hoped it had conferred on itself by its declaration of independence in 1988. A pragmatic stance was eventually struck by the Palestinians, who were keenly aware that it was the internal struggle, the intifada, which had put them back on to the international agenda. For the moment at least, the intifada would not be abandoned, and the struggle would continue on two fronts, resistance on the ground on the one hand, and diplomacy on the other. Later the role of the intifada would come to be re-examined.

Madrid Convenes

The Madrid conference was opened on 30 October by President Bush, who laid down both the general objectives and the ground rules under which talks were to be held. He pleased the Palestinians and unsettled the Israelis when he spoke about territory: cutting across Yitzhak Shamir's known preoccupation with the idea that the clash between Israel and the Palestinians was not a territorial issue. What was needed from the talks, said President Bush, was a "stable and enduring settlement". But to achieve that, he added, "territorial compromise is essential for peace". The United States leader went on to stress that talks must be held on the basis of UN resolutions 242 and 338, which require the return of land taken by Israel in the war of 1967. Those resolutions may or may not call for the return of the whole of the Occupied Territories, a question which pivots on the precise interpretation of the text (see the Appendix), but certainly call for the exchange of land for peace. President Bush said the objective was not "to end the state of war in the Middle East and replace it with a state of non-belligerency". This, he said, would not last. President Bush also revealed that his aim was an idealistic one. What he wanted to see, he said, was this: "A Middle East where vast resources are not devoted to armaments. A Middle East where young people no longer have to dedicate and all too often give their lives to combat. A Middle East no longer victimised by fear and terror. A Middle East where normal men and women lead normal lives."[11]

When the delegates began to make their speeches, the Palestinians won a victory over the Israelis in terms of their rhetoric, which gave them an impact on the conference and through the media on the world at large that Israel could not match. Faisal Husseini and the spokeswoman, Hanan Ashrawi, because of their residence in East Jerusalem, were not allowed to front the Palestinian delegation. Israel had not merely affected unconcern with the Palestine National Council's deliberations, but had also insisted that the Palestinian delegation should in no way claim any connection with the PLO. The delegation was actually headed by a figure hitherto almost unknown outside Palestinian circles, Haidar Abdel-Shafi: a doctor from the Gaza Strip, and a man with an immense reputation for probity and for fidelity to the Palestinian cause. Aged 72, Haidar Abdel-Shafi was chairman of the Red Crescent Society in Gaza, and a supporter of Yasser Arafat, who served three years in detention for his PLO links.

The faith shown by Arafat and other Palestinian leaders that the symbolic impact of the meeting in Madrid would transform the world's view of the Palestinians was in the event fully justified, thanks to Haidar Abdel-Shafi's oratory. The head of the Palestinian delegation made his debut on the stage of world politics with a simple but well-constructed plea which made an eloquent appeal to all its listeners. He turned first to the international delegations and to the wider international audience he knew was listening to his words:

> We, the people of Palestine, stand before you in the fullness of our pain, our pride and our anticipation. For too long the Palestinian people have gone unheeded, silenced and denied – our identity negated by political expediency, our rightful struggle against injustice maligned and our present existence subsumed by the past tragedy of another people. This is the moment of truth. The people of Palestine look at you with a straightforward direct gaze, seeking to touch your heart, for you have dared to stir up hopes that cannot be abandoned.

Haidar Abdel-Shafi also directly addressed the Israelis themselves:

> We wish to directly address the Israeli people, with whom we have had a long experience of pain. Let us share hope instead. We are willing to

11. Text from *The Times*, 31 October 1991.

live side by side on the land and promise of the future. We have seen you at your best and at your worst, for the occupier can hide no secrets from the occupied, and we are witness to the toll that occupation has exacted from you and yours. We have seen your anguish over the transformation of your sons and daughters into instruments of blind and violent occupation – and we are sure that at no time did you envisage such a role for the children you thought would forge your future. We have seen you look back in the deepest sorrow at the tragedy of your past and look on in horror at the disfigurement of the victim turned oppressor.[12]

The gathering of powers and participants, the impact of the speech, the presence of the Palestinians at the international negotiating table, and the legitimising and empowering circumstances of the conference: all conspired to give an unmistakable signal of the entry of the Palestinians as a national entity into international life. One journalist commented: "It was a crucial event, laden with diplomatic authority."[13] If it lived up to Palestinian hopes, the meeting also confirmed Israel's fears. Yitzhak Shamir frowned sternly during the Palestinian address, and his delegation looked uncomfortable. The Israeli leader's own speech, in contrast to that delivered by Haidar Abdel-Shafi, concentrated on Israel's past as a justification for its present unwillingness to compromise. "The rebirth of the State of Israel," he said, "so soon after the Holocaust has made the world forget that our claim is immemorial. We are the only people who have lived in the land of Israel without interruption for four thousand years, we are the only people who have had an independent sovereignty in this land, we are the only people for whom Jerusalem has been a capital, we are the only people whose sacred places are only in the land of Israel."

Shamir's tone seems with hindsight to have been an error, in contrast to the more open and optimistic approach taken by the Palestinians, but it was not a surprise. Shamir's attitude to the talks had been made clear enough in the weeks before they opened. He refused to acknowledge the Palestine National Council's approval, since the PLO was not in Israel's view a participant in the peace process. And he picked a team of hard-liners to accompany him to

12. Quoted by Michael Sheridan, "A nation steps out of the shadows", *Independent on Sunday*, 3 November 1991.
13. Ibid.

Madrid, with Binyamin Netanyahu, now Likud's leader, to sit at his elbow. In his speech, the Israeli leader looked back into history to justify Israel's stand, and made demands without offering concessions. Haidar Abdel-Shafi on the other hand had looked forward, to the possibility of a new dispensation which would be able to satisfy both Israeli and Palestinian needs. In reality a situation as intractable as the dispute between the Palestinians and the Israelis can only be solved, as the negotiators in Oslo were to find two years later, by looking resolutely forward and by refusing to refer to the past. That combined with the next phase of the Madrid meeting, which was to consist of a head-on clash and an exchange of insults between the Israeli and the Syrian delegations, to give the impression that the peace process could founder on Israeli intransigence and that its first session might be its last, like the Geneva conference of 1973.

In fact the talks were to go on in Washington, into a total of eleven rounds of bilateral meetings, between negotiators whose support was drawn from the widest field of expertise that each side could muster. The Palestinian team was sustained by a panel of academics and other experts of Palestinian background drawn not only from the Occupied Territories and from the ranks of PLO sympathisers but from the Palestinian diaspora round the world. A newspaper photograph in the Spanish newspaper *El Pais* taken at Madrid seemed to some observers to sum up the situation, and to indicate that in spite of the intransigence of the Israeli principals there might be hope for the peace process. The picture was of the Palestinian team-member Saeb Erakat, talking in the conference chamber to Elyakim Rubinstein of the Israeli delegation.[14] It seemed that perhaps the future of the talks, and of hopes for peace in Israel and Palestine, lay with men like these and not with the older generation of leaders.

As a prelude to the bilateral talks which were to stretch out over the next year and a half, the Israelis met the Palestinian delegation and the other Arab delegations separately at a hotel in Madrid on 3 November for a preliminary round of direct negotiations. It was a historic moment, since the meeting was the first between Israeli and Palestinian representatives since 1948. Yitzhak Shamir had already left Madrid and headed back to Israel, and the atmosphere was altogether more promising and less hostile than that in the main negotiating chamber. In Shamir's absence, seven Israeli negotiators led by Elyakim

14. Ibid.

Rubinstein kept a rendezvous with the Palestinians and Jordanians together for what both sides described as a satisfactory and even cordial meeting. "We are very happy that the opening of the bilateral negotiations took place in such a positive manner," said Hanan Ashrawi, the Palestinian spokeswoman.[15]

Among the topics that came under discussion were ways in which the talks could be made to relate to the UN resolutions 242 and 338, and the need to negotiate about the nature of an interim Palestinian administration. As always with Shamir and his Likud administration, the government succeeded in pouring cold water over the negotiators' enthusiasms and achievements. In his opening speech, he had flown in the face of reality by insisting that the conflict between the Palestinians and Israel was not territorial, and he repeated that assertion in Jerusalem a week later, during the visit of the South African President F. W. de Klerk, when famously he said that there is no room for two states between Jordan and the Mediterranean, and that Israel needed the Occupied Territories because "its dimensions are small".[16]

Throughout November Shamir kept up his pugnacious tone towards the Americans, who were eager to maintain the momentum of the peace talks now that they had begun, and to avoid the fiasco of opening negotiations with no follow-up, as had happened at the 1973 Geneva Conference. Shamir continued to warn the Americans that they should not link economic aid to Israel's participation in the talks. Israel made a bid to get reconvened talks sited in the Middle East, in a move to oblige the Arab states to accept the degree of recognition of Israel which would be implicit if the talks were held in Jerusalem, or if an Israeli delegation were to be invited to an Arab capital. In the absence of agreement between Israel and the Arab states on a venue, Washington acted to have them resumed on neutral territory. The United States eventually laid down 4 December as a definite date for the resumption of talks in Washington, which one Israeli minister described, in terms which almost defy belief, as an "impertinent ultimatum".[17] But impertinent or not, the American invitation was not to be disregarded and it was in December, just a week after the target date of 4 December, that the peace talks reassembled in the American capital.

15. *Le Monde*, 5 November 1991.
16. AFP, 12 November 1991.
17. Richard Beeston, "Israelis challenge impertinent US", *The Times*, 25 November 1991.

CHAPTER 5

HARD TALKING IN WASHINGTON

The Treadmill Begins

No less than eleven rounds of bilateral peace talks in Washington, in which Israeli negotiators faced the Palestinian delegation, were to follow the Madrid conference. Separate bilateral talks were also held between Israel and the three Arab states involved in the negotiations: Syria, Lebanon and Jordan. The Jordanian delegation, which provided an umbrella for the Palestinians at Madrid, was soon to be separated from the Palestinians, at first in practice and then in principle. But the negotiations with Yitzhak Shamir's Likud government were blighted by the failure of his coalition in early 1992, which reduced the Likud administration to the status of a caretaker and deprived it of a real mandate to negotiate. In spite of this there were some apparent glimpses of progress as well as many disappointments for the Palestinians in the first half of 1992. When Yitzhak Rabin's Labour-led coalition took over in July there were at first great hopes of progress, but as we shall see these too began to evaporate by the spring of 1993.

Meanwhile in a separate development most inauspicious for the talks, relations between the Palestinians and Israel were dealt a blow which was at least temporarily devastating, by the sudden deportation by Israel in December 1992 of 400 Palestinian activists from the militant Muslim Palestinian movement, Hamas. That seems to have been an ill-considered and intemperate decision by Labour Prime Minister Rabin, who, in his anger at the abduction and murder of an Israeli soldier, failed to calculate the consequences of the deportations. The Palestinians viewed it as catastrophic for the prospects of peace. It seems as if the Israeli government had expected the Palestinian delegation with its basically pro-PLO orientation, to be unconcerned by an Israeli clamp-down on Hamas, which was essentially the PLO's rival for support in the Occupied Territories, and was developing an alternative agenda for the shape of a liberated Palestine. But in the event, the rash Israeli move brought about what almost became a reconciliation between Hamas and the PLO, with public expressions of support from Tunis for the Hamas deportees. Though efforts were made by both sides in 1992 to rebuild the possibility of progress at the talks, the effect of the deportations was to cast a continuing pall and to block the efforts of those on both sides, the technocrats rather than the politicians, who were desperate to get on with the business of making peace.

The course of the other strands of the bilateral negotiations was as tantalising as the Palestinian talks. Flashes of optimism would occasionally illuminate an otherwise discouraging landscape of futile words. Hopes which sprang up in the autumn of 1992 that Israel might be able to reach an early agreement with Syria were dashed, and may have been little more than the product of excessive optimism on the Israeli side. Israel's Foreign Minister, Mr Shimon Peres, the veteran Labour politician and one-time Prime Minister of Israel, seems to have been guilty throughout the talks of attempting to anticipate reality by putting an excessively hopeful gloss on events. The stumbling block was Syria's unwillingness to contemplate a territorial compromise in the Golan Heights. The return of the whole of Golan was Syria's basic demand, on which Damascus was not prepared to negotiate. While Syria was unable to make progress, Lebanon was also not able to resolve its own dispute with Israel, which mainly turned on the issue of Israel's military presence in southern Lebanon and its control of a further strip of Lebanese territory which Israel described as its "security zone". Finally, while Jordan had little territory to negotiate with Israel, it was as unhappy as were the Palestinians at the continued Israeli settlement policy. Amman was unable to move towards resolving its own relations across the River Jordan while the Palestinians still vainly sought the fulfilment of their aspirations.

The Palestinians: Early Optimism

In November 1991, at the beginning of the bilateral process, as the Madrid talks ended and the delegations dispersed, there was no doubt which side believed it had come out of the meeting as the moral victor. The Palestinian delegation was overtly jubilant. They were aware of the impact made by the speech given by their leader, Haidar

Abdel-Shafi, and their press spokeswoman Hanan Ashrawi knew she had impressed the world's media. Faisal Husseini, the real head of the negotiators, often regarded as Yasser Arafat's representative in the Occupied Territories, was aware that his presence at Madrid had enhanced his status, and had scored a real victory over the Israeli government, which objected to him on the grounds that he was a resident of East Jerusalem, regarded by Israel as sovereign territory, and also that he was an acknowledged figure within the PLO, who had several times been imprisoned. All the members of the delegation had become, virtually overnight, political personalities on the international stage, and the Palestinian cause had benefited from that. While Yasser Arafat, in his military uniform and kefiyyeh, had provided one kind of leadership and image for the Palestinians, the civil and persuasive demeanour of the delegation from the Occupied Territories gave a new and at this stage welcome dimension to the Palestinian identity.

On the other hand, the Israeli delegation went home disconsolate. Yitzhak Shamir's tone had been relatively conciliatory: American pressure behind the scenes had left him little alternative. But he bitterly resented having to stand in front of the representatives of the great powers, and the television cameras, in order to acknowledge publicly by his very presence at the conference that aspects of the relationship between the Israeli state and the Palestinians were negotiable.

Shamir went home early, ostensibly to keep the Sabbath on Saturday 2 November, leaving the Israeli delegation to be led by Deputy Foreign Minister Binyamin Netanyahu, now Likud's leader in opposition. Once Shamir was back in Jerusalem, however, his spirits picked up, and he appeared to come to believe he had won some kind of victory in Madrid. At any rate, the evidence is that he and his advisers decided that by deploying a sufficiently agile, evasive and disputatious strategy the peace process could be spun out indefinitely, while Israel continued to create "facts on the ground" with the establishment of new settlements and the expansion of old ones. Meanwhile the old Israeli goal of achieving legitimacy in the eyes of its enemies was still there. Binyamin Netanyahu summed up: "Our purpose is to get beyond the biggest obstacle – the Arabs' opposition to Israel's very legitimacy. Once the obstacle of legitimacy can be overcome, peace can follow very, very quickly."[1]

1. David Watts, "Mr Israel sees way to peace", *The Times*, 27 November 1991.

Getting Started

Difficulties over getting the talks restarted after Madrid began to surface even before the conference came to an end. Shamir's first ploy was to ask for the talks to be reconvened in Jerusalem, or in an Arab capital. He argued that the talks should alternate between Israel and each of the capitals of the Arab states concerned, Damascus, Amman and Beirut. The disadvantage of this to the Palestinians was obvious: with no capital to which to invite the Israelis, their lack of sovereignty and the difference between their status and that of the participating states would be obvious and to their detriment. While Israel stood out against the participation of the PLO, it would be out of the question for the Palestinians to use the good offices of the Tunisian government to host a round of talks in Tunis. But the Palestinians were in no mood to be trifled with. From Madrid they flew to Amman for meetings with PLO officials, and then re-entered the Occupied Territories across the Allenby Bridge, the sole land route that connects Israel with Jordan. In Jericho they were given a rapturous reception by the local population, inaugurating a week of fevered debate about the prospects for peace and the tactics to obtain it. The Palestinian people of the Occupied Territories, who had on television seen their own representatives at Madrid, seemed to leap back to life after the stifling years of the occupation and the intifada, when the means of expression had seemingly been reduced to a stultifying simplicity: the stones thrown at Israeli soldiers by the youths and children, the closed shops, and the sullen atmosphere.

There were some in Israel who strongly resented the mood of celebration, and did their best to mar it, and with it the prospects for more talks, with a threat to prosecute spokeswoman Hanan Ashrawi for meeting PLO officials abroad. This seemed to emanate not from the government as a whole, however, but from the Ministry of Police; a government spokesman, Health Minister Ehud Olmert, soon admitted she was most unlikely to face any action. President Bush made his mood clear when he told a group of Arab-Americans in Washington: "Please know that Hanan is on my mind and I'm paying very close attention to what is happening over there."[2] But those like Hanan Ashrawi, who had espoused wholeheartedly the peace process, were

2. Richard Beeston, "Israel threatens to prosecute Ashrawi", *The Times*, 17 November 1991.

too determined now to be deterred by what was easily seen as petty action by some Israelis. Nonetheless, there were ominous signs about the real prospects for peace. Yitzhak Shamir is said to have told officials that they should "spin out the autonomy talks over ten years, so that by the time an agreement is reached there will be half a million Jews resident in the Occupied Territories."[3]

Not only the Israelis wanted to minimise the achievement of the Palestinian delegation. Some in the Territories believed the group of Palestinians who went to Madrid were not representative, and were selling out the Palestinian people: this was a view prevalent among Habash's PFLP but also held by Hamas, the Islamic resistance movement. Even some old PLO supporters were sceptical. One of Yasser Arafat's veteran PLO representatives in the West Bank said this to a journalist in December 1991: "They can talk. We approve of that. But they will get nothing. For 40 years we have talked and fought, talked and fought. So now is the time for talking: fine. But believe me, my son and his son will both carry a gun. The time for fighting will come again." Others felt a new era was beginning, or at least that the potentiality for change was there. Hanan Ashrawi herself, on the other hand, took a predictably sanguine view: "There is no time for old ideologies. Everybody has paid their dues. All of us have a long history of political work. This is the moment for political articulation and discussion."[4] She was also optimistic: "For us, Madrid will remain as the first real sign announcing the inevitable birth of the Palestinian state." But her optimism was prudently tempered with realism: "This is only the first stage in a difficult journey."[5]

Settlements: Obsession and Downfall

Yet another sign of trouble to come, both for the peace process and for Yitzhak Shamir himself, was the continued drive to settle Jews in the Occupied Territories, in the face of the express desire of the

3. Peretz Kidron, "Pocketfuls of goodies", *Middle East International*, 432, 21 August 1992.
4. Michael Sheridan, "A woman of her time", *The Independent on Sunday*, 15 December 1991.
5. Jean-Pierre Langellier, "Les Palestiniens racontent Madrid", *Le Monde*, 9 November 1991.

United States and President Bush that settlement should be suspended for the duration of the peace process. It is hard to disentangle the threads of the settlement movement, and to distinguish whether the pressure to continue was coming from the Likud government or from the settler movement. The answer seems to be that both were the case. In the case of the ideological and religious settlements it was the settlers themselves who made the running. The ideological wing of the settler movement itself, at the same time, needed little encouragement to go on expanding. These were the settlers who believed they had a religious duty to occupy Eretz Israel or whose Zionist convictions drove them to want to annex the ancient Jewish territories of Samaria and Judaea, as Israelis call the West Bank. Meanwhile the government promoted other settlements which it wanted to encourage for security reasons, such as the developments which now surround Jerusalem inside what Israel regards as its sovereign territory.

What is certain is that Shamir's government was strongly reluctant to oppose settlements as the Americans wanted. In spite of the successful American move in September to choke off pressure from Congress to push through Israel's ten billion dollars in loan guarantees, the Israelis still appeared to believe that with the Madrid meeting behind them they could continue building settlements and still hope for American support to be forthcoming in due course. Within the context of the Israeli coalition, and even inside the spectrum of Likud itself, which was still in some ways more of an alliance of different factions than a political party, there was strong pressure for continued Jewish settlement in the Occupied Territories which would eventually put Shamir's government under severe strain and would be a factor leading to the elections of June 1992. Certainly in November 1991 some of Shamir's more right-wing cabinet colleagues were pressing very actively for more settlements to be started, in a government which since the collapse of the coalition with Labour had depended on the extreme right and the religious parties.

Bush Takes a Hand

On 22 November President Bush, in the absence of any sign of an agreement between Israel and the Palestinians about the date and venue of the next round of talks, chose to precipitate the next stage of the process. He sent the Palestinian delegation and the Israeli government a definite invitation to a new round of talks to be held in Washington on 4 December, the date Washington had set at Madrid. Aware that the Palestinians would not agree to a Middle Eastern venue, the United States chose to ignore the Israeli government's contention that the talks should be held in the region. Almost incredibly, Israel reacted with fury to the American initiative. Though Yitzhak Shamir was well aware that he had been unable to resist the American pressure to go to Madrid, it was as if the government, as well as right-wingers in the population at large, had still failed to understand the change in the nature of the relationship between Israel and the United States. The right-wing Police Minister, Ronnie Milo, who had initiated the move to prosecute Hanan Ashrawi, called the invitation an "impertinent ultimatum". Another member of the cabinet, Ehud Olmert, was equally cool about the Americans, but more careful in his language: "There is no doubt we are speaking of an administration that does not try or pretend to show ... some amount of friendship or an effort to coordinate, as was common with other administrations." The Israeli cabinet, collectively, was clearly suffering from nostalgia for the palmier days of President Reagan.[6]

The First Round

The Palestinians arrived in Washington on time on 4 December, announcing that they were ready and able to begin negotiations. According to Hanan Ashrawi: "We have come in good faith to discuss matters of substance. We have not come to buy time nor to waste it ..."[7] The Israelis did not turn up to begin the talks until almost a week later. Once again, American pressure had to be exerted to shift the intransigent Israeli cabinet, which had begun to believe that the safest way to avoid making concessions was to stay at home. Binyamin Netanyahu said the delay had been because Israel refused to be dictated to by the United States, which had not consulted the Israelis

6. Richard Beeston, "Israelis challenge impertinent US", *The Times*, 25 November 1991.

7. Simon Tisdall, "Palestinians hurl the gauntlet", *The Guardian*, 4 December 1991.

in advance before announcing the date of 4 December. In Israel, while the government was making up its mind, the newspaper *Ma'ariv* said that the government had to "make it clear that Prime Minister Shamir isn't in Bush's pocket".[8] On the other hand, there was some embarrassment in Israel about the way the government was dragging its feet. Labour and left-wing politicians were critical, and the large-circulation daily *Yediot Aharonot* said: "Who in the world will believe that our government is committed to peace?"[9] Finally on 10 December, the first round of the Washington bilateral negotiations got under way, but Israel's fears of being rushed into unwanted concessions still ruled its policy. Defensively, Israel deliberately sought to entangle the talks in procedural wrangles almost as soon as they started. Israel's central dilemma was pinpointed by analyst Lawrence Freedman: "Because recognition is the main thing Israel wants from its neighbours, it has tried to shape the negotiations to achieve this without major territorial concessions. It is such a small country, and has so little confidence in the trustworthiness of its neighbours, that it sees every territorial concession as a high risk to its security. But without concessions of land, the Arabs will not concede full recognition."[10]

The issue which caused the procedural breakdown was also connected with the vexed issue of recognition, this time of the recognition of the Palestinians by Israel. Israel had got its way at Madrid, and had avoided recognition of the Palestinians' separate existence by having them come to the talks as a joint delegation with Jordan. But in Washington the Palestinians wished to be alone with the Israeli delegation to talk about matters which concerned them alone, and did not affect the Jordanians. Israel would only agree to this in the context of specially constituted sub-committees. The Palestinians were reluctant to agree to this. Hanan Ashrawi said: "We will not be treated as a sub-committee. It is perfectly respectable these days to talk to Palestinians. It is quite kosher. We are no longer the pariahs of the world, and we are a perfectly harmless people." The result of the stand-off was that the talks remained, literally at first, in

8. Michael Sheridan, "Israel twists on horns of dilemma over peace talks", *The Independent*, 29 November 1991.

9. Ian Black, "Israel climbs down to fill empty seats", *The Guardian*, 5 December 1991.

10. Lawrence Freedman, "An empty gesture for Israel", *The Independent*, 3 December 1991.

the corridor, as the delegations refused to agree whether to meet in one room, as Israel wanted, or in two, with Israel talking separately to Jordanians and Palestinians, as the Palestinians demanded. It is tempting here to suggest that Israel was not alone in reducing the talks to a confrontation over procedure. The Palestinians' touchiness sits uneasily with their professed claim that all they wanted to do was to talk about matters of substance. But the Palestinian delegation at this point was interested in beginning the way it intended to continue: that is to say, talking about Palestinian affairs without the presence of the Jordanians and as a full negotiating party in their own right.

The talks broke up on 18 December, with no substantive progress made. While the Palestinian and Jordanian delegation failed to reach a compromise with Israel over their procedural disagreement, the Jordanians were also unable to talk. Jordan's territorial concern is limited, however, to a few square kilometres of territory on the border between the two countries to the south of the Dead Sea, and was to present little difficulty when it eventually came under discussion. However, the parallel talks with Syria and Lebanon had also remained bogged down. At first the Syrians would not even shake hands with their interlocutors, but at least they had met. Nonetheless, though the two sides had met round a table there had still been little in the way of a meeting of minds. While the talks were going on, Syria underlined its entrenched opposition to everything Israel stands for by voting against the repeal of the UN General Assembly motion equating Zionism with racism. Furthermore, at this early stage there seemed little hope of any flexibility on either side over Syria's main demand from the talks, the return of the Golan Heights in their entirety. In the third strand of the talks, with Lebanon, the atmosphere was at least described by negotiators as "cordial", but Lebanon would be unable to reach agreement with Israel without Syrian approval.

"Came Forth Fingers of a Man's Hand"

Prescient commentators had already suggested that Shamir's agreement to go to Madrid might already have sounded the knell for his government. Likud had been going it alone, with its right-wing and religious coalition allies, since the breakup of its coalition with Labour in March 1990. That was itself connected with problems in the peace process, and was directly precipitated by Labour's discontent with Shamir's reluctance to accept the make-up of a Palestinian delegation to talk about his own autonomy plan. At the time of the Madrid conference the Likud-led coalition could command 64 seats in the 120-seat Knesset, but 18 belonged to minority religious and right-wing parties which could if they chose threaten the Prime Minister with the withdrawal of their support. The absence of a Labour counter-weight in the cabinet meant that Shamir was gradually drifting to the right, which in Israeli terms means a tougher policy towards the Arabs. This pleased the right-wing constituency in the country, half the electorate, but stitched Shamir into a strait-jacket. Now, the sudden change of direction involved in Madrid and its follow-up were upsetting that right-wing electorate on which Shamir depended. The need to reassure its right-wing supporters was at least part of the explanation for the rhetoric of indignation with which the Israeli leadership reacted to United States pressure to negotiate. In the longer run, as we know, Shamir was indeed not to survive, but the portents of his political collapse were already to be seen in December 1991. There was due to be tough talking in the Israeli cabinet before the government agreed to send a delegation to Washington, but even so Likud's far-right coalition partners were already unhappy. For the moment the government survived, but in mid-January the axe would fall when two extreme right-wing parties, Tehiya and Moledet, with five Knesset seats between them, pulled out of the coalition, destroying Shamir's Knesset majority, and effectively crippling the peace talks until the Israeli election on 23 June 1992 and the new Labour government, which took office on 13 July.

The second round of the Washington talks again opened a week late. Planned to resume on 7 January 1992 they in fact did not get going until 13 January. This time, after the frustration of the first round, with its unresolved clash over protocol and failure to address any substantive issues, it was the Palestinian delegation that was reluctant to show up. Israel was more enthusiastic than before, in a move that seemed to be aimed at getting the sympathy of the US Congress, which was now about to debate the granting of the much discussed ten billion dollars of loan guarantees, discussion of which had been delayed by President Bush until after Madrid. A Palestinian who was close to the peace process, Yezid Sayigh, offered this analysis: "Israel . . . will seek to portray the bilateral talks as progressing satisfactorily, in order to persuade Congress that there is no need to link the housing loans offer directly to the peace process."[11] The Palestinians' reluctance was based on their unwillingness to re-enact the charade of December, and their fear that the United States might lean on them to make concessions, in order to keep the talks going. They also looked very unfavourably at Israel's proposed deportation of a group of twelve Palestinian activists from the Occupied Territories, in a familiar manoeuvre whose illegality in international law was customarily disregarded by Israel: which also presaged the much larger-scale deportation by the Labour government a year later that almost brought the peace process to a halt.

Nevertheless a meeting in Washington did take place and this time succeeded in resolving the procedural problem, if not to the satisfaction of both sides then at least sufficiently to permit them to sit down and talk together. The Palestinians would from now on talk separately to Israel, with only a token Jordanian presence, but would accept a subsidiary status in what would be called "general meetings" of the Israeli, Palestinian and Jordanian delegates. This was virtually all that was achieved in this round, which broke up on 16 January, and to the disappointment of the Palestinians the encounter failed once again to broach any substantive issues. The Palestinians were later to become in effect a separate delegation on their own operating independently from the Jordanians, as even Israel found the fiction of the joint delegation too cumbrous to manage. Israel's refusal to talk about the continuing process of Jewish settlement in the Occupied Territories was threatening the continuation of the talks, the Palestinians said. Echoes of Camp David and Yitzhak Shamir's own 1989 autonomy plan were raised, when Israel's Ambassador in Washington, Zalman Shoval, was reported to have said that "the key purpose of these negotiations was to agree Palestinian interim self-government in the Occupied Territories, not territorial matters," and added that "the settlement question should be decided when the final status of the territories is negotiated in another three years." The spectre was raised again of the apparently unprecedented status envisaged for the Palestinians by Likud: autonomous but with no territory. Further, it was clear that Likud intended to pack the Occupied Territories with settlers, creating facts on the ground that would limit Palestinian autonomy to a very residual status.

11. Yezid Sayigh, "The peace negotiations: dim hopes for 1992", *Middle East International*, 416, 10 January 1992.

All Likud's plans began to seem less relevant as soon as the small extreme right-wing parties inside the Likud coalition decided to sink Shamir's government. One of these parties, Tehiya, was unhappy about even the limited progress which had been made at the peace talks, and discontented with the Israeli negotiators' reluctant agreement to talk separately to the Palestinians. It therefore determined that there should be no Palestinian autonomy of even the restricted kind Likud might have envisaged. The Tehiya leader Yuval Ne'eman, who held the science and energy portfolio, announced his imminent resignation on 15 January, while the talks were in progress, and Moledet, the other extreme right-wing group in the coalition, followed suit. The resignations were offered and took effect at the next cabinet meeting on 19 January.

The withdrawal of the five Knesset votes the two parties commanded was enough to demolish Shamir's Knesset majority, reducing his voting strength to 59 in the 120-seat house, and he announced he would go to the polls rather than struggle on with what would obviously have been highly conditional left-wing support. Shamir's supporters guessed that he would not be sorry to go to the country in order to boost his party's electoral standing, and as soon as 20 January he effectively began his electoral campaign with a widely publicised promise to the settlers, guaranteed to appeal to Israel's right-wing, that the process of expansion into Eretz Israel would continue. Speaking at the West Bank settlement of Betar he said: "We see the building here and all over Judaea and Samaria. This building will continue and no force on earth will stop it."[12] As the electors were to show in June, however, Shamir had wrongly judged the mood of the country.

The Phoney War

The undermining of the Likud government and the effective destruction of its mandate was to give an unreal air to the process of negotiation which continued throughout the first half of 1992, up to the Israeli election. Likud continued to insist it was the proper

12. Ian Black, "Shamir says settlements will continue", *The Guardian*, 21 January 1992.

negotiating partner of the Palestinians, but the hope and likelihood of a Labour government in Israel was more and more taken into the Palestinians' calculations. One major and significant development that did take place however was the first session of the multilateral talks in Moscow, where Israel, the Palestinians and the delegations from Syria, Lebanon and Jordan were due to meet with the sponsors of the peace talks, as well as with other concerned nations including the remaining Arab countries, to talk about regional issues of international concern. The first session of the multilateral talks took place in Moscow at the end of January 1992, and this time it was the Palestinians' turn to refuse to attend, in protest at the Israeli refusal to meet a team chosen by the Palestinians themselves rather than a delegation vetted by Israel.

The Palestinians named a delegation of eight, none of whom were formally members of the PLO hierarchy, who in the end went to Moscow but did not go to the talks. Israel's objection was to breaches of their rule that only Palestinians from the Occupied Territories should participate. The Palestinians wanted to include members from the diaspora, and also from East Jerusalem. Syria and Lebanon also stayed away from Moscow, as well as some other Arab states. Though the usefulness of the talks was gravely limited by the absence of the Arab delegations, apart from Jordan, and the associated boycott of the talks by some other Arab states, the Moscow meeting nevertheless at least served to initiate the five international forums in which regional issues were to be discussed in later coming talks, where the Palestinians would in due course cooperate. The five subject areas were security and arms; economic development and cooperation; water resources and use; the environment; and refugees. In later rounds of multilateral talks, the Palestinians would attend, but the clash over representation continued. For example, at the talks on regional economic cooperation which were held in Brussels in May, Israel refused to attend because of the membership of the Palestinian delegation.

Contrasting Plans

By March, two more sessions of talks had taken place, but no real progress had been made and the Palestinians had begun to suspect that what Israel was now aiming to get from the talks, reverting once more to its time-honoured policy, was a solution to the Palestinian problem based on agreements made with the Arab states which would enable it to turn its back on the Palestinians' grievances. Meanwhile, pressure was being put on the Palestinians by the United States to remain engaged in the talks and not pull out. Some comfort was given to the Palestinians, on the other hand, by America's sternness over the issue of the loan guarantees Israel continued to want, in order to be able to house the expected influx of Russian Jews. By mid-March 1991, that conflict had reached a head, and on 17 March the Israeli cabinet formally announced that it no longer required the loans, if that meant there must be no more new settlements in the Occupied Territories. The proposals which the two sides had put on the table by this time could not have been more contradictory. The PLO had not been slow to formulate a plan for autonomy, and in January had produced a text, which was presented by the official Palestinian delegation. By late February Israel had countered with its own text, which, unsurprisingly was wholly incompatible with the Palestinians' ideas.

The Palestinian plan called for the establishment of a Palestine Interim Self-Government Authority (PISGA), whose jurisdiction would extend to all the Palestinian inhabitants of the Occupied Territories. This would comprise an executive council of 20 members, a judiciary authority, and an elected council of 180 members which would represent the West Bank, the Gaza Strip, and East Jerusalem. The Palestinians said their plan would provide for the peaceful transfer of power to a Palestinian authority in the Occupied Territories and set the scene for negotiations on the final status. As the Palestinian authority took over, the Israeli military and civil administration would withdraw. The Israeli army, according to a text given to Agence France Presse, would "withdraw from all the populated regions, immediately before the beginning of the electoral process".[13] The army was to "withdraw by mutually agreed steps to points on the frontiers of the occupied Palestinian territories" at the moment the PISGA began to operate. The Palestinians envisaged that the United Nations would be called on to provide security during a transitional period.

The Israeli plan, which Israel insisted was a serious offer, was dismissed by the Palestinians as wholly inappropriate. Its main lines were that the authority of an interim self-governing authority (ISGA)

13. AFP, *Le Monde*, 24 January 1992.

would apply to the Palestinian inhabitants of Judaea and Samaria (i.e. the West Bank) and the Gaza Strip, and the ISGA's powers would be administrative, rather than judicial or legislative. The interim arrangement, Israel's plan made clear, would concern the status of the people but not the land. The existing links between the Occupied Territories and Israel would be kept intact, and links between the Palestinians and Jordan would be fostered. Meanwhile Israelis would continue to settle as of right wherever they wished in the Occupied Territories, and Israel would have sole responsibility for all security matters. There is no mention either of the withdrawal of Israeli troops or of elections for the Palestinians.[14] On the other hand, the Israelis were later to demonstrate that they were still proposing Palestinian municipal elections, as they had done before. This February plan was evidently the direct descendant of Yitzhak Shamir's autonomy plan of 1989 and of Camp David, and the Palestinians were unable to take it seriously as a basis for negotiations, but Israel was earnest in putting it forward. Little trace of it is left in the document produced in Oslo during 1993, but elements of the Palestinian counter-plan have clearly survived.

Noises Off

While the sterile confrontation between Israel and the Palestinian negotiators continued, two events took place in the margin which may have had a fundamental effect on the peace process. First was the challenge mounted in February by the Israeli Foreign Minister, David Levy, for the leadership of the Likud, which may have been the fatal blow to Yitzhak Shamir's electoral prospects. The clash between Levy and Shamir was partly personal and partly political. The Prime Minister had excluded him from the Madrid conference because he feared the Foreign Minister was more likely to favour offering the Arabs concessions. Levy represented a different constituency in Israel. He was from Morocco, and had been born into a relatively poor and powerless family. He was not an English speaker, and therefore seemed in some ways less sophisticated than other Israeli leaders,

14. Lamis Andoni, "Conflicting proposals for self-government", *Middle East International*, 420, 6 March 1992.

though too much has been made of this by American reporters who failed to appreciate Levy's educated use of French. His rise to high office was unprecedented for someone of his background, and it gave him enormous leverage in Israel's Sephardic community, the so-called oriental Jews, many from Morocco or Yemen. The orientals often felt they had little in common with the Ashkenazim, of broadly European origin, or their descendants who were by now Israeli-born so-called Sabras, who had occupied the commanding positions in Israel for so long. Many of the oriental Jews were conservative and anti-Arab in their politics, and they were an important source of support for the Likud government. Without Levy's backing, Yitzhak Shamir could not feel so secure in calling for their support. Levy failed to wrest the leadership from Shamir, and later resigned from the cabinet. The resulting split in the loyalties of Likud supporters could have been enough to tilt the electoral balance.

The second upset was the air crash which almost removed PLO leader Yasser Arafat from the scene in April 1992. Arafat's plane crashed in a sandstorm in the Libyan desert on the night of 7 April 1992, and for a few hours the Palestinian leader was feared to be dead. Arafat had no clear successor as head of the PLO, and while the possibility remained that he had disappeared from the scene, minds on all sides were concentrated on the effect his disappearance could have on the peace process if the Palestinian movement split into factions in the course of a struggle for the succession. Strong emotions were aroused in the Arab world, and the Palestinians, though sometimes ready to criticise Arafat for his autocratic ways, were alarmed. From the point of view of the peace process, however, it seems that the exercise of formulating contingency plans for managing without Arafat concentrated minds in Washington on his centrality to the diplomatic picture. Even in Israel the possibility of Arafat's death served to emphasise his importance as the real interlocutor on Palestinian affairs, and brought to the surface the realisation that the Israeli leadership had consistently tried to ignore, that Arafat was the interlocutor to whom Israel would ultimately have to turn. This was not a new idea, indeed it had been canvassed from the first by such relative doves as Yossi Beilin of the Labour Party and Yossi Sarid of Meretz, the far left-wing alliance. But the sudden possibility that there was no more Arafat may well have brought even the Israeli right to realise how essential their bitterly hated foe had in fact become to the achievement of peace.

Keeping Up Appearances

One more round of talks took place before the Israeli election, opening on 27 April, and this time all the delegations took part without demur. The mood at the fifth round was described as more hopeful than before, though it could hardly have been less hopeful, given the hostility which had characterised the talks since January. So far, the Palestinians on the one hand had spurned Israel's limited proposals, while on the other hand Israel refused either to accept the Palestinians' ideas about who should represent them at international forums like the multilateral talks, or to listen seriously to the more far-reaching Palestinian ideas about independence. In April, however, the Israelis formally tabled their proposals for municipal elections in the Occupied Territories, which were meant to be a partial answer to the Palestinian demand for democratic representation. The Palestinian delegation did not reject the idea outright, though it met with little favour in Tunis. Of course, municipal elections were precisely the level of democratic representation which was consistent with Israel's contention that Palestinian autonomy should be about the representation of people rather than the independence of territory: municipal authorities claim no sovereign rights. This is why the idea was rejected by the PLO, because of the danger that elected municipalities might be seen to weaken the case for the elected Palestinian body the PLO wanted.

By May, all eyes in Israel were focused on the imminent elections, and the lack of progress in the talks was beginning to be reflected in a new upsurge in the intifada, which by now had taken an angrier turn. Casualties in the war of the stones continued, as Israeli troops reacted with either live ammunition or the often lethal rubber bullets to aggression by gangs of Palestinian youths and children. But a higher level of violence was now in evidence. At the begining of April for example, an army post in Rafah, at the southern edge of the Gaza Strip, was hit by a grenade thrown from a car, and an army jeep was pelted with petrol bombs. Israeli troops opened fire on stone-throwing onlookers, killing four. The grenade which began the exchange was the responsibility of an armed group, one of several now at the hard core of the insurrection. In a selection of the increasing tide of incidents in the spring and summer of 1992, an Israeli girl was stabbed to death in a Tel Aviv suburb in May, and the same day three armed Palestinians and an Israeli solder were killed in a fierce gun battle in

Gaza. A few days later a rabbi from a settlement in the Gaza Strip was stabbed near his home. Israeli soldiers shot a middle-aged Palestinian woman after stones were thrown at their bus at Jenin in the West Bank, and a 65-year-old woman died when a tear-gas canister was thrown into her home in Gaza City. In early May, two young Palestinians were shot dead in a village near Hebron. The violence went on right up to the brink of the elections, and after them: in the first three days after the polling on 23 June three Israelis and three Palestinians were killed in the Occupied Territories.

But both at the level of the Palestinians in the streets of the Occupied Territories and in the diplomatic sphere inhabited by the Israeli delegation and the PLO, there was beginning to be hope that there could be a more peaceful future after the Israeli elections. The hope for the Palestinians was that Yitzhak Rabin and the Labour Party could topple Likud in the coming elections. Opinion polls in Israel were starting to show a tilt towards Labour, and in spite of the renewed intifada violence, or perhaps because of it, it began to appear as if the Israeli electorate were favouring Labour because they saw a chance of better progress in the peace talks. The endless violence was taking a toll in Israel, and while it served to strengthen the determination of the entrenched right-wing, and especially of the settlers and their supporters, other Israelis, especially the crucial middle-of-the-road voters, were beginning to swing behind the idea of giving peace a chance.

CHAPTER 6

THE ROAD TO OSLO

Rabin Takes Over

In the event, Rabin's victory was bigger than many had anticipated, and represented a clear defeat for Likud and a positive mandate for Labour. The Israeli people had decided that they were tired of the strong-arm policy of the right, and that they wanted to try the experiment of making peace with the Palestinians. Yitzhak Shamir, who himself thrived on conflict, and who was described even by his friends as permanently in the grip of a mood suspended between truculence and mistrust, had failed to grasp that what a significant section of Israel's people had come to value in the 1990s was peace, rather than war. Under Israel's proportional representation system, where the number of Knesset seats precisely reflects the size of the popular vote, Labour took 44 seats out of the Knesset's 120. Labour's firm ally, the newly formed Meretz, which was formed to bring together left-wingers in a single grouping, took twelve. This gave Labour 56 seats on which to build its alliance, and the five seats which went to Arab members were enough to ensure that Labour would be able to get its policies through the Knesset, and especially that any move towards peace would not be blocked by the legislature.

Likud's showing, on the other hand, was unexpectedly poor, with only 32 seats. In general, the right suffered. The hard-line Tsomet party, led by Rafael Eitan, took 8 seats, and must have gained seats from Likud, but the number of seats held by the two far-right parties which advocated extreme measures in the Occupied Territories fell to 3, held by Moledet: the Tehiya party got too few votes to qualify and was eliminated. The remaining 16 seats were taken by various religious parties, who are inclined to the right but pursue their own arcane agendas. Rabin refused to rely on Arab support, and wanted to form a broad coalition, so in the end he took the religious party Shas into his government, which took office on 13 July. This was a move which was to cause Rabin some political trouble later, since the Shas leader Aryeh Deri, who held the portfolio of Interior Minister, was under investigation for alleged corruption while he was in the Likud government.

While Rabin was forming his government, the Palestinians were assessing the chances of a better atmosphere at the peace talks. There were positive signs. Labour in opposition had become less inclined to favour Likud's ideas about a Greater Israel, and was better disposed towards making peace with the Palestinians as the longer-term solution. On the other hand, Labour was not necessarily historically committed to returning Arab land: from 1967 to 1977, Labour had held on to the Occupied Territories it had captured from Jordan and Egypt when it could perhaps have divested itself of them, and 1974 to 1977 had been Yitzhak Rabin's first term of office as Prime Minister. But even though Yitzhak Rabin was known as a hawk, the signs seemed clear that he had now come round to recognising the unavoidability of making peace. A further good augury was that he had no choice but to ally himself in government with Meretz, the party of Shulamit Aloni, Amnon Rubinstein and Yossi Sarid: politicians who were committed out of their strong left-wing principles to peace with the Arabs. The left-wing element in the new Israeli government was in due course to prove to be very important, as it emerged that the Deputy Foreign Minister, Yossi Beilin, an energetic 45-year-old from a diplomatic family, was the moving spirit behind the Oslo talks which have given the new impetus and direction to the peace process.

Yet another indication that peace was on the cards was that Israeli voters had shown in opinion polls that they were in favour of trying to put an end to the conflict with the Arabs, and were willing to consider an exchange of territory for peace in order to do so. Since the intifada began, the conflict has begun to sap the energies of Israel, though right-wingers would scoff at the idea. Young Israelis had to serve in the army, and reservists were obliged to do their regular periods of service, and most saw duty in the Occupied Territories. That meant every family had its experience of the conflict. Worse still, with violent incidents spilling out from the Occupied Territories across the so-called Green Line into Israel proper it was coming closer to home. Israel had had enough of fighting, and this seemed especially to be true of many of the generation too young to have adult memories of Israel's wars against the Arab states.

Talking to Labour

Though Oslo was in due course to take over the peace process, for the moment the conventional talks between the official Israeli delegation and the Palestinians in Washington continued to appear to be the forum in which the peace talks were primarily located. The Labour Party's early signals to the Palestinians indicated that they should in Israeli terms be "realistic" about the talks: in other words that they should not hope for too much. Yitzhak Rabin, in his first speech to the Knesset about the peace process, said that the Palestinians should not expect to get everything they wanted. After 14 years of Likud rule Rabin was anxious to remind the Palestinians that there was a high degree of national consensus in Israel, and that though there might be differences in emphasis between Likud and Labour, both parties were at bottom and in the last resort the guardians of Israel's security, and the custodians of the country's old Zionist idealism. The difference lay in how the identity of Israel and the requirements of its security were interpreted.

Nevertheless a partial freeze on Jewish settlement activity seemed to be part of Labour's thinking, though Rabin drew a distinction between "security" settlements and "political" settlements that the Palestinians found it hard to accept. As Rabin's ideas were translated into practice, it looked as if even Labour's ideas about restrained settlement would have led to an increase of 50,000, in other words nearly half, in the settler population in the West Bank. And as the summer wore on, there was an even bigger blow for the Palestinians: President Bush decided to revoke his opposition to the loan guarantees wanted by Israel and to let Congress vote them through, without asking for an end to new settlement in the Occupied Territories as a condition.

All this sharply diminished any early optimism the Palestinians might have felt. In the early days of Rabin's new government the US Secretary of State, James Baker, had been to Jerusalem to talk to both sides. The Palestinian delegation told him of their concerns, which now included not just the need to progress to autonomy with an elected Palestinian body, but also developments which had come up since the peace talks began. These included the need to curb Jewish settlement activities, worries about human rights in the Occupied Territories, and the representation of the Palestinian community as a whole in the peace talks, with voices to speak for East Jerusalem and the worldwide diaspora as well as the Occupied Territories themselves. When the sixth round of the talks opened in Washington on 24 August 1992 there was still an unmistakable mood of optimism, but as the talks continued the Palestinians and the Arab national delegations were forced to reassess their optimism over what could be expected from Labour. And after the loan guarantees went through, Palestinian optimism drained away.

Hamas Flexes its Muscles

The old cycle seemed to have resumed, in which a return of the intifada in the Occupied Territories, in its new and more violent form, accompanied a failure to make progress in the talks in Washington. A new phenomenon was the increasing role played by the Islamic militant movement Hamas. Hamas had existed for some time, and was taking a stronger grip over opinion in the Occupied Territories as the mainstream PLO appeared to be demonstrating its impotence by failing to make any headway in the peace talks. The ordinary population began to feel increasingly ignored, circumvented, tricked and despised by the Israeli and American politicians who they blamed for their plight. They also began to doubt the competence of the Palestinian delegation, which further undermined their credibility and that of the mainstream PLO which backed them. Arafat himself said at the end of 1992 that the result of fourteen months of talks after Madrid had been "zero": this was the kind of pessimism that opened the door to Hamas.[1] Yitzhak Rabin may have been more subtle in his rhetoric, but has in practice been as unbending as Shamir. The circumstances were the classic ones in which the slogan that "Islam is the solution" begins to appeal to people who have despaired of other remedies for their grievances. It is a fact that Islam is enjoying a popular resurgence across the Muslim world, but circumstances of resentment, disillusion and deprivation give it more fertile ground in which to take root.

During the autumn of 1992 there were more talks, and a seventh

1. David Hirst, "On the edge of the divide", *The Guardian*, 21 December 1992.

round took place in October and an eighth in December. Little progress was made at the talks. But the most significant event of late 1992 was the precipitate deportation across the Lebanese border on 17 December of 417 alleged Palestinian supporters of Hamas, in what seems to have been an impulsively angry gesture by Prime Minister Rabin, in response to the death of an Israeli border guard kidnapped from his home and found dead on 16 December. Hamas was understandably secretive, but guesses were that it had the support of at least a quarter of the population of the Occupied Territories, perhaps more in Gaza; though probably less in the West Bank. The armed wing of Hamas, known as Izzedin al-Qasim, took the responsibility for the death of the border guard, Sergeant Nissim Toledano, aged 29.

The degree of frustration that Yitzhak Rabin and his government must have been feeling is underlined by a report written before the deportations took place: "Sergeant Toledano is the fifth Israeli serviceman to be killed by Hamas within a week. Four others died in ambushes in Gaza and Hebron. Mass arrests, curfews and sealing off the Occupied Territories have failed to find the gunmen and highlight Israeli impotence."[2] Rabin decided that if he could not find the gunmen, at least he could deport all those suspected of supporting Hamas. The trouble was that Hamas was a nebulous organisation, and it seems likely that, though Israel had picked out some Hamas sympathisers, many of those picked up and promptly deported, in what soldiers themselves said was a haphazard and chaotic operation, were simply the visibly pious.

The effect of the deportations was to threaten to kill the peace talks, since the PLO reacted to them with what the Israelis may have seen as an unexpected anger. Rabin may have believed that the PLO would turn its back on the deportations, reasoning that Hamas was its rival for support in the Occupied Territories and that a blow against Hamas could only in the end benefit the PLO. It was not to work out like that. The PLO made the contrary calculation that if it was not seen to support Palestinians who were suffering adversity as the result of Israeli actions, it would redound to its discredit. PLO leaders were also straightforwardly incensed at the blatant disregard of the Fourth Geneva Convention, which governs the administration of conquered territories by an occupying power. Israel had consistently ignored

2. Ian Black, "Hamas makes its mark . . .", *The Guardian*, 16 December 1992.

aspects of this convention, as for example in the deportations of 12 Palestinians a year before by the Likud government. But the sheer number of these deportations made them hard to ignore. Rabin may also have expected Lebanon to absorb the deportees, instead of leaving them for a year at Marj el-Zuhour in the inhospitable border region between Israel and Lebanon to languish in the full light of international publicity, surviving on aid from the Red Cross and from sympathetic local Shi'ites.

A Sea Change in America

The other event which took place in the autumn of 1992 was the election in the United States of President Bill Clinton, who denied George Bush his second term as US president and gave America its first Democrat government in twelve years. Just as the Palestinians had to make a fresh calculation about what they might expect from the peace talks when Israel's government changed over from Likud to Labour, so they also needed to make careful estimations of the effect that would follow from such a fundamental political realignment of the talks' main sponsor. The object of bringing peace to the Middle East had been a personal ambition for President Bush, and had been the result of his own assessment of what was the best way to achieve American policy aims in the region in the context of the changes in international circumstances. The pressure he and his officials had brought to bear on Israel was something new in Israel's experience and unique in American foreign policy. Bush's Republican administration had dismissed the pressure of the Jewish Zionist lobby in the United States in the run-up to the election, since they regarded the pressure groups as in any case primarily composed of Democrat voters.

By the same token, the Palestinians felt some apprehension over the potential Israeli influence on the Clinton administration. At the most pessimistic estimation, the Palestinians feared that Bush's even-handed stance and the new-found sympathy to Israel shown by Washington might have been a one-off, which would not be repeated again in Washington. After all, an understanding of the Arab point of view was a new phenomenon in Washington. President Bush's predecessor Ronald Reagan had showed a total commitment to Israel and had been described as the best friend that country had ever had. Meanwhile, sympathy for Israel was also traditional in the Democratic Party, from President Truman, who was the first to recognise the new state, to John F. Kennedy who had struck up a friendship with Israel's first Prime Minister David Ben Gurion in 1962 when Ben Gurion visited America for the first time, and had reassured Israel then that there would continue to be a special relationship between the two countries.

Without President Bush, the Palestinians reasoned, they might lose even the modest amount of support for the Arab case that Bush's Republican administration had shown. In the event there were reasons why the change was not to be so drastic. The US State Department officials who had implemented President Bush's Middle East policy and served as his special advisers were for the most part Democrats in their political sympathies and would stay in office. And Clinton had already decided that the adjustments President Bush had been trying to achieve in the Middle East were beneficial to the policy of the United States. A last round of talks under the Bush administration, round eight, took place in Washington in December, in the context of American assurances meant to pave the way for more talks when the new administration was installed in January.

In spite of the ambient pessimism, the Washington talks were to go ahead in 1993, as the United States managed to convince the Palestinians, probably against their better judgement, that they could attend negotiations without betraying the approximately 400 deportees still huddled in their tents on the Lebanese border with Israel. The Israeli government itself also alienated the Palestinians and risked the complete breakdown of the talks by seeking a judgement from the Israeli supreme court sanctioning the deportation of the Palestinians. All this distracted attention from a very important move initiated by left-wingers within the Labour-led coalition. This was the passage through the Knesset of a piece of new legislation, dear to the hearts of Labour's left-wing and of their Meretz allies, legalising contacts between Israelis and the PLO. This came into effect in January 1993 and was in due course to pave the way for the later contacts between Israel and the Palestinian leadership.

The United States was desperate to reassure the Palestinians at this point of its concern to keep the Washington talks in existence. A first prudent move was a condemnation of Israel's deportation of the 400 Palestinians. In February President Clinton's Secretary of State Warren

Christopher held talks with Palestinians in East Jerusalem, where he met a group of Palestinians centred on the delegation to the peace talks. Christopher listened to a letter from Yasser Arafat, read by Hanan Ashrawi, reiterating the PLO's interest in achieving peace, and at his meeting with Palestinian representatives Warren Christopher produced six points designed to explain the new administration's attitude to the peace process. These were a continuing American commitment to UN resolutions 242 and 338, an assurance of Washington's commitment to making progress at the talks, support for the commitments made by President Bush, and an assurance that the United States understood the Palestinians' views. Later in 1993, in another gesture designed to underline the American commitment to the talks, the American administration also gave the assurance that the United States would play a full part as a participant in future rounds of talks.

Oslo

But what was happening now on the peace front was not taking place in front of the cameras in the diplomatic cockpit of Washington. Movement was taking place, but it was going on in secret, in clandestine meetings and secret channels, which were to lead ultimately up to the scene of 13 September on the White House lawn. Hints and suggestions indicate that there was more than one secret channel of contact between Israel and the Palestinians open during 1993, as Rabin and Peres on the one hand, and Arafat on the other, attempted to supplement the increasingly sterile Washington talks. Abu Ala has said that Arafat was involved in other channels of contact.[3] In public, though Rabin introduced a note of realism in April when he announced that Faisal Husseini would be allowed to take part directly in the talks, and would no longer be barred as a resident of East Jerusalem, there was little progress in the official talks. Round nine began on 27 April and went on into May 1993, round ten in July, and round eleven started in September, without reporting any marked progress. The characteristic atmosphere at the talks had become one of obfuscation, complexity, and an almost retrograde

3. Panorama, BBC1, 13 September 1993.

movement as issues were defined and redefined. The action was elsewhere.

The United States administration appeared embarrassed, when the Oslo breakthrough was announced, by the continuing emphasis it had put on the Washington talks. To save its face it was at great pains, when the Oslo process had become public knowledge, to claim that it had not been unaware of what was going on. This seems however unlikely to have been wholly true. One report suggests that when Secretary of State Warren Christopher was told about the Oslo channel and its success on 27 August 1993 he was "amazed". The account continues: "Washington had been aware since the outset that secret talks were taking place, but had little idea of the pace and scope. The US knew about four secret channels that the Israelis were operating with the PLO and believed Israeli diplomats who said, in the words of a senior US official, that nothing 'had particularly jelled'."[4] There certainly had been other contacts: among others Yossi Sarid, Israel's Environment Minister and a Meretz party member, had been talking to Nabil Shaath, the PLO official attached to the Washington talks; and Haim Ramon, the left-wing Labour Health Minister, had held his own conversation with Ahmed Tibi, a Jerusalem doctor who had stood for election in Israel on the Meretz ticket and is now an Arafat aide.

On the other hand, another account affirms that after each of the meetings in Norway, Deputy Foreign Minister Egeland made a report to the US State Department, while State Department official Dan Kurtzer was also monitoring the talks, so that the Americans must have known the detail of what was going on.[5] The truth may be that while Washington may have had some notion about contacts in Oslo, the Norwegians had been limiting the amount of information they passed on after May, when unguarded remarks by Americans during the multilateral talks indicated that the Americans' discretion was not entirely to be counted on. Officials in Washington may also have dismissed reports from Oslo as no more than indications of another of the "freelance" schemes which they knew Israel's Foreign Minister Shimon Peres was trying out. Certainly Peres, a veteran Labour politician with as long a pedigree as Yitzhak Rabin, who has also

4. Kevin Fedarko, "Swimming the Oslo channel", *Time*, 13 September 1993.

5. Christophe Boltanski et. al., "Israel–OLP: sept mois pour un accord", *Libération*, 9 September 1993.

served his turn as Israel's Prime Minister, has long been Rabin's rival as well as his colleague, and might have been suspected of exaggerating the value of the Oslo talks of which he became, behind the scenes, the patron. He was beginning by 1993 to acquire a reputation in the context of Israel–Palestinian negotiations as an optimist, a speculator, and a kite-flier. But on this occasion the Oslo channel, certainly one of the ventures of which Peres was the patron, was to come good in the most spectacular way, as the Americans were to discover.

There was a certain amount of action in 1993 in the Washington talks but it did not concern the Palestinians. While little moved in the Palestinian bilateral talks, there was a flurry of interest and concern as it began to seem that Syria might be preparing in its bilateral talks with Israel to reach an agreement on the future of the Golan Heights. That speculation proved to be premature, partly because Israel had not taken into account how determined Damascus was to recover the whole of the Golan with no territorial compromise, and partly because Syria decided not to run ahead of the Palestinians, who were apparently making no progress. Indeed the whole Syrian episode could be put down to Israeli wishful thinking, and might be seen as another outbreak of Israel's earnest desire to reach peace settlements with its other Arab neighbours, on the lines of the peace treaty with Egypt, while avoiding the inconveniences which would arise from having to settle with the Palestinians first. These Syrian manoeuvres also appear in a new light after the revelation of the Oslo negotiations between Israel and the Palestinians, and the new climate of opinion explains the movement which again seemed to be getting under way in talks between Israel and Syria in January 1994.

There have now been some revelations about how the Oslo talks were initiated, and the course they took, as some of the participants and facilitators, Israeli, Palestinian and Norwegian, have begun to talk to the media. Much of the praise has gone to the Norwegian Foreign Minister, the late Johan Joergen Holst, whose death in January 1994 at the age of 56 was tragic and may have robbed him of the Nobel peace prize for which his name was being suggested. Holst's role was important, but he was himself aware that he took the credit for an enterprise in which a number of Norwegians, diplomats and others, had played a vital role.

It is also strongly arguable that the credit for initiating the Oslo channel, as it became known to its participants, should go to the

Israeli Deputy Foreign Minister, Yossi Beilin. But also the acknowledgement for sanctioning it should go on the Israeli side to Foreign Minister Shimon Peres, whose conviction was very firm that Israel's future could only be assured through peace. As the Oslo negotiations developed, Peres increasingly threw his weight behind them. It is questionable how much credit Yitzhak Rabin can take: though he was happy to back the Oslo channel when it looked like succeeding, and by the time it began to look as if Oslo might work he was being fully consulted by Peres, his conservatism and caution might have restrained him from the gamble which Peres was confident enough to approve. Meanwhile for the Palestinians the main participant was Abu Ala, who shared with Yasser Arafat the job of managing the PLO's finances. His activities were in turn sanctioned by Mahmoud Abbas, known as Abu Mazen, the Palestinian foreign affairs specialist, and by Arafat himself.

Shimon Peres has published his own account of the secret negotiations, in his new book: *The New Middle East.*[6] Peres tells us that the Oslo channel was to last eight months until the deal was clinched on the morning of 18 August 1993. It was two weeks earlier, on 4 August, that Peres decided that all the remaining differences between Israel and the Palestinians over the limited autonomy agreement at which they were aiming had at last been ironed out. On that day Peres sent a message to Johan Joergen Holst to say that in his view the differences had been bridged, and that the time for an agreement had come. Shimon Peres said he felt the time was coming close when he received a letter in June 1993 from the PLO spokesman Bassam Abu Sharif, one of Yasser Arafat's close associates, assuring him of the PLO's anxiety for peace and asking for official Israeli government recognition. Bassam Sharif's letter expressed the Palestinian perception of him as the Israeli politician most likely to be able to make peace: "We admire you for your clear vision of the future, your ability to grasp new ideas, and your authentic vision of the creation of a new Middle East. That we share with you. When we look in depth at the position of various Israeli ministers, you emerge as the one with the necessary historical dimension to build a better future."[7] The letter no doubt signified that the PLO in Tunis felt the time was coming for the talks that hitherto had been held in Norway to develop into a

6. Shimon Peres, *The New Middle East*, Element, London 1993.
7. Ibid.

discussion at the level of principals, between the PLO and the Israeli cabinet.

Peres details how he and Rabin kept everything to do with Oslo scrupulously secret, in order not to have to cope with domestic criticism or interference from Israel. This was the last thing they wanted, especially as the Israeli government was in increasing trouble over maintaining its majority. The problem was the Shas party, where leader Arye Deri finally led his members out of the coalition, after an Israeli court ruled that he could no longer serve as a minister because of earlier corruption scandals. Unbelievable as it might seem, it was on the night the agreement with the Palestinians was signed, 13 September, that Shas left the coalition, thus putting in jeopardy Yitzhak Rabin's ability to push through a vital Knesset vote backing his actions. In the event, Labour got through with 61 votes against 50, after the abstention of the Shas members and three Likud members who defied their party by refusing to vote against the peace plan.

The Actors

Further details of the Oslo channel have come from Norwegian sources and from the participants in the talks, confirming the date of mid-December given by Shimon Peres for the beginning of the talks, but also detailing the level of Norwegian participation. Journalists have laboured to uncover what detail the participants are willing to divulge of the Oslo channel: the book by BBC reporter Jane Corbin is very informative about what happened at the talks, which she has derived largely from extensive conversations with the Norwegian negotiators Terje Larsen and Mona Juul, as well as other interviews, and the account given here relies heavily on it.[8] On the other hand, though they give invaluable information, the early accounts may have exaggerated the degree to which the chance encounters and personal enthusiasms of the first unofficial Norwegian intermediaries influenced the outcome. In fact Shimon Peres had already contacted Norway's

8. See especially Jane Corbin, *Gaza first: the secret Norway channel to peace between Israel and the PLO*, Bloomsbury, London 1994. Jane Corbin was the television reporter who made the BBC Panorama programme cited elsewhere and her book is an invaluable primary source.

former Foreign Minister, Thorvald Stoltenberg, in 1992 to see if Norway could act as an intermediary to get clandestine talks going, in order to try to circumvent what seemed to have become the intractable blockage of the Washington talks.[9] The PLO had also contacted Norway at least four times during 1991 and 1992, according to Jan Egeland, Deputy Foreign Minister, in order to try to get Norwegian mediation between themselves and Israel.[10] Stoltenberg himself had been long interested in what Norway could do for the Middle East peace process. The Norway channel was the outcome more of the consistent policies of Israel, the PLO and the Norwegian government than of personality and historical accident, romantic though that theory might seem.

There was a Scandinavian tradition of international peace-making, in which Stoltenberg was anxious to follow. The first Secretary-General of the United Nations, Trygve Lie, who served from 1946 to 1953 also had his roots in the Norwegian Labour Party, and that tradition was still alive. Stoltenberg was also a veteran Norwegian Labour politician who had served as Norway's Ambassador to the United Nations and had briefly been UN High Commissioner for Refugees before returning to the Norwegian government in 1990. In his first stint as Foreign Minister in 1987, Stoltenberg had set in train a systematic involvement of Norway in Palestinian and Israeli affairs. Labour returned to power in Israel, the international links between the Norwegian and Israeli Labour parties were quickly exploited by both Peres and Stoltenberg. In 1992 Stoltenberg was able to use his young assistant, diplomat Mona Juul, to make discreet unofficial contacts and get a channel of confidential negotiations moving under Norwegian auspices, but it would be giving too much responsibility to Mona Juul or to her husband Terje Larsen to suggest that they were ever the prime movers, though they played an important part.

Norway is a small country, whose population is actually less than that of Israel, and personal links in political, diplomatic and academic circles are strong. Another way in which the country resembles Israel is that the informal links of long-standing friendship help to oil the wheels of politics and business. The younger Norwegians who helped to initiate the Oslo channel all knew each other. Stoltenberg's deputy, Jan Egeland, was an idealist who had worked with Amnesty

9. Kevin Fedarko, loc. cit.
10. Boltanski, loc. cit.

International and the International Red Cross in Geneva, as well as doing a stint at the Hebrew University in Jerusalem, and he was a friend of Mona Juul, the wife of Terje Larsen, who was himself the go-between who initially brought together the participants in the Oslo channel. Larsen himself was not a professional diplomat, and Mona Juul should be the one who is given full credit for realising and reporting the potential importance of Larsen's contacts. Terje Larsen was a social science researcher, working for the Norwegian Institute for Applied Social Sciences, FAFO, whose sociological survey in the Gaza Strip and the West Bank had been funded by Stoltenberg. One of Larsen's research assistants was Stoltenberg's daughter, and Larsen's academic co-worker was Marianne Heiberg, the wife of Johan Joergen Holst, who became Foreign Minister in April 1993. Mona Juul herself, a young diplomat who had served in Cairo, as Stoltenberg's assistant, completed the circle. It was through this tight nexus of acquaintance that the contact Terje Larsen made with Yossi Beilin, Israel's Deputy Foreign Minister from July 1992, was quickly drawn to official attention in Oslo, and may indeed have been prompted by the Norwegian Foreign Ministry. It was also after an approach to the Norwegian Foreign Ministry by the Palestinian financial expert Abu Ala that Mona Juul and Terje Larsen were able to bring the Palestinians and the Israelis into contact in what was to prove so fruitful an encounter.

If the Norwegians provided the means for the initial contacts to take place, the motive force, however, came from Yossi Beilin, who in turn was the faithful henchman of Foreign Minister Shimon Peres. Beilin was increasingly aware that the official talks in Washington were going nowhere. As round succeeded round, what was developing was becoming almost ritualised. Each delegation would group in its own quarters, meeting only relatively briefly and in the most stylised way to exchange and reject the details of mutually incompatible proposals. There was no openness of discussion, and little opportunity for the delegations to exchange ideas informally. The blockage in Washington made Beilin anxious to find an alternative way of allowing responsible Israelis and Palestinians to talk about the issues. Shimon Peres was also keen to find a way of revitalising the negotiating process. Beilin himself had set up a think-tank to look into ways of promoting peace through direct contacts with the Palestinians. One of Beilin's two associates was Yair Hirschfeld, of the University of Haifa, who had already made many contacts with Palestinians in the Occupied Territories.

Tentative Contacts

Larsen was told in May 1992 that Beilin, then an opposition Knesset member, could be a useful contact, and no doubt fed that information back via his wife to the Norwegian Foreign Ministry, who would themselves have been by this time assessing who the policy-makers would be in a likely Israeli Labour government. Beilin was aware of Larsen, who had been studying Palestinian issues in the West Bank and Gaza, and was interested in peacemaking between the Arabs and Israel. The Norwegian Foreign Ministry must certainly have been aware of Larsen's intentions when he met Beilin in an encounter snatched during Beilin's campaign for the June 1992 election. Beilin knew he was destined for office if Labour won the election, and the opinion polls were beginning to point that way. He knew of Larsen's ministry connections, and was interested to see if Norway could use its good offices to get a second track of negotiations going, in secret, where Palestinians and Israelis could get down to the discussion of their differences away from the stultifying effects of protocol and publicity.

Larsen seems to have been empowered to make early promises that Norway could use its good offices. Other meetings swiftly followed, at first between Beilin, Larsen and Feisal Husseini just before the Israeli elections; and, after Labour had come to power and Beilin was installed as Deputy Foreign Minister, another on a more official level between Beilin, Egeland, Juul and Larsen. On this occasion, on 12 September 1992, Egeland agreed Norway would organize secret contacts between Israelis and Palestinians. Norway wanted to make clear that it would be willing to host any kind of meeting the Israelis were able to set up, and would use its diplomatic capacity to make any arrangements that might be necessary. Between then and December, when the first contacts arranged by Larsen were to take place, Stoltenberg took the precaution of telling the US State Department what he was proposing to do.

Meanwhile on the Palestinian side, developments were also taking place. The PLO hierarchy in Tunis was as strongly aware as were the Israelis that the Washington talks were getting nowhere, and were just as anxious to develop other contacts. The PLO's foreign affairs specialist, Mahmoud Abbas, known as Abu Mazen, discreetly contacted Egypt in October 1992, to ask if the Egyptian Foreign Minister, Amr Moussa, could arrange a meeting between the PLO and Israel. The answer was no: Yitzhak Rabin felt the approach was premature, and

Abu Mazen's initiative went nowhere. On the other hand, Shimon Peres confirms in his account of the talks that contact between the Israeli Foreign Ministry and the PLO was also maintained through the intermediary of the Egyptian government, where President Mubarak, Foreign Minister Amr Moussa, and adviser Ousama el-Baz were all involved in tentative contacts between Israel and the PLO from the autumn of 1992, and were later aware of the secret talks in Oslo. Peres says he was convinced by the Israeli author and intellectual Amos Oz that in the last resort no progress could be made without direct contact between Israel and the PLO.

But it was through the Norwegian connection that the Palestinian overture was to succeed, and that the Palestinians were to be brought into effective contact with Israel. Mona Juul and Terje Larsen's crucial meeting with Abu Ala was in February 1992, when the Palestinians had come to Norway. The purpose of his visit was to try to get funding from the Norwegian government for the PLO and he approached the Norwegian Foreign Ministry. No doubt the issue of informal contacts with Israel was again raised. Abu Ala soon became aware that Larsen and Juul had direct contact with Israel, and indicated that he might be interested in meeting Israeli doves. The Norwegians were to capitalise on that meeting in December 1992, when they were at last able to bring Abu Ala, a senior Palestinian, into contact with Yair Hirschfeld, who acted as a proxy for Yossi Beilin. Abu Ala had conveyed to Larsen that if Israel wanted to contact the PLO leadership, the result would not be disappointing: as he put it, "This is not a game."[11] This was the meeting which Shimon Peres rightly counts as the real beginning of the Oslo channel. The contacts painstakingly made by Juul and Larsen on Stoltenberg's behalf had begun to pay off.

11. Ibid.

CHAPTER 7

OSLO COMES OF AGE

The Talks Begin

What could be called the preliminary phase of the exchange was also the most tentative and the least formal. Yossi Beilin was in London for the multilateral talks on regional economic development, and had brought with him his researcher Yair Hirschfeld so that Hirschfeld could make contacts among the Palestinian participants in a less formal way than would be open to Beilin. Terje Larsen was also in London: his ostensible reason was to discuss research funding with Hirschfeld. On the Palestinian side, Abu Ala was naturally present for the economic talks. All the actors were able to be in London simultaneously, each for good reasons. The meeting was the result of months of patient preparation, by Beilin and Larsen, with the knowledge and backing of the Norwegian Foreign Ministry.

Hirschfeld and Abu Ala met discreetly over a late breakfast at Larsen's London hotel, the Cavendish, for what was still for Hirschfeld a technically illegal meeting. Abu Ala arrived accompanied by Afif Safieh, the PLO's London representative, for an encounter whose potentiality the Palestinians clearly wanted to explore. The Palestinians wanted to know who Hirschfeld represented, and though he stressed his independence he also indicated his links with Beilin. The other member of Yossi Beilin's research team, Ron Pundak, recalls how unlikely it had seemed at the time that the meeting could be the seed of the major change in Middle East politics that has resulted: "Nobody believed that out of this funny meeting in London, involving an academic and someone who is not a high-ranking politician, something big would happen."[1] Hirschfeld met Abu Ala again later the same day, but before that second meeting he was debriefed by the American official in charge of the US delegation at the multinationals, Dan Kurtzer. Kurtzer had already been told by Jan Egeland in

1. Kevin Fedarko, loc. cit.

November 1992 that Norway was contemplating opening an informal link between Israel and the Palestinians. The United States apparently gave its blessing to the opening of another informal channel.

From that exploratory meeting, more purposeful contacts soon developed. At the PLO headquarters in Tunis Abu Ala reported to Abu Mazen, who handled all contacts with Israel. Abu Mazen reported to Arafat, who gave his approval for the contacts that were being made. Larsen visited Tunis two weeks later, in late December 1992, ostensibly to discuss his survey of the Occupied Territories. With full PLO backing for his tentative contact, Abu Ala now asked for confirmation that Yair Hirschfeld represented Yossi Beilin, and asked in direct terms whether Norway could facilitate further meetings. What he wanted was secret meetings, and he proposed that Larsen's research institution, FAFO, could provide a front. Larsen was told that Abu Mazen was aware of the contacts that had been made, and he was received by Arafat: a clear sign that the Palestinian leader, who would otherwise have had little time to spare for an obscure Norwegian sociologist, was aware of Larsen's role. Larsen gained the impression that Arafat was asking for Norway's help. Yossi Beilin quickly agreed to Hirschfeld's participation in talks, but insisted that everyone involved must agree not to divulge his connection with what would take place. Just as, in London, Yossi Beilin had maintained the fiction of being unconnected and not responsible when he sent Hirschfeld to make the initial contact, Beilin now wanted, for the moment at least, not to be identifiable as the progenitor of the Oslo channel. The breaking row over the deportation of the alleged Hamas activists made Beilin's position still more sensitive.

Nonetheless, the Oslo process went ahead. FAFO became the cover, and the Norwegian Foreign Ministry agreed to pay the bills. Norway's Prime Minister gave her own go-ahead to the process. Secrecy was built in to the operation. In Tunis, only Abu Ala, Abu Mazen, and Arafat himself knew what was happening. The official Palestinian negotiating team in Washington was kept in the dark throughout, until the Oslo process was almost at an end. In Israel, for the time being only Yossi Beilin knew: it seems that Shimon Peres was not told the details about Oslo until late January after the end of the first meeting that took place in Norway, when Peres also informed Rabin of what was happening. In Norway, only Larsen, Juul, Egeland and Stoltenberg knew what was to take place. Even Holst's wife, Marianne Heiberg was not told, and Holst was not fully aware of what was happening until he took over the Foreign Ministry in April when Stoltenberg returned to the United Nations.

The secrecy was maintained throughout the duration of the talks. A news agency report which was to appear in June to the effect that there were clandestine negotiations taking place in Norway, published by a sharp-eyed AFP reporter in Washington, who had evidently heard a rumour from US State Department sources, was swiftly discredited by denials and disclaimers from the Norwegian Foreign Ministry. The AFP report mentioned the State Department official Dennis Ross as the initiator of the talks, which might indicate how seriously they were now being taken by the Americans. It could also have reflected an offer which was said to have been made by Norway in January to involve the Americans directly in the talks, if they wished. That offer was probably made to Ross via Dan Kurtzer. The same rumour that talks were taking place was resuscitated later by the Israeli press, with a report in *Ha'aretz* on 12 July that a high-level Israeli negotiator was talking to the Palestinians somewhere in Europe. Again this was dismissed as groundless, this time by the Israeli government.

The participants in the first round of the Norway channel arrived in Oslo on 20 January, to be installed by Larsen in a country house belonging to a wealthy industrialist at the country town of Sarpsborg, 80 kilometres south of Oslo. In what were deliberately informal circumstances the two delegations were encouraged to exchange ideas. The Israelis were represented by Yair Hirschfeld and his colleague Ron Pundak. The Palestinian team was Abu Ala, accompanied by a colleague and fellow economist Maher el-Kurd, who was nominated by Arafat, and a third man, Hassan Asfour, who was to report to Abu Mazen. Asfour was a former communist from Gaza who had studied in Moscow and in Baghdad, and of the three was the most unlikely interlocutor for the Israelis. His role was to keep a precise record of the talks, for the Palestinian participants and for the leadership in Tunis. The working language of the Norway channel was from the beginning English, and English was the language in which texts of agreements and other documents were drafted.

The two days of talks began on 21 January with a briefing by Marianne Heiberg on the Gaza and West Bank project run by FAFO. She was unaware of the real aim of the gathering, and the intention was to provide a disguise: Heiberg would return to Oslo and tell colleagues an academic meeting was taking place. Once the talking began in earnest, what the two delegations decided to do was try to produce a "declaration of principles": an achievement which had eluded the official talks in Washington. This would be a document which would set out the aims of negotiation, and also define what each side regarded as negotiable and what was not open to discussion. It seemed to the two sides that it was vital not to recriminate about the past, and that an attempt to aim at a comprehensive agreement in which all the outstanding problems would be tackled was probably doomed to failure. These two errors had contributed to the stalemate of the Washington talks. The idea of an interim accord was quick to surface: to agree on what could be agreed on and set the rest aside for later. In addition, early in the proceedings, Abu Ala mentioned the idea of an early Israeli withdrawal from Gaza: an idea he knew would be attractive to the Israelis, since it had been widely canvassed in the Israeli press. Hirschfeld seems to have listened attentively to that idea, which he and Abu Ala both knew was close to Shimon Peres's own thinking. -

When Yossi Beilin heard about what had happened in Norway, he immediately briefed Peres, who was satisfied to hear that "Gaza first" was on the table and in the minds of the PLO. Peres took Rabin fully into his confidence within the next two weeks. Rabin was sceptical, and had other irons in the fire, just as Yasser Arafat did in Tunis. But he was willing to let the Oslo channel continue and sanctioned a further meeting. This second encounter began on 12 February, once again at Sarpsborg. Both sides had developed the tentative plan that had been drawn up in January, adding their own elaborations and glosses, and in the process making the document less acceptable to the other side. A joint document was once again produced by the end of the meeting. Following the February meeting a third encounter took place in March. "Gaza first" remained a central proposal, but many of the other ideas discussed in Norway were unacceptable to Israel or to the PLO, or were simply too crude, taking insufficient stock of reactions and consequences. But for both Israel and the Palestinians the most important thing was the growing sense that the other side was prepared to do a deal: a contrast with the stagnation in Washington.

The talks in Oslo were on the brink of taking a more serious turn, and were about to be transformed from exploratory conversations into a more serious channel of negotiation. Thorvald Stoltenberg had briefed US Secretary of State Warren Christopher on talks so far, and had given him a copy of the document produced at Sarpsborg. Dan

Kurtzer, the State Department official contacted by Jan Egeland at the beginning of the whole process, part of whose brief it was to monitor informal Israeli–Palestinian contacts, was also kept in the picture. Kurtzer felt it was unlikely the Oslo channel could come to fruition unless Yitzhak Rabin himself was involved, as he told Beilin and Hirschfeld when he met them in Jerusalem in April. But though he was apparently privately sceptical about their chance of success he encouraged them to continue. On 13 April the new Norwegian Foreign Secretary, Johan Joergen Holst, took office. Holst was already part of the social circle which had instigated the Oslo channel: his wife was, of course, Larsen's colleague, and Holst himself was a good friend of Terje Larsen and Mona Juul, as well as incidentally being Thorvald Stoltenberg's brother-in-law. He decided to upgrade Norway's interest in the talks and, while keeping them secret, to give the Norwegian Foreign Ministry a more direct role.

To match the American interest and Norwegian concern with the talks, a new subject area was introduced which also raised the interest of the talks a further notch. This was the idea of adding a town in the West Bank to Gaza as part of the area to be first granted autonomy. That had been proposed to the PLO by Peres through his Egyptian contacts as long ago as the end of 1992, as the first meetings of the Oslo participants were taking place in London. Arafat now decided he wanted a West Bank city to be involved in any interim arrangement and instructed Abu Ala to raise the question of Jericho in Norway. The attraction of this for the PLO was enormous. It would signify that Israel had no intention of offering the Palestinians the Gaza Strip while retaining the West Bank, and indeed as it has eventually found its way through into the interim agreement; the inclusion of Jericho gives an authenticity to the declared intention to extend the agreement to the rest of the Occupied Territories, that an initial agreement which covered only Gaza would, from the Palestinian point of view, have lacked.

The Oslo Channel Takes Centre Stage

At the end of April, the Oslo talks began again, this time at a hotel on the outskirts of Oslo, with a senior Norwegian diplomat, Geir Pedersen, in attendance to signify the Foreign Ministry's more direct concern. The ideas the participants were now working on were centred round three main principles. These were "Gaza first"; the idea of stage by stage withdrawal; and economic cooperation. But as each side began to take the idea of the Oslo channel as a possible means of real communication between Israel and the PLO, which could hold out the hope of a real resolution of the long conflict between them, with the benefits that would bring, what they became more concerned about was to establish the bona fides of the other side. The Palestinians wanted to know to whom Hirschfeld and Pundak were reporting back: was it to Beilin, to Peres, or to Rabin himself? On the other side, the Israelis wanted some demonstration from Abu Ala of the influence he was able to wield within the PLO. Abu Ala was able to show at the multilateral talks on refugee issues held in Oslo from 11 May 1993 that he was able to influence Palestinian policy, and the Palestinians in their turn became convinced of the high level at which Hirschfeld and Pundak were reporting.

The next stage came on 15 May, when Peres and Rabin met privately to discuss the question of upgrading the Oslo channel. According to one account, Peres wanted to go to Oslo himself to meet Abu Ala, but Rabin overruled him. Instead, however, they agreed to send Uri Savir, a young career diplomat who had just been appointed director-general of the Israeli Foreign Ministry: the highest non-political figure, who was answerable directly to Peres. Hirschfeld and Pundak would continue, in order to provide continuity and maintain the Palestinians' confidence, but Savir would fly to Norway to join the talks. Looking back on the Oslo channel, Peres himself waxes almost lyrical with praise for the role of Norway:

> Norway is a magnificent country – beautiful scenery, extraordinary people. A close-knit group of top government people made itself available for passing messages between ourselves and the PLO. . . . They acted with absolute discretion. When discussion began to intensify, they spared no logistical or other effort to keep the momentum going and shield us from the curious. As soon as I knew the talks were to be taken seriously I gave the Prime Minister the background information and then kept him informed of every detail. Together we worked out the directives to the Israeli delegation. . . .[2]

The talks which continued in May were still aiming at the

2. Peres, op. cit., p. 14.

production of an agreed declaration of principles, and the two main items Savir wanted to bring up were Jerusalem, which the Israelis wanted to be kept firmly off the agenda, and Jericho, which Israel wanted to discuss. Savir was anxious to persuade the Palestinians to set Jerusalem on one side, so that the idea of interim agreement over Gaza and Jericho could be pursued. Israeli intransigence over Jerusalem was too strong to permit it even to come up for discussion at an early stage. Savir was therefore keenly pushing for the Palestinians to agree to allow it to be put aside for later discussion. He was highly gratified to find that when Abu Ala contacted Abu Mazen in Tunis to ask him for guidance, that Abu Mazen agreed to leave the issue of Jerusalem on one side. At the same time at the official peace talks in Washington, where the ninth round of talks was in progress, the Israelis were also pressing the Palestinians to accept their own text of a declaration of principles, which in the event the official Palestinian delegation rejected. But in Oslo the auguries were more propitious. Uri Savir's verdict was favourable: "I can do business with him. I will try and sell it."[3]

Back in Israel, he confirmed Peres's feeling that the Oslo channel could be taken seriously, and said the same thing to the more sceptical Rabin. In his view, Israel should negotiate seriously with Abu Ala as the PLO's representative. At around the same time, in Washington, Faisal Husseini was giving an interview to the East Jerusalem newspaper *al-Quds* in which he said that "sooner or later there will be no escaping direct talks with the PLO and with PLO leader Yasser Arafat."[4] Husseini added that the boycott on talks with the PLO had already been broken, thus raising the question whether the PLO members of the team in Washington, if not the others, knew something about Oslo by this stage. Meanwhile, at the end of May Holst briefed Warren Christopher about developments in Oslo, including the news that Israel was now involved officially and at the highest level.

The talks were again upgraded with the arrival of yet another Israeli negotiator to join Uri Savir and the two academics. This was Joel Singer, a Washington-based lawyer of Israeli nationality, who was a

3. Corbin, op. cit., p. 86.
4. Hillel Kutler, "Israel presents Palestinians with informal declaration of principles", *The Jerusalem Post, International Edition*, 15 May 1993.

trusted friend and former associate of Yitzhak Rabin, when Rabin had been Minister of Defence in the Likud-led coalition government in 1988. His first meeting with the other negotiators was on 11 June. Singer brought a lawyer's eye to the document which the negotiators in Norway had been trying to produce, and also gave Rabin a voice in the negotiations and a means of monitoring their progress. As the talks were upgraded and became more serious, with more participants and more vested interests involved, there was a corresponding danger that they could become bogged down in the same kind of difficulties that had beset the talks in Washington. But Singer also gave both the talks and his own position an immediate boost by confirming that he represented Prime Minister Rabin. Singer first participated in the session of talks which began on 11 June, when participants recall that his technique was to ask interminable questions, pinning down the Palestinians on points of detail, in a way that made them suspect there would be hard bargaining to come. Singer appeared aggressive and aroused resentment. The Norwegians had grave misgivings, fearing that their carefully cultivated channel of negotiation might be about to be torpedoed, and was certainly in danger of becoming as unproductive as the talks in Washington.

Singer's participation was welcomed in Tunis as evidence of Rabin's commitment to the talks, and the Palestinian leadership was in no doubt about the need to go ahead. June 23 was the date of the letter to Peres drafted by Arafat's aide Bassam Abu Sharif. Meanwhile, Rabin and Peres gave Singer the job of drafting a proposal for an agreement, to take the place of the declaration of principles the Oslo channel had so far been working on. The document Singer was to work on would take into account the impressions he had gained from Abu Ala during his questioning of what the bottom line would be for the Palestinians: the things they would not negotiate away. It would also take account of the public position taken by the Palestinians in Washington, which they could not afford to repudiate. But it would also make sure that the Israelis' fundamental demands were not ignored. In the end, the purpose of the document was the same as the purpose of the whole negotiating process, namely to offer the Palestinians enough to get their cooperation in bringing the conflict between the Palestinians and the Israeli state to an end, the key to the normalisation of Israel's position in the region, while safeguarding Israel's security and its own vision of its integrity.

On 3 July talks re-opened in earnest in Norway. The Norwegians tried to keep the atmosphere informal, though at this stage they brought in for the first time the Norwegian security service to mount guard. Another large country house had been found by Deputy Foreign Minister Jan Egeland, this time at Gressheim, an hour's drive north of Oslo. The Israeli delegation now consisted of Uri Savir and Joel Singer, as well as Yair Hirschfeld and Ron Pundak. Abu Ala still had with him Hassan Asfour, but Maher el-Kurd's place was taken by Mohammed Abu Koush, a lawyer and a Palestinian official resident in Germany. The Norwegians were represented by Geir Pedersen, the official earlier drafted to look after the talks, as well as Terje Larsen and Mona Juul, and Jan Egeland himself came to join the session. The meeting seemed pregnant with possibility, but broke up with no conclusion after the proposal drafted by Singer had been thoroughly examined by the Palestinians. Each side went back to base for further consultations. Five major points still needed substantial discussion. These were the acceptability of "Gaza and Jericho first", the inclusion of UN resolutions 242 and 338 as points of reference, the framework for later negotiations on the permanent status of the Occupied Territories, the status of the refugees from the 1967 war, and the participation of East Jerusalem in elections.

The talks re-started within a week, on 10 July, this time at yet another venue, a hotel at Halvorsbole. Tunis and Jerusalem were both apparently keen to keep up the momentum. The Norwegians were optimistic that the differences could be ironed out and that an agreement could now be achieved. They perhaps failed to appreciate how much new material would be added to the competing drafts in Israel and by the PLO. Much work in fact still remained to be done. The five points outstanding from the previous talks were still on the table, but they were augmented by the further concerns of the Palestinian leadership and the Israeli government. Yitzhak Rabin wanted security to be discussed in detail. But the Palestinians had a long list of further points for discussion, of which the Israelis regarded several as very important, which had been added by Arafat and the PLO's legal advisers. The meeting again broke up quickly, after the Israelis failed to persuade Abu Ala to return to the draft they had agreed at the previous session, with only the five outstanding questions to discuss.

This time Norwegian Foreign Minister Johan Joergen Holst himself took a hand. Fortuitously, he had a long-standing engagement to visit Tunis and talk to his Tunisian opposite number Habib ben Yahyia set up by his predecessor Thorvald Stoltenberg. That meant that without attracting undue attention he was able to visit PLO Chairman Yasser Arafat on 13 July, where he was easily able to convince himself that the PLO Chairman was fully *au fait* with the negotiations which had been carried out so far. Holst had taken Mona Juul with him to Tunis, and was able to send her to Jerusalem to convince the Israelis that the PLO were in earnest, however obstructive they might for the moment seem to be, and that Arafat himself was fully behind the Oslo channel. She and her husband were met by all the Israeli negotiators, headed by Shimon Peres himself, who were anxious to assess the value of proceeding, given what they perceived as deliberate obstruction by the Palestinian side in adding new conditions at this stage. This may have been the most important moment in Norway's participation in the talks: at any rate the diplomat Juul, and her husband the facilitator of the talks, succeeded over the next two days in persuading the Israelis that all was not lost. After a further meeting in Tunis it seemed as if the Palestinians would agree to abandon their new document and return to the one negotiated at Gressheim.

Agreement Nears

Though agreement was now in fact close, there were to be more moments of anguish before the two sides were finally brought together. At the next meeting in Norway on 24 July there was instant disappointment for the Israelis when they realised that the Palestinians would insist after all on talking about the document they had produced at Halvorsbole, with its unacceptable conditions. There were confrontations and manoeuvres. In the end the clash was solved by the recognition by each side of the other's central concern. For the Israelis this was security. For the Palestinians, it was the acquisition of the initial segment of territory, in Gaza and Jericho. The Israelis also introduced a new element: the mutual recognition by Israel of the PLO, and by the PLO of Israel's rights and existence. The last-minute wrangling to achieve compromise on the issues the two sides still needed to compromise on took on a cliff-hanging quality. Abu Ala threatened his resignation as the Palestinian negotiator, but retracted. Savir's suggestion was for each side to select, from the sixteen points which remained to be resolved at this stage, the eight on which it believed it could most easily compromise, and to attempt to persuade Jerusalem and Tunis respectively to come up with modified proposals.

The Oslo channel had by this time become the negotiating route on which both sides were placing the greatest reliance, as the official talks lurched from one empty encounter to the next. It was the virtual collapse of the official talks which saved Oslo, when otherwise the problems that had come up might have made it seem to the principals more trouble than it was worth. The necessary compromises were at least in part forthcoming, and Israel was satisfied about the arrangements for its security as they appeared in the document; while the Palestinians felt they would get the territory in which they needed to base themselves and were satisfied with the promise that their extent would spread over the rest of the Occupied Territories. It was becoming urgent to press on quickly with Oslo if news of what was happening was not to leak out, with all the problems that would bring, as factions both in Israel and the PLO would become involved.

Some idea of what was happening in Oslo was also beginning to be more widely known. News of what was happening in Norway was also beginning to be disseminated through official channels. On 3 August Rabin admitted to Warren Christopher that there was the possibility of an early deal on Gaza and Jericho. The Americans had not been fully briefed since May, and Christopher evidently suspected that the talks in Norway were running into a blind alley, as the official talks also were. What was apparently a more serious breach of confidence came in early August in Cairo, when Abu Mazen had asked Egyptian intermediaries to discuss with Warren Christopher, on the Egyptian leg of his Middle East tour, proposals which were in effect those under discussion in Oslo; these involved a preliminary deal over Gaza and Jericho, with the issue of Jerusalem postponed for later. Two of the official negotiators, Faisal Husseini and Saeb Erakat, as well as the spokeswoman Hanan Ashrawi, felt so let down by what they suspected were manoeuvres behind their backs that they flew to Tunis and tried to offer their resignations.

The next meeting in Norway on 13 August 1993 again brought problems. Mutual recognition by Israel and the PLO, which had appeared to the Israelis as a proposal the Palestinians would welcome, had itself become fraught with difficulties, as the Palestinians brought a new demand, that the renunciation of violence by the PLO which Israel was asking for should be matched with a parallel renunciation on Israel's part. Foreseeing difficulties, the Israelis asked if that could now be put aside while the declaration of principles was refined to the point where both sides could accept it. Then, in a final consultation with Tunis, Arafat told Abu Ala to call the talks off if more concessions could not be wrung out of the Israelis. The frustrating feeling of having failed at the last fence, combined with a mounting panic that the talks might not be completed, cast a cloud over both negotiating teams, as well as over the Norwegians. In addition, Shimon Peres was due to make an official visit to Sweden and Norway beginning on 17 August, and this was beginning to loom with the force of a deadline in the negotiators' minds.

In the event, Peres decided to take a personal hand in the talks. When he arrived in Stockholm on 17 August, he asked Norwegian Foreign Minister Johan Joergen Holst to come to meet him there. Holst was accompanied by Mona Juul and Terje Larsen, and Peres had brought with him Joel Singer as well as his own staff. Peres explained that he wanted to end the negotiations himself, and as soon as possible, by speaking directly to PLO Chairman Arafat. For Peres, this was to put into practice at last his conviction that Arafat's position at the heart of the Palestinian movement was unassailable, and that in the end Israel could only achieve its aims by talking to him directly. Norwegians telephoned Arafat in Tunis, and put the proposition to him. The PLO leader agreed that it would be possible to negotiate on the telephone, and a dialogue was set up, with Abu Ala at the Tunis end of the telephone link, with Arafat, Abu Mazen, Hassan Asfour, and two others who were by this time aware of the channel, Arafat's aide Yasser Abed Rabbo – who had conducted the PLO dialogue with the United States – and another PLO lawyer, Muhsen Ibrahim. From Stockholm, Johan Joergen Holst spoke for Peres and Singer. The crisis phone call was protracted, but in the end the outstanding points of difference were settled.

Peres himself details in his book the points he believes were crucial for Israel in the final agreement, and the concessions Israel gave:

> We got concessions without which we would never have been able to sign an agreement. These include responsibility for security against threats from outside our borders and responsibility for the security of every Israeli in the territories. Jerusalem remains outside the autonomy accord, although its Palestinian residents will be able to participate in elections for autonomy. The settlements stay where they are, and settlement security stays in the capable hands of the Israeli Defence Force. We promised to continue negotiations on autonomy for other

areas within Judaea and Samaria after the elections, which were targeted for nine months from 13 October 1993, the day the declaration of principles went into effect. Until then, Israel would transfer five important areas of administration – health, education, welfare, tourism and taxes – to the Palestinians.[5]

Letting the Cat out of the Bag

The final accord was signed in Oslo in the small hours of the morning on 20 August, at a private ceremony during Shimon Peres's official visit. Even at this late stage, small verbal amendments were still being made in the text of the agreement. The signing itself was an emotional occasion. Peres tells the story:

> That night in Oslo, I had celebrated my seventieth birthday. In Israel it was still dark, in Norway the early northern dawn was just beginning to show through the mist. Here was a small group of Israelis, Palestinians and Norwegians – partners to one of the best-guarded diplomatic secrets ever, a secret whose imminent revelation would mark a watershed in the history of the Middle East.[6]

The rhetoric was hopeful. Johan Joergen Holst complimented the participants: "In order to create history, you have to have a sense of history, and having a sense of history means making possible that which is necessary. This is what you have done here tonight. You have lived through years of confrontation. Now you are entering a new era of cooperation."[7] Uri Savir expressed the sentiments of liberal Israeli thought: "We Israelis have no desire to dominate the lives and fate of the Palestinians. Therefore with this agreement we are fulfilling not only a political interest, but also a moral predicament of our people. We would like our meeting to be a moral high ground: an encounter of peace, democracy and economic prosperity."[8] For the Palestinians, Abu Ala's speech was more practical: "We do not want the victims of war to become the orphans of peace, and we regard the signing of this

5. Peres, op. cit., p. 28.
6. Peres, op. cit., p. 1.
7. Corbin, op. cit., p. 168.
8. Corbin, op. cit., p. 169.

declaration of principles as a new chapter of hope for them, and as a new important page of our history... Both our people and your people have enough potential and efficient resources if real peace takes place, and cooperation and stabilisation materialise."[9]

The next step was to let the United States know what had been happening. Since May, the briefings given to the State Department had been deliberately sketchy, to avoid damaging leaks. Shimon Peres and Johan Joergen Holst went to the United States to break the news to Warren Christopher in California, where the US Secretary of State was on vacation. Holst was accompanied by Larsen and Juul, and Peres brought with him Joel Singer and his own staff. When they met Christopher on 28 August Peres made a brief but impassioned speech explaining the importance to Israel of what had been negotiated, and Holst stressed that Norway had kept the United States as well informed as it believed possible during the talks it had helped to bring into being. Joel Singer then talked Christopher and his aides through the agreement. Christopher and Dennis Ross were quick to agree that what they had seen was a major breakthrough, of a quite different kind to anything that could now be expected from the official Washington talks. Mutual recognition then seemed to be the only remaining step to be taken. The strategy was to make a public announcement soon, and then hold a signing ceremony which would be conditional on both sides making the act of mutual recognition envisaged by the original document which Savir and Singer had agreed to set aside in the interests of completing the declaration of principles.

The decision when to make an announcement was taken out of the diplomats' hands. On 28 August the Israeli papers carried the news that Peres had met someone from the PLO in Norway, and the government spokesmen had not denied the story. In Tunis, an official had said that Israel and the PLO had reached an accord. By Sunday morning *Ha'aretz* was carrying a text of the agreement. Both the Palestinian and the Israeli negotiating teams were furious at discovering that their own efforts had been superseded, and that they had in effect been duped, by being allowed to struggle on, ploughing their own unrewarding and unproductive furrow, while their respective leaderships had turned their attention and their hopes elsewhere. The problem of the role of the Washington talks, and their

9. Corbin, op. cit., p. 169.

relationship to the agreement which had been made in Norway, was one that remained to be solved. But with the news now definitely out, the Americans confirmed the story, and the Norwegian Foreign Minister gave a news conference, giving his version of how the talks had unfolded and of the Norwegians' role.

Mutual Recognition

But the last element of the negotiations was not yet in place. The mutual recognition documents still needed to be signed. Israel had to accept that the PLO was the legitimate representative of the Palestinian people, and the PLO needed to accept Israel's right to exist, and to renounce those clauses of its charter which recognised the use of violence. The leap for Israel was one of substance. Though the Israeli Labour Party had lifted the ban on contacts between individual Israelis and the PLO, it was a big leap to recognise, and recognise in public, the organization's legitimacy, even though the negotiations which were almost complete had been held with the PLO behind closed doors. Some had long ago taken that step: indeed many on the left in Israel had for many years believed no progress could be made unless Israel talked directly to the PLO. Others, like Shimon Peres, had relatively recently come to see its logical unavoidability. Israel's Prime Minister, Yitzhak Rabin, though a veteran Labour man, was also a hawk, and was in the process of bringing himself with great reluctance to cross the Rubicon of official recognition of the PLO. The problem on the Palestinian side was a different one: of devising a formulation which would not appear to many members of the PLO from different factions and at all levels like a surrender to Israel's demands. At different times and in different contexts, Arafat had already recognised Israel's right to exist, accepted UN resolutions 242 and 338, renounced the use of violence, and had said the clauses of the PLO charter advocating violence were defunct. But to put all this succinctly and acceptably on paper was a different matter.

Negotiation went on, in Oslo and also in Paris, to get a mutually acceptable formulation of the two letters of recognition to be signed by Yitzhak Rabin for the Israeli government and Yasser Arafat for the PLO. Arafat had difficulty with the wording of the part of the letter in which the relevant clauses of the Palestinian Charter were to be repudiated. Arafat eventually settled for the formulation that the wording of the charter was now "not operative and invalid". According to the sections of the charter which Israel wanted removed, Palestinians must work for "the retrieval of Palestine and its liberation through armed struggle", while the text of one key clause contains the exhortation: "Armed struggle is the only way to liberate Palestine." Another controversial issue was Israel's demand that the PLO should repudiate and undertake to quell the intifada. Here Arafat's resistance was stronger, since he realised that this could be fatal to his support in the Occupied Territories where the intifada had since 1987 become an important element in the lives of young Palestinians. The letter he eventually drafted contained an undertaking that the PLO would "renounce the use of terrorism and other acts of violence", and in a separate clause he said he would seek the "normalisation of life" in the Occupied Territories. The PLO, Arafat said, would also recognise "the right of the State of Israel to exist in peace and security". Rabin's reply was simple. His letter simply said that "the government of Israel has decided to recognise the PLO as the representatives of the Palestinian people."

Not only the wording of the letters of recognition had to be settled, but also the agreement of the leaders to write and sign them had to be ratified in Israel by the Knesset and in Tunis by the PLO executive committee, acting on behalf of the Palestine National Council. Arafat faced a hostile PLO executive committee, some of whose members had already stepped down because of what they regarded as the Chairman's excessively conciliatory stance towards Israel. The PLO Chairman was determined to push through the accord which had been reached in Oslo, as well as his proposed recognition of Israel, and he pushed his ideas through the Palestinian forums by a combination of political acumen and force of personality. In the end, only those who felt the most extreme misgivings voted against: others voted for Arafat or abstained because they believed that splitting the Palestinian movement would be a worse danger than accepting the Oslo agreement.

Arafat's own Fatah central committee approved the moves, with six voices against out of a membership of 18, and Arafat also got a majority in the Palestinian executive committee. Of the 18 committee members, two, Shafiq al-Hout and Mahmoud Darwish, had ceased to take part in executive committee decisions in August, while another was ill. George Habash and Nayef Hawatmeh refused to come to the meeting from their bases in Damascus because of their opposition to the agreement. Two committee members, the hard-liners Abdallah Hourani and Mahmoud Ismail, stood out strongly against the proposal, and in the end Arafat won through with nine votes to four. Finally, the Palestinian Central Council, the Palestinians' ultimate body in the absence of a full convocation of the Palestine National Council, voted by 63 votes to 8, with 11 abstentions, in favour of the Oslo agreement and mutual recognition. Some of Arafat's hitherto closest associates were nevertheless very doubtful about the wisdom of what was in effect the renunciation of the Palestinian national struggle in its old form, in exchange for a foothold in Palestine which was of limited extent, both in terms of territory and in terms of jurisdiction. One such was Farouk Kaddoumi, in effect the PLO's foreign minister, who was of course also deeply hurt that he had been kept unaware of the Oslo negotiations. Other doubters, senior in the hierarchy of Fatah and the PLO, were Khalid el-Hassan and Hani el-Hassan. On the other hand, Arafat had important allies, such as Abu Mazen, who was by now deeply committed to the agreement, and Yasser Abed Rabbo, who in terms of his political constituency is the leader of a moderate faction of the DFLP.

In Israel, Rabin also faced political problems. His own Labour Party backed the agreement unquestioningly. Though some hawks on Labour's right-wing may have had reservations, the agreement had the backing of both Rabin and Peres, Labour's two old rivals, and Rabin's own credentials as a patriot who will put Israel's interests first were beyond question for Labour. Labour's left-wing Meretz rivals were even more enthusiastic. The Shas party, in the throes of its own internal difficulties and on the brink of withdrawing from the coalition, nevertheless expressed its support for the agreement. Even within the opposition Likud party, now led by Binyamin Netanyahu rather than the embittered and defeated Yitzhak Shamir, there were some who spoke in favour of the agreement and even a few who would vote for it in due course. But as a whole Likud, under Netanyahu's leadership, was vehemently opposed to the accord, raising the question whether Likud would ever have attempted to reach an agreement with the Palestinians through the Washington process, or if Netanyahu and his political friends would always in the last resort have tended to sabotage peace. On the far right in Israel, the adherents of extremist parties such as Moledet, and Tehiya, the latter now unrepresented in the Knesset, as well as hard-liners like

Rafael Eitan and Ariel Sharon, were beside themselves with rage over what they saw as a betrayal. The more extreme members of the settler movement, as distinct from the less political settlers, were also incensed.

The signing of the mutual recognition documents was completed on 10 September 1993, after the week of anxious exchanges between Tunis and Jerusalem and the last flurried meetings between the negotiators. This eventually opened the way for the meeting in Washington and the public signing of the accord, in the full glare of international publicity, which was welcomed by its supporters as the opening of a new era of great potentiality for peace, but condemned by others, both in Israel and in the ranks of the PLO, as a political mistake which would lead only to disaster. The Israeli critics were concerned with the abandonment of the ideal of Greater Israel, which had during the years of Likud rule from 1977 come to be identified with the ideals of Zionism. Across a spectrum of right-wingers in Israel of different backgrounds, the agreement signed with the Palestinians was seen as a mistake. These ranged from hard-headed soldiers who believed that any Arab presence west of the Jordan was a danger, to political right-wingers who wanted Israel to be able to exploit the land of the Occupied Territories, to a fringe of religious settlers who sincerely believed that the land of Judaea and Samaria, as they preferred to call it, had been given to the Jews by God.

On the Arab side, the opponents again covered a spectrum. Ordinary Palestinians were at first preponderantly in favour, but later began to have misgivings about the degree of control and lack of territory inherent in the new agreement. Political opposition came mainly from the ideological left, mainly from those who had built their lives within the struggle against Israel. There was a very real fear that what the Palestinians had done was not to set their feet on the road to statehood, as many of the younger intellectual supporters of the agreement hoped, but had on the other hand submitted to Israeli and international pressure to accept a poor deal. Finally, on the Palestinian side entrenched opposition came from the religious movement, Hamas, which was growing in influence, which had put an Islamic interpretation on the Palestinian struggle and had its sights, however unrealistically, on the establishment of a Muslim state in the whole of Palestine. Hamas had in common with the ideological left that it would prefer to continue the struggle rather than accept what they saw as the wrong conclusion. In the early enthusiasm in Gaza for the agreement, Hamas seemed to have lost some of its support, but it has been flowing back during the following frustrating months.

Though the determination of the political leaders to press the agreement was enough to get the agreement signed, in spite of the build-up of increasingly vocal opposition from each side's extremist wing, it was sadly not enough to press it through to its intended conclusion on time. The problem was not opposition, it was once again the difficulty of negotiation between the two sides. A Palestinian team led by the senior PLO figure Nabil Shaath, who had been the PLO spokesman attached to the Washington talks, sat down at the Egyptian resort of Taba in Sinai just across the Israeli border, to talk to Palestinian negotiators led by the retired general Amnon Shahak. Their purpose was to put flesh on the Oslo agreement's bones, and to work out the fine detail of Israel's proposed military withdrawal, and the transfer of authority to the Palestinians in Gaza and Jericho.

But in the event, the virtues of the accord also proved to be its failings. The Oslo negotiators had succeeded by looking for points of agreement, and by leaving on one side for later generations of negotiators the interpretations and timetables which could have led to discord and bogged the process down. But that in itself meant that the leeway available for disagreement was still very wide. The negotiators in Taba quickly found points on which they could not agree, and the negotiations there and in el-Arish and in Cairo looked as if they were blighted by the same curse as the failed Washington negotiations. Meetings between Arafat and Rabin, and Arafat and Peres, restarted the talks when they faltered, but progress still seemed alarmingly slow and fraught with problems. We return to that ongoing process of unravelling the implications of the Oslo agreement in the conclusion to this book.

III

The Parameters of Peace

CHAPTER 8

INTERNATIONAL ATTITUDES

America's Present Need

America's bloodless victory in the Cold War, with the fall of Communism and the disappearance of the Soviet Union, has been the most crucial of the factors behind today's new style of negotiation between Israel and the Arabs. The climate of opinion on issues of peace and war altered, and so did the context within which policymakers worked. Through immense economic pressure, exerted by obliging the Communist bloc to compete in a cripplingly expensive arms race which it could not hope to win, the West fulfilled the prophecy that Communism would not be able to satisfy the needs and aspirations of the people of the Eastern bloc. The result is that the world today, with only one superpower, is a very different place from that in which earlier discussions of Middle East peace took place. Political scientists are already reflecting on how the changes that have taken place at the beginning of the 1990s will affect the next century: "The ending of the Cold War has created a remarkable fluidity and openness in the whole pattern and quality of international relations."[1]

The New World Order is a key concept in the new dispensation. The idea of the so-called New World Order was formulated by President Bush on 11 September 1990, in the address to Congress he made as he constructed his Gulf War plans. What he called for was:

A new world order ... a new era – freer from the threat of terror, stronger in the pursuit of justice, and more secure in the quest for peace, an era in which the nations of the world, East and West, North and South, can prosper and live in harmony. . . . Today, that new world is struggling to be born, a world quite different from the one we have

1. See, for example, Barry Buzan, "New World Realpolitik", *International Affairs*, July 1991.

known, a world where the rule of law supplants the rule of the jungle, a world in which nations recognise the shared responsibility for freedom and justice, a world where the strong respect the rights of the weak.[2]

These ideas were more fully developed later, after the end of the Gulf War fighting.[3] It is true that almost four years later the fruition of the new order is still awaited, but one thing is nevertheless certain: the old order is no more.

For the first time since the end of the Second World War, in other words since the moment when Israel came into being, there is a world without polarised conflict between two great power blocs. Such a world is necessarily a very different place, and the change must pervade and influence every crevice of international politics. The United States is able today to pursue policy goals of its own choosing, rather than those crudely thrust upon it by the perceived need to combat Communism on the global stage, and Middle East peace has been one of those goals. In addition, the United States had in President Bush a very different leader from his predecessor, President Reagan. Not only was Reagan the American president who carried to the greatest length the reduction of American foreign policy to a simplified doctrine of opposing Communism, but also his commit-ment to Israel was more absolute and less qualified than that of any other United States president, before or since.

It may be that America is making a new adversary out of militant Islam now that it has beaten Communism. It might be too optimistic to say that American foreign policy is now free from external constraints. The United States may not be able to avoid the need to organise its policies around opposition to an adversary. The United States may step into the role of the Great Satan designated for it by the revolutionary regime in Iran, if it opts to view militant Islam as the new anathema, replacing Communism in America's demonology and in the rationale of its foreign policy.[4] Politicians of the right in Israel have sought to get the United States to continue its unconditional support, on the grounds that Israel, having for so long been a bastion against Communism, now stands out against the new enemy of Islamic fundamentalism. Before Likud lost power in June 1992, that was the

2. US Department of State Current Policy Document No. 1298, 1990.

3. T. B. Millar, "A new World Order?", *The World Today*, January 1992.

4. See, for example, the analysis offered by Edward Mortimer in "Christianity and Islam", *International Affairs*, January 1991.

line taken by the party's ideologue, now its new leader, Binyamin Netanyahu.

The United States has in the event resisted up to the moment the temptation to make Israel its champion in a new battle against militant Islam. On the contrary, America's new freedom to choose foreign policy goals is what enabled Washington to decide to cease to make unquestioning support for Israel a central plank of its policy in the Middle East. This does not mean that the absolute guarantee America has always offered to Israel that it will maintain Israel's integrity and independence as a state no longer exists. But it does mean that America is now in a position to make demands on Israel it has never made before; different demands from those it formerly imposed. When it became clear to the Israeli leadership that President Bush's invitation to peace talks was not one that could be declined, the Israeli leadership was stunned. As one report from Jerusalem put it: "Shamir and his ministers have sounded by turns angry and subdued, defiant and conciliatory. But mostly they have appeared dumbfounded by a series of events that has seemed to upset decade-old assumptions by Israeli leaders about the politics of their relationship with the United States."[5]

The support offered to Israel by the United States had its roots in Israel's origins. The creation of Israel was in some senses made possible by the United States. President Truman offered his approval, and the powerful Jewish community of the United States, whose political backing was largely behind Truman's Democratic Party, gave Israel money and moral support. American succour for the state of Israel could be viewed as a recompense for the Holocaust, the death of millions of Jews in Europe during the Second World War, which was offered to the Jewish people by the government of the United States. This support had the effect of polarising the Middle East. The Communist countries of the Eastern bloc, led by the Soviet Union, saw that Israel's existence was important to the United States, and therefore offered their own friendship to the Arabs, in the knowledge that help against Israel would be welcome. In that sense, the existence of Israel opened the Middle East to the Communists, by allowing the Communists to make an appeal to governments which otherwise themselves might have preferred American help.

---

5. Jackson Diehl, "Israelis shaken by Bush's resolve", *Guardian Weekly*, 29 September 1991 (from the *Washington Post*).

This was not how the United States saw it. American policy makers did not interpret Communist influence in the Middle East as a reaction to Washington's support of Israel, on the contrary, they rationalised their support of Israel by regarding it as a bastion against encroaching Communism, which was a threat in some Arab countries. Syria and Iraq in particular flirted with the Soviet bloc, though Jordan and Lebanon remained conservative societies where the threat was only one of potential Communist subversion. The United States did not criticise Israel's own policies towards the Arabs inside and outside its frontiers, which were seen as Israel's own affair, though occasionally, as at the time of Suez, Washington was not wholly in agreement with Israeli policy. This was the case for so long, that it is hard even for the more realistic Labour government which is in power in Israel today to accept that there has been an irreversible change.

Today, however, the United States asks more of Israel than it has ever done before. In order to get American support, Israel has to fall in with Washington's policy aims. When the nature of the new demands first became clear, the then Likud Prime Minister Yitzhak Shamir was reportedly furious, and said that President Bush was, as he put it, "creating euphoria in the Arab world", by encouraging "the conception that the US is on their side".[6] Yitzhak Rabin, now Israel's Prime Minister, contented himself with saying that in his view Israel had lost the battle with the American administration and should have avoided confrontation. In return for the certain continuation of its support for Israel, America has asked for a change in Israel's policies towards the Arabs, in order to bring about an overall pacification and normalisation of the region.

The change of American view has been the result of the end of the Cold War. But if the lifting of Cold War constraints has allowed America to change its views of Israel's role, then a further factor has been influential in giving the United States a new set of strategic priorities in the Middle East. This was the upheaval in American thinking about its traditional foreign policy alignments brought about by the Gulf War in 1991. The effect of the Gulf War has been to add to America's changing view of Israel's importance a new perception of the significance to the United States of new alliances with Arab states, and of good relations with the Arab world. The question was put

6. Michael Yudelman, "Shamir blasts US tilt against Israel", *The Jerusalem Post International Edition*, 28 September 1992.

trenchantly by a journalist, writing days before the start of the Madrid talks: "The question has not yet been addressed, but sooner or later will be: what can Israel offer the Americans that cannot be provided by their Arab friends?"[7] That question was also being asked in Israel in the summer of 1991 by a thoughtful member of an extreme-right party, the ex-minister and former leader of the Tehiya party Yuval Ne'eman, who wrote a long article in the newspaper *Davar* expressing the fear that "as the Soviet Union declines, leaving a unipolar world, the US may prefer 21 Arab states and their oil to Israel and its problems".[8]

The United States reacted to the Iraqi invasion of Kuwait in August 1990 with a rapid decision to move against Iraq and restore the status quo. The United States wished to reassure states in the Gulf that it would not stand by and see legal regimes displaced in an area of vital geopolitical importance, nor governments toppled by force. In addition, for the strategic interests of the United States, a secure and reasonably priced supply of oil from the Gulf was and is of immense importance. Though at present America still has substantial reserves in its own oil fields, as the century progresses it is likely that the United States will need to use more and more Gulf oil. Gulf oil is also of great importance to America's allies in the industrial world, in Europe and also in Japan, where supplies from the Gulf make up ten per cent of the country's oil usage. The American administration reasoned that if the Gulf's oil resources were to fall into hostile hands, the United States, its allies and the world economic system could seriously be threatened. Washington could hardly under the circumstances have failed to act against Iraq, but it also chose to assemble an alliance whose *raison d'être* was largely political rather than military.

American military force would itself have been a sufficient lever to do the job of removing Iraq's forces from Kuwait, given the fulcrum of a base for action in Saudi Arabia, but the United States wished to be seen to be acting in concert with its allies in Europe, and in the Middle East, in order to avert the accusation of peremptory unilateral action. The cooperation against Iraq of Syria, Egypt, and the rest of the Gulf States was centrally important to American policy. As we saw

7. Brian Whitaker, "In America's own interest", *Guardian Weekly*, 27 October 1991.

8. Julia Slater, "The Middle East and the new Soviet Union", *Middle East International*, 409, 27 September 1991.

in the last chapter, Washington set its Arab allies on a par with Israel, in the context of the Gulf War preparations and of the battle which came in February 1991. In the aftermath of the war, the United States wanted and still wants to keep its newly forged links with the Arabs intact.

The end of the Cold War on the one hand, and the politics of the Gulf War on the other, are two phenomena which are closely intertwined. The disappearance of world polarisation, the end of the Cold War, the disintegration of the Soviet Union, and the disappearance from the world scene of organized Communism as the guiding principle of a power bloc opposed to the United States, have all been factors in bringing about the restructuring of American attitudes to the Middle East. The Middle East was one of the main arenas where the Cold War was fought out, and the conflict was to a considerable extent kept alive by the Cold War strategies of the two superpowers. While America supported Israel as a bastion against international Communism, the Soviet Union linked itself with Syria and Iraq. At an earlier stage, the Soviets had penetrated Egypt, until that country's dramatic switch of allegiance under President Sadat after the 1973 war.

The United States today has no counterbalance, in the world in general and the Middle East in particular. The old Communist structures of influence in the Middle East have disappeared. Russia has had no ideological impetus, after the fall of Communism and the old Soviet regime, to keep up the network of foreign relations established by the Soviet Union. Meanwhile, it became clear that a new and pauperised post-Communist regime certainly could not afford to patronise and support client states. The new regime in Moscow has therefore been relatively uninterested in maintaining the expensive alliances and treaties with the Arab world set up by its predecessor. Meanwhile the Soviet Union, with ample oil supplies of its own, lacks the motivation of the United States and other countries in the West to secure their oil resources by keeping up ties with the Middle East.

Mikhail Gorbachev, the last Soviet leader, had already perceived that there was no advantage to be gained for him from opposing the United States-led alliance and Washington's determination to reverse the Iraqi invasion of Kuwait, even though Iraq had formerly been closely linked with the Soviet Union. President Gorbachev saw that the Soviet system was tottering, and calculated that his best advantage lay in aligning himself with the West, or at least in adopting a stance of positive neutrality. That was the message that emerged from the summit conference between President Bush and President Gorbachev in Helsinki in September 1991, when Gorbachev clearly indicated that the Soviet Union would not oppose the proposed American military move. The United States did not find itself involved in an ideologically expressed conflict with the Soviet Union in the Gulf, and therefore Israel's significance was marginal.

Why has the pressure for a resolution of the Palestinian problem been a necessary concomitant of the American desire to bring peace between the nations of the Middle East? What President Bush and his advisers saw was that it was impossible to have one without the other. Washington perceived that if there were to be an end to the hostility between Israel and the neighbouring Arab states on the one hand, then there must also be a resolution of the simmering antagonism between Israel and the Palestinian population of the Occupied Territories, where the internal uprising known as the intifada had been under way for almost four years. The commitment of all the neighbouring Arab states to a just outcome for the Palestinians was sufficiently strong that no approach to international peace could be made without tackling the Palestinian question.

Justice for the Palestinians was also an aim of American statesmen: it would be harsh to say otherwise. But the main consideration was nevertheless the desire to regulate Israel's relations with its neighbours, and thus to ease tension in an area of the world where the United States would frankly prefer to be able to give priority to the more pragmatic goal of protecting its oil interests. In the past it has been the existence of those hostile frontiers between Israel and the Arabs which has meant that the United States, to fulfil the duty of supporting Israel as expected by both Jewish and non-Jewish citizens of America, has had to expend diplomatic effort, military vigilance, and above all enormous amounts of cash to ensure Israel's economic viability and military supremacy in the area.

The United States will save no resources in the short run, since in return for Israel's demonstration of its willingness to make peace, Washington has guaranteed the stepping up of arms supplies. But in the longer term, in a non-hostile Middle East bound together by trade links and treaties, the investment currently demanded from Washington, moral, physical and economic, would be sure to fall. However, given the commitment of the Arab states to seeing justice for the

Palestinians, each for its different reasons, and because of their common Arab identity, the desired result on the international plane cannot be achieved without also solving the internal problem of the Palestinians, and settling an acceptable future for the people of the Occupied Territories.

The View from Brussels

Europe has taken a leading part in the search for Middle East peace. European and other nations also have their own interest in seeing a Middle East solution, and the new concern of the United States to pacify the region has allowed other nations' policies more scope. Though only the United States itself has had the power to move and shake the political structure of the Middle East, other states have exerted their own pressures to bring about a settlement. The European Union and its member states, including Britain, have played a key part. American foreign policy is active and manipulative. It is made by the US administration, tempered only after the event by Congress, and has a decisive and executive quality. European policy in contrast emerges from the collective mechanisms of the European Commission and is today of a more bureaucratic nature. Europe is taking a strong interest in the shape of the new Palestine and Israel which may emerge, and especially in their economic development. In the past Europe has taken political initiatives, such as the Venice declaration of June 1980 which added to a call for peace Europe's view that the Palestinians must participate in any negotiations.

Europe may again take a more overtly political stand over the Middle East in the future, as the provisions of the Maastricht treaty come into force and Europe moves towards the adoption of a common foreign policy, which will include the formulation of policies on the Middle East and the Palestinian issue. Foreign policy formulation is at an early stage within the European Union, and it will be some time before Europe is in a position to take real initiatives. Nevertheless it has been clearly perceived in Europe that the key issue is the clash between Israel and the Palestinians, and that other aspects of Middle East peacemaking could follow from a resolution of that central issue. A sketch of the European view of the issue of Middle East peace is given by Gerd Nonneman, in a study published for the

European Commission research body, the Federal Trust, who writes: "The Arab–Israeli dispute remains in many ways the central issue in the complex and inter-connected obstacles to peace and security in the Middle East."[9]

Europe's interest is not a new phenomenon: from its vantage point closer to the potential trouble spots of the Middle East, Europe has always been interested in approaches to peace. For the United States government, though it has taken an active interest in the Middle East, the region is psychologically far-off. For Europe, on the other hand, the Middle East is a near neighbour, and European views of the Middle East are coloured by the close relationship. With the relatively limited nature of direct American experience of the Middle East, it was easy during the eight years of the Reagan administration for American policy, in the Middle East as elsewhere, to be regulated on the uncomplicated basis of unquestioningly supporting Israel on the one hand and of frustrating the supposed intentions of the Communists on the other. But Europe's views have always been both more complex, and more concerned.

History is a reason for European concern. We have already heard much about the British mandate over Palestine. Britain also held the League of Nations mandates over Jordan and Iraq, as well as having the closest links with Egypt, over which the British government exercised tight political control up to the end of the Second World War. France's mandates over Syria and Lebanon have given that country strong cultural links with Beirut and Damascus, and France's former colonial relationship with Algeria, as well as its protectorates over Tunisia and Morocco, have bequeathed a strong French concern with the Arab Maghreb. Italy had its colony in Libya, and Germany has always had a special interest in Turkey. All these historical links, and the continuing human involvements to which they have given rise, have sharpened Europe's concern for the fate of the Middle East.

Geography also exerts its influence. For the states of the European Union the danger of war, were it again to threaten in the region today, would be uncomfortably close to home. The contrast between the American and British attitudes to the Gulf War makes this clear. For the United States, the Gulf War was an overseas adventure, while

9. Gerd Nonneman, ed., *The Middle East and Europe: the Search for Stability and Integration*, Federal Trust for Education and Research, EC Commission, London 1993.

for Europe it felt more immediate. During the months of the Gulf crisis, Europe's skies were full of unaccustomed activity by military aircraft, and air routes were disrupted. That sensation of immediacy was absent in the United States. Similarly, popular opinion in America was perhaps more easily lulled than that in Europe by the press reports of smart bombs and surgical strikes, and by the sanitisation of the news from the war front, while Europeans were and are more sceptical.

Two vital European Commission documents issued in September 1993 coincided closely with the first meeting between Yasser Arafat and Yitzhak Rabin on 13 October, and underline the interest of the Commission in the Middle East, as well as that of the other organs of the European Union. The first of these, published just before the 13 September ceremony in Washington, is a Commission Communication, on relations between the European Community and the Middle East. Commission officials stress the importance of the economic role Europe may be able to play, and the importance of economic aid and cooperation in the encouragement of the peace process.

> The Community's own experience demonstrates that war between previously hostile parties can be made unthinkable through economic integration. While this model cannot easily be transposed to the Middle East, it does suggest that the development of economic cooperation can be a powerful tool in reducing the level of conflict, making peace irreversible and encouraging the people of the region to learn to live in peace.[10]

The second document acknowledged the importance of the White House meeting: "With the breakthrough represented by the signing of the Israeli–PLO Agreement the Middle East peace process has reached a critical phase. The relationship between Israel and the Palestinians is at the core of the Arab–Israel problem. The difficulties between Israel and the Arab neighbours may now begin to be resolved. A comprehensive peace settlement could be within reach if negotiations are pursued in all tracks of the Madrid framework."[11]

---

10. "Future relations and cooperation between the Community and the Middle East", Communication from the Commission, Commission of the European Communities, COM(93) 375 final, Brussels 8 September 1993.

11. "EC Support to the Middle East Process", Communication from the Commission, Commission of the European Communities, COM(93) 458 final, Brussels, 29 September 1993.

The document goes on to indicate the future approach Europe is likely to take: "On the economic front the time is now right for the EC, together with the international community and especially the Gulf countries, to embark on an ambitious cooperation programme, which would embrace the economic development of the West Bank and Gaza, bearing in mind the need also for international efforts in favour of the region as a whole."

The Wider World

Russia has been just one of the other states involved in the search for peace in the Middle East. The West, United States and Europe, do not have a monopoly. Moscow has played an important part, especially as it has inherited the Soviet Union's seat at the Security Council table and has taken on some of its international role. Though Russia recognises the limitation of its resources, it keeps an interest in the areas of the world in the old Soviet diplomatic hinterland. As an analyst of Russian foreign policy recently explained: "Russia's present foreign policy is an extension of the policy pursued in the last two or so years of Mikhail Gorbachev's rule."[12] Russia has continued its joint sponsorship of the Middle East peace talks held in Madrid and then in Washington, of which Gorbachev, as president of the Soviet Union, had been an original sponsor.

Russia's new foreign policy makes a cornerstone of cooperation with the United States, and Moscow would not now seek to compete with Washington as a centre of influence. The modesty of Russia's new role is marked, in contrast with the historically high profile of the Soviet Union. When Moscow jointly sponsored the brief Geneva Conference which followed the war of 1973, the then United States President, Richard Nixon, and his Secretary of State, Henry Kissinger, were extremely wary of Moscow. They feared that the Soviet Union under the leadership of Leonid Brezhnev might seek to disrupt the conference for its own purposes. The principal Soviet contribution to the Madrid process has been to host the multilateral talks on arms control, one of the five multilateral working groups whose meetings

12. Mohamed el-Doufani, "Yeltsin's Foreign Policy: a Third World Critique", *The World Today*, June 1993.

have run in parallel with Israel's bilateral negotiations with the Palestinians and the three Arab states involved in the talks.

Russia now has diplomatic relations with Israel as well as with the Arab states, and may yet return to play a larger part in the Middle East, especially if it can resolve its own internal conflicts and turn its attention confidently to the outside world. Fred Halliday offered this speculation in early 1993, before the clash in October 1993 between President Yeltsin and the Russian Parliament partially resolved the power struggle between them in the President's favour: "If the Russian Federation undergoes greater crisis, perhaps even civil war as some fear, this will have enormous negative implications for the Middle East, as for Europe and the Far East. If Russia can, over five or ten years, reorganise itself, then it will play an independent role in the Middle East. The problem is that no one can now say how long all this will take."[13]

Japan has also shown concern with the Middle East, to a level which is perhaps surprising. Japan's motives are economic, and it has shown itself to be a keen observer and a willing participant in the peace process. Tokyo has already promised a major contribution to the economic fund for the new Palestinian entity in Gaza and Jericho, and the Japanese Finance Ministry closely monitors developments. Japanese banks and businesses are also taking care to keep themselves well informed on developments in the Middle East. Japanese research groups such as the Nikko Research Centre, which monitors information of economic relevance to Japanese business, stay in close touch with the evolving Middle East situation. Tokyo was the venue for a crucial session of the multilateral working groups in December 1993, which took the decision to move on from collecting data to the more active role of designing and recommending economic and social projects.

Japan has a general concern to promote stability in the Middle East, on which the country depends for ten per cent of its oil supplies as well as other products of the petrochemical industries which are being increasingly developed in the Gulf. Japan's economy is facing problems in 1994, and Japanese business observers reason that any disturbance in the region could disrupt the supplies on which Japanese industry depends, if there is the remotest possibility that a

13. Fred Halliday, "New uncertainties in Russia's foreign policy", *Middle East International*, 444, 19 February 1993.

Middle East conflict could include any new clash in the Gulf. In the words of one oil analyst: "Military conflict in the Persian Gulf thus remains Japan's Achilles heel. Unless it is willing and able to transform its economic might into military strength, Japan remains just as vulnerable to the loss of its oil supplies as it was in 1990."[14] The Gulf will of course remain Japan's primary focus, but a resolution of the Arab–Israeli problem will also continue to be something Japanese observers bear in mind.

The Third World

Third World relations with Israel and the Arabs are also in a state of flux. An end to the Middle East conflict will be a relief to many developing countries, committed to the Palestinian cause by old fraternal ties, but anxious to exploit the help Israel may have to give. This is especially the situation in Africa. Again, the change springs ultimately from the end of the Cold War and the new unipolarity of international relations. There is no Communist alternative to which Third World countries in Africa and elsewhere can now turn. In theory, Israel is still seen as an oppressor by countries which have for the most part endorsed the Palestinian cause, but in practice attitudes to Israel are more ambiguous. Countries which are anxious to take advantage of the technological expertise which Israel has to offer, as well as to buy arms from Israel's developed arms industry, welcome the chance to make such contacts openly and legitimately.

The Third World's opposition to Israel is historic. Many reasons have conspired to promote it: Israel's apparent status as a usurper, its location within the Arab lands, the support offered to it by the United States and by the former colonialist powers. All these brought the anathematisation of Israel by newly independent states. In the years after Israel's foundation the international diplomacy of the Arab countries, through the medium of the United Nations and elsewhere, helped to foster that attitude. Arab statesmen took a high profile role. Egypt's former President Gamal Abdel Nasser played a leading part in the non-aligned movement which crystallised at the Bandung Conference of 1955, and King Hassan II of Morocco was a guiding

14. Paul McDonald, "Japan: energy security", *The World Today*, January 1993.

spirit at the formation of the Organization of African Unity (OAU) in 1963.

Black African countries largely broke off relations with Israel after the OAU ban imposed in 1973, though Israel did better at keeping its lines open to countries in Asia and Latin America. In 1974, the General Assembly of the United Nations passed a resolution on the subject of Palestine, which extended the General Assembly's recognition to the rights of the Palestinians, and asked for world support to enable the Palestinian people to "regain its rights", in the resolution's words. Then in 1975 Third World disapproval of Israel culminated in the formal opprobrium heaped on the country's head by United Nations General Assembly Resolution 3379, when the General Assembly formally endorsed the proposition that Zionism is a form of racism, by a majority of 72 votes to 35, with 32 nations abstaining.

That situation was destined to change. The resolution of 1975 was rescinded by the UN General Assembly on 16 December 1991, as part of the general revision of positions which followed the opening of the Madrid talks. Votes against the resolution were cast by no fewer than 111 members of the world body, including old opponents of Israel as diverse as Vietnam and Zambia. Black Africa also began to move back towards recognition of Israel. Change had been in the pipeline in fact for some time. Though isolated on the diplomatic front, Israel nevertheless began in the 1980s to find ways to forge links with Africa and with other Third World countries. The editor of *Without Prejudice*, a Washington-based journal on racial discrimination, has commented: "The broad support for the resolution in the mid-1970s may be, in part, a function of diplomatic solidarity among Arab states and other Third World countries which for various reasons has deteriorated considerably since then."[15]

Energetic Israeli diplomacy has been one reason for the change that has been coming for a decade in the attitudes of Third World countries to Israel. Throughout the 1970s and 1980s, Israel continued to use every stratagem at its disposal to make connections with countries round the world, in a policy of constructing international links wherever possible. Writing in 1988, the Israeli analyst Benjamin Beit-Hallahmi of the University of Haifa argued that Israel's foreign policy effort was not a side issue. On the contrary, it was vital to the

15. Jospeh Schechla, "The Zionism is Racism resolution", *Middle East International*, 410, 11 October 1991.

country's survival: "Israel's global involvement is by this time a necessity, not a luxury. Israel's survival is tied to global processes and global structures. The rise of the Third World is the real threat to Israel's future, because in a world where liberation movements win, Israel's future looks bleak."[16] Israeli foreign policy makers made the decision that in the bid to insert Israel into the world network of international relations, it would develop ties with any state which was willing to reciprocate.

Not all Israel's diplomacy has been of equal value: it has sometimes made what even its friends regarded as doubtful moves in its eagerness to make links with other nations outside the United States and the Western nations which have been its traditional sources of support. Unfortunate friendships may at one time have done Israel as much harm as good. When few states were willing to speak to Israel, it forged links with so-called pariah states, such as South Africa and Chile. This certainly tarnished Israel's image. There were some advantages, for example the South African ties enabled cooperation in the field of nuclear development to take place: Shyam Bhatia writes: "Far more significant is the strategic cooperation between Israel and South Africa, which many believe led to the joint testing of a bomb."[17] Israel did not give these ties up, at least until Likud left office: President de Klerk of South Africa visited Israel in November 1991, immediately after the opening round of the Madrid talks. Other diplomatic efforts were more orthodox, such as the efforts made by Israel to establish ties with a ring of states just beyond the Arab world, notably Iran and Turkey. Israel's relationship with Iran was active during the Shah's regime, but has now deteriorated to open hostility between Israel and the Islamic government in Tehran.

Israel has also had important and semi-clandestine contacts with China and India. Those two countries have been among those to move recently towards establishing normal relations with Israel. Israel has had a long-standing and unadvertised relationship with China based on cooperation in the field of weapons. This has led in the past to strain between the United States and Israel, because of alleged Israeli leaks of American weapons technology to the Chinese. Here

---

16. Benjamin Beit-Hallahmi, *The Israeli Connection*, I.B. Tauris, London 1988, p. 246.

17. Shyam Bhatia, *Nuclear Rivals in the Middle East*, Routledge, London 1988, p. 45.

again the opening of the peace process greatly emboldened Israel, and a visit by the Defence Minister, Moshe Arens, to China in November 1991, which would hitherto have been left discreetly unmentioned, was well documented by the Israeli press.

Israel's policy of striving incessantly to make international links has certainly paid off. Even at a time when much of the world appeared to disapprove of its actions, the country never gave up its efforts to make international connections and links. All of these have now been of great assistance to Israel as it moves towards full international acceptance in the light of the peace negotiations begun at Madrid, continued in Oslo, and endorsed in Washington. The suggestion made by Benjamin Beit-Hallahmi, that Israel's international ties are a necessity rather than a luxury, has been vindicated by the use Israel has been able to make of its existing international links to enhance its standing. The United States pushed the Likud government unwillingly to the conference table, but Israel has been able to present itself in the negotiations as a sovereign state basking in the full approval of international recognition, rather than as an anomalous state principally dependent on the United States. The international recognition Israel has already won is one reason the Palestinians must secure their own future by coming out of these talks with an agreement that will stick. Israel has made itself a member of the community of nations. The Palestinians must also in due course be allowed to join that community.

CHAPTER 9

THE ARAB STATES AND ISRAEL: A HISTORY OF CONFLICT

Arab Unanimity: a Question Mark

Palestine, and its liberation, have been at the heart of the ideological programmes of the Arab states over the last 45 years. But perhaps in changing international circumstances the Arab states have begun to tire of the Palestinian issue, and of its effect on their own international orientation. Once again, the root cause of the change is the end of the Cold War. With a single superpower, there is nothing to be gained from being opposed to Israel and therefore to the United States. No reward will be forthcoming from the Soviet bloc, which has melted like Prospero's visions into thin air. Just one example is Syria's new-found rapprochement with the United States. The already visibly crumbling influence of the Soviet Union was one consideration for Syria's decision to join the American-led alliance in the Gulf War.

The poorer Arab states need money and aid, while the richer ones need defence and security, and the United States is the potential source of all these benefits. There are therefore many goals which Arab states wish to achieve, which would today only be hindered by a continuing hostility to Israel. Partially this is because compromise with Israel would buy American support. But it is also because an end to the Arab–Israel conflict would allow Arab states to redeploy scarce resources hitherto devoted to warlike preparations: the Arabs would enjoy a peace dividend. For all these reasons the Arab states came willingly to the opening conference over Middle East peace at Madrid in 1991, even though Syria chose to make the opening session the venue for an ideological diatribe.

Even for Syria, change is on the way, even though it has been the most unbending of the Arab states concerned in the peace process. The possibility of getting back the Golan Heights has roused even the stern regime in Damascus to an awareness of the possible benefits of peace. Syria has always seen itself as the patron of a potential state in Palestine fashioned in its own image and run by its own Palestinian allies. In reality, however, the possibility of adding Palestine to Lebanon in the sphere of Syrian influence was always an unlikely prospect, and has now receded farther into the realms of fantasy. Syria's more pragmatic ambition was to control a Palestinian movement in exile which would serve as a political instrument throughout the Arab world. That too is now a less viable aim, as the rejectionist Palestinians fostered by Damascus seem doomed to lose their influence when a settlement in the Occupied Territories takes shape. Just as Jordan and Lebanon would like to work out the details of their own settlements with Israel, in order to live in peace and tackle their own problems, Damascus appears to be coming round to the idea of abandoning the permanent confrontation with Israel.

Israel's birth was perceived by the Arabs, with much truth, as a great injustice done to the whole Arab nation, and this was a factor of crucial importance in forging Arab identity in the latter half of the twentieth century. Today it may be that if the Palestine problem is resolved, then the Arabs will need to look for new principles. Identity has been a central concern of Arab political theorists, and there has been a search for a unifying principle around which the Arabs can coalesce. The Arab states share the Arabic language and the Muslim religion, though some Arabs are Christians, and some Muslims who inhabit Arab lands, especially in the Maghreb, speak other languages in addition to Arabic. Arab nationalism has a long history, running back to the days of the end of the old Turkish empire. More recently, secular theorists like the Baathists and Nasserists have erected their own philosophy of Arab nationalism based on earlier ideas. Meanwhile, there has been a struggle to define an Arab socialism, while other movements have tried to make religion the unifying force.

But Palestine and its redemption have so far featured in the programmes of all. Were the Palestinian problem to begin to approach a solution, it could now be that this unifying principle would lose its force. Under those circumstances it has been suggested that the Arab world might split along different lines, and conflicts of interest between richer and poorer states could flare into hostility. The dividend of peace could be lost, if the problem of Palestine were to wither away. That has been one interpretation of the Gulf War, where Iraq, though itself an oil state, succeeded in presenting itself, to the satisfaction of some, including the Palestinians, as the champions of the have-nots. Nonetheless, the resolution of the Palestinian question remains a moral imperative.

Palestine and the Evolution of Arab Politics

The unrighted wrongs of Palestine have historically provided the spur for revolutionary Arab regimes to topple supposedly ineffective bourgeois ones, and have also served as a justification for the autocratic nature of some Arab political regimes. There would be time enough for liberalism and democracy, the argument has tended to run in some Arab states, when the nation's problems have been solved; and those problems awaiting solution have included social reform, economic development, and the issue of Palestine. This was one way in which the Palestinian issue was mobilised, in the context of Arab politics and ideological thought. Another way in which the Palestinian problem focused international politics, and therefore the politics of the Arab states, was in the context of the Cold War, where America's unquestioning support for Israel brought corresponding Russian support for the Arabs. Here again, the issue of Palestine became articulated to an ideology. But if Palestine was a factor which divided the Middle East, as between Arab and Israeli, it unified the Arabs, so that even the conservative Gulf states supported the Palestinian cause. This produced a complex situation fraught with contradictions, which for the United States was difficult to manage, with its interests in the Gulf and its support for Israel to reconcile.

   The involvement of the Arab states in the Palestinian dispute over the last 45 years, since the foundation of Israel, has transformed the confrontation between Israel and the dispossessed Palestinians into a general confrontation between Israel and the Arab world as a whole. That opposition, between the Arab states and Israel, was for long periods in danger of displacing the Palestinian conflict itself as the essential issue in the Israel–Arab dispute. As recently as 1991, the prominent Palestinian scholar Walid Khalidi felt he had to issue this reminder:

> The crux and the kernel of the Arab–Israeli conflict is the Palestine problem. The Arab–Israeli inter-state conflict is derivative from the non-resolution of the Palestine problem. The crux of the Palestine problem

is the struggle between two national movements: on the one hand the Zionist movement (and, since 1948, Israel), and on the other, the Palestinian national movement. The crux of this struggle had been and continues to this day to be, the issue of the control or sharing of the land of Palestine.[1]

Israel as an Issue for the Arab States

What Walid Khalidi was concerned about was that the Arab states had come to see their own grievances against Israel as paramount, and had almost begun to lose sight of the injustice to the Palestinians that was the root of the quarrel. That this had happened was not so surprising, since the foundation of Israel had brought about the immediate, spectacular and public humiliation of the Arabs, who were unable to live up to their promise to lose no time in destroying the Zionists' self-proclaimed state and in restoring the Palestinian Arabs to what was deeply felt was their rightful position in Palestine. From 1948, the struggle has not only been about getting justice for the Palestinians, but also about restoring Arab pride and the dismantling of the alien Zionist state implanted in the Arabs' midst. Since then, the fate of Palestine has been the direct or indirect cause of two further general wars between Israel and its neighbours in the Middle East, in 1967 and 1973, and has been heavily implicated in three other regional conflicts, Suez in 1956, Lebanon in 1982, and the Gulf in 1991.

Arab losses and humiliations, incurred in the fight against Israel, and the determination of the Arab states to achieve restitution, were enough to commit the Arabs ever more deeply to the struggle. That antagonism has fed off itself, with bitterness creating yet more hatred, until the reassessments of very recent years. In addition, the Arab world has been subject to profound political upheavals and bitter internal antagonisms, many of which can be traced back to the hostility between the Arabs and Israel and the failure, and apparent inability, of the Arab governments to impose their will. It would not be an exaggeration to say that the entire shape of politics in the region has pivoted on one single issue: the opposition between Israel and the Arab states. That opposition came in turn to overshadow and distort

1. Quoted by Donald Neff, "The long struggle for recognition", *Middle East International*, 459, 24 September 1993.

its original cause, the oppression, exile and disappropriation of the Palestinians.

Jordan, Syria, Lebanon and Egypt have been centrally concerned in the confrontation with Israel, because of their borders with it. But all the Arab states have to a greater or lesser extent been involved. The most vehement in their rejection of Israel in the 1960s and 1970s at one stage were the so-called rejectionist states, who repudiated every suggestion that they might compromise. These were Syria and Iraq, and farther afield Marxist South Yemen, post-revolutionary Algeria, and Colonel Gaddafi's Libya. But until President Sadat's great volte-face in 1977, Egypt was Israel's chief antagonist, and its principal opponent in the two wars of 1967 and 1973, while the conservative Gulf states were happy to enforce the trading boycott against Israel, and to bankroll the PLO. That link between the Gulf and the PLO, which Yasser Arafat is now assiduously trying to rebuild, was cemented after the PLO was recognised by the Arabs as the Palestinians' sole legitimate representative, at the Rabat conference on 28 October 1974. The far-flung geography of the Arab world, with 21 members of the Arab League including the Palestinians themselves, has been no impediment to Arab unity on the Palestinian issue, though two of the states farthest from the scene of the action, which are also two of the most pro-Western in their political orientation, Morocco and Oman, have been less vehement against Israel than some other Arab states.

The War of 1948

The new Israeli entity was attacked in 1948 by the armies of Egypt, Lebanon, Jordan, Iraq and Syria. This was the first stage in the process of widening the conflict and transforming it to a general opposition between Israel and the Arab states. The sharp defeat inflicted on them by the Jewish forces was a surprise to the world, though in fact the Arab armies were not well organized, and the Arab governments must have been advised by their intelligence services of what might be the outcome of a clash with the Jews. The Jewish militias organised by the Zionist leaders were well-trained and well-equipped, and the myth that a small but determined Jewish army defeated a far superior Arab force is probably untrue: in fact the Jews were strong and well-organized, while the Arabs were relatively weak, apart from Jordan's Arab Legion.

The Israeli historian Simha Flapan quotes contemporary estimates to that effect. Sir Harold Beeley told American experts just before the end of the Mandate that "for some time at least the Jews, strengthened by recruits entering by sea, could withstand and possibly defeat the poorly organized and badly equipped Arab armies." Meanwhile, Richard Crossman said that the Haganah, the Jewish self-defence force, was "the mightiest fighting force in the eastern Mediterranean, since it is not a private army but the whole Jewish population organised for self-defence."[2] The Palestinian Arabs themselves had never organised in the same way as had the Jews, and took little part in the fighting.

The bitter experience of defeat was the outcome for the Arab states. In the undeclared civil war between the Jewish militias and the Palestinians which lasted from the end of 1947 until the declaration of the state of Israel, many Palestinians became refugees. From the declaration of Israel's statehood in May 1948 until the truce which came a month later, the Jewish force, now officially called the Israel Defence Force, was on the defensive, and the Arabs may have imagined they could have beaten the IDF. Egypt seems to have believed that it was in its interest to break the truce. But with the arrival of arms and men from abroad the balance was tilted in the other direction, and Israel went over to the attack. Israel bought weapons in the United States, France and Britain, and used an airfield built by Czechoslovakia to import its needs. Egypt opened its armistice talks with Israel in January 1949, and the other Arab states had all officially ended the fighting by July. The catastrophe, as the events of 1948 and 1949 became known to the Arabs, was etched deeply in the Arab consciousness. The problem of Palestine was no longer a local issue, but one which concerned the Arab world as a whole. The inability of the Arab governments to overcome the Israelis and retrieve lost Palestinian territory added fuel to an already smouldering fire of resentment.

The Arabs, both the Palestinians and their neighbours, felt that the existence of the Jewish state was in itself representative of a terrible injustice. The Arabs deeply resented the Mandate which established a Jewish nation on Palestinian soil. They saw the new self-proclaimed state of Israel as the continuation of the Mandate by other means, and

2. Beeley and Crossman are quoted by Simha Flapan, *The Birth of Israel: Myths and Realities*, Croom Helm, London 1987.

as a way of depriving the Palestinians of their land. That revulsion against the Jews was exacerbated by the news of massacres, like that at the village of Deir Yassin near Jerusalem in April 1948, as 250 Palestinian villagers were killed by Jewish forces, mainly from the Irgun Zvai Leumi. The attack spread panic among the Arab population, many of whom fled. The massacre was condemned by some Jewish leaders, but others, especially from the Irgun, attempted at the time and afterwards to deny what had happened at Deir Yassin, but the historical reality of the deliberate killing now seems beyond doubt.[3] Israeli historians, who seek to show that both sides used unacceptable violence, cite a reprisal attack, in which 77 Israeli medical staff were killed when a convoy was ambushed in Jerusalem. But the depth of the antipathy of the Arab governments against Israel after the conflict, which sprang from incidents like that at Deir Yassin, could scarcely be overestimated. The result was that their commitment against Israel was absolute.

Suez: 1956

Suez was the next episode in the confrontation. The Suez crisis had worldwide implications, for the old colonial empires of Britain and France which were coming at last to an end, and for Anglo-American relations. For the Arabs, it was also a phase in their experience of Israel, which involved itself in the British and French plan to invade Egypt and repossess the Suez Canal in 1956, after its nationalisation by President Nasser. The effect was to exacerbate Egypt's existing hostility to Israel. The aims of the British and the French were to regain the Suez Canal and to humiliate President Nasser of Egypt, who was seen in Europe as a serious menace to the future of European influence in the region. As we know, the main effects of the Suez adventure were in the event detrimental to European interests. Suez actually enhanced Nasser's already powerful attraction for the Arab popular masses in the Middle East, as the sympathy aroused by

---

3. Benny Morris, *The Birth of the Palestinian Refugee Problem, 1947–1949*, Cambridge University Press, Cambridge 1987, p. 114; Noah Lucas, *The Modern History of Israel*, Weidenfeld and Nicolson, London 1974, p. 251.

the Anglo-French attack was followed by the calling off of the operation and what was in effect a diplomatic victory for Nasser. It also drove a wedge between Britain and the United States and opened the door to Soviet influence in Egypt. Israel's role in the operation was to invade the Sinai peninsula, which would provide Britain and France with an excuse to act, in order, as it would appear, to safeguard the Suez Canal. But from the point of view of the Palestinian issue, what Suez did was to prejudice the centrality of the injustice to the Palestinians and to move the international situation another step towards assuming the form of a state-to-state conflict between Egypt and Israel.

Nasser's discomfiture was one benefit Israel hoped it would get from the Suez adventure. That hope was to be disappointed. But in more pragmatic terms, Israel got the demilitarisation of Gaza, since the Egyptian army did not return when the zone was handed back to Egyptian administration, and the opportunity to use the Straits of Tiran for ships bound for Eilat. On the other hand, from the point of view of the Arab–Israeli conflict, the effect was to heighten Egyptian resentment of Israel. The conflict became a more direct one, between Egypt and the still new Zionist state, while the grievance of the Palestinians, and the affront to all the Arabs which it represented, still smouldered in the background.

Israel's temerity in invading the territory of a neighbouring Arab state had escalated the conflict out of the more limited arena of Palestine in the practical sphere, as well as the moral one. Egyptians were also conscious of the new dimension of Zionist ambitions which the Sinai expedition of 1956 opened for Israel. When Israeli troops reached Mount Sinai, the site of the turning point in the life of Moses as recounted in the Bible, and therefore of religious significance for the Jews, Ben Gurion said the operation was the "greatest and most glorious one in the annals of our people", and when speaking to the Knesset about the campaign, said that Israel's armed forces had "brought us back to that exalted and decisive moment in our ancient history, and to that place where the Law was given, and where our people were commanded to be a chosen people".[4] From this point, Zionist ambitions appeared as a direct threat to Egypt as well as a threat to Palestine.

---

4. Quoted by Michael Ionides, *Divide and Lose*, Geoffrey Bles, London 1960; from a report in the *Manchester Guardian*, 6 November 1956.

The June War: 1967

The Suez expedition had already gone some way towards the internationalisation of the Arab–Israeli conflict. It undermined Western influence in the Middle East, and contributed to the collapse of the Baghdad Pact in which Western nations had allied themselves in a regional security pact with pro-Western governments. It also endangered the Hashemite regime of King Hussein in Jordan and in the longer run brought about the fall of the Iraqi Hashemite regime. Though it was the United States which ended the Suez expedition, Washington's decision to back Israel's demands for the demilitarisation of Sinai and access to Eilat helped to confirm the impression that American policy was also formed in the light of Israel's demands. Suez also opened the way to Communist influence in the area. One of the precipitating factors in the Suez conflict had been the decision of the United States to withhold the finance for the Aswan High Dam project, conceived by Nasser, with his revolutionary colleagues and political advisers, as the cornerstone of a plan to transform the Egyptian economy, to make prosperous the peasants who had benefited from the land reforms, and to build a new society in Egypt. The Soviet decision to finance the Dam, followed by the so-called Czech arms deal which gave Nasser the arms he needed to modernise Egypt's forces, were the key to growing Soviet influence in the whole Middle East in the following years.

But it was 11 years later, with the war of 1967 and its disastrous outcome for the Arabs, that the Arab–Israeli conflict was truly elevated to the international status of a war between nations. The war of 1948, with the failure of the Arab armies, had been a set-back, but the defeat of 1967 was a reverse of truly cataclysmic proportions for the Arab states. This time it was not the Palestinians who were the principal victims, though another wave of them became refugees in Jordan: the brunt was borne by the Arab states themselves. The war was the result on the one hand of the mounting Arab sensation that Israel's existence in what had hitherto been a part of the Arab world was intolerable, and on the other hand of Israel's growing fears for its security. For each side, there was by 1967, after years of angry confrontation, a strong consciousness of the approach of a clash which might resolve the conflict between Arabs and Israelis one way or the other. Each side believed it could win. Both the Israelis and the Egyptians were at the same time reluctant to precipitate the fateful eventuality, but also eager to use it to influence the course of subsequent history. In the event, war sprang inevitably out of the continuing border confrontations which followed the Suez clash. Tension on the frontier between Israel and Egypt steadily mounted, and in response to a decision by Egypt to close the Straits of Tiran, and to ask for the removal of the United Nations troops from Sinai, Israel mounted a pre-emptive strike.

That the war was "avoidable" was the verdict of a former US diplomat, Richard B. Parker, who was serving in Cairo at the time of the June 1967 war, but he offers this analysis of events following the Egyptian closure of the Gulf of Aqaba:

> The Egyptians took this step in full awareness of the Israeli position, but evidently thought that while the Israelis might undertake a punitive strike, they would not launch a general war, and, that if they did strike, the Egyptians would be more than a match for them. It was a tragic miscalculation on their part. The Israelis struck with overwhelming force on 5 June and demolished the Egyptian air force within a matter of hours. Routing the Egyptian army took a little longer, but it was all over by 8 June.[5]

The capture of the West Bank and East Jerusalem, and the establishment of the Israeli foothold in the Golan Heights took a brief while after the Egyptian front was settled, but the whole campaign was over in six days. Israel's military superiority was established beyond question, to an extent which took the Israelis themselves aback, though some analysts argued then and now that Israel will only ever be capable of fighting a quick war. In a conventional war, if Israel cannot win in a few days, its lack of strategic depth and its inability to replenish lost resources would tell. That, of course, was and is the rationale behind Israel's drive to acquire nuclear weapons.

It could be argued that in 1967 Israel had won a military victory, but sowed the seeds of a diplomatic defeat. Prominent military figures such as Yitzhak Rabin and Moshe Dayan quickly saw that the extent of the territory now held by Israel, and the number of Arabs living within it, would now be a problem. At the same time the then Prime Minister, Levy Eshkol, made clear three principles to which Israel would attempt to stick. These were that it would not return to the pre-war frontiers; that peace would be the price Israel would exact for

5. Richard B. Parker, "The June 1967 war: some mysteries explored", *Middle East Journal*, 46:2, Spring 1992, p. 180.

withdrawal from any territory; and that negotiations with the Arab states would be direct. The Security Council passed its Resolution 242 on 22 November 1967, where Israel succeeded with American help in removing the word "the" from the English version so that what they were called on to accomplish was a "withdrawal from territories occupied", rather than from "the territories". This diplomatic manoeuvre has always enabled Israel to argue that the UN resolution only obliges it to withdraw from some part of the Occupied Territories: indeed it has been claimed that by withdrawing from Sinai, Israel has already fully honoured its obligations. Within Eshkol's principles there was already clearly visible the idea of resolving the Palestinian problem over the heads of the Palestinians by coming to agreements with neighbouring Arab states.

Egypt's Recovery: 1973

Anwar Sadat succeeded Nasser after his death in 1970, and he soon began to plan Egypt's counter-attack on Israel. This was accomplished on 6 October 1973 when Egyptian forces crossed the Suez Canal in a long-planned and carefully concealed surprise attack, and drove the Israelis back into Sinai. Though Israel successfully counter-attacked, crossing the Canal itself into Egyptian territory farther south, and also consolidated its position in the Golan Heights, it was shaken by the realisation that it was not invincible. The government of Mrs Golda Meir fell in the aftermath of the war, and the post of Prime Minister was taken by Yitzhak Rabin, who had been Chief of Staff in 1967.

Israel entered the American-sponsored indirect negotiations which were to lead in the short run to the disengagements with Egypt. Egypt no doubt had the Palestinian issue in mind, but perhaps by this stage it had become secondary to those of recovering Egyptian territory and Egypt's national dignity. In the longer run the outcome was comprehensive for Egypt, and included the Camp David Accords of 1978, the peace treaty with Israel of 1979, and the removal of Israel's settlements from Sinai as part of the complete hand-back of the peninsula to Egypt. This war was the turning point which brought Israel to bite the bullet and negotiate with Egypt, since it was not until this point in the aftermath of the 1973 war that Israel was disposed to listen to Arab demands.

Israel emerged with a peace treaty with its most populous neighbour, and the state which had presented it with its most serious military challenge. The immediate ostracisation of Egypt by the other Arabs meant that Israel was not in the short term able to use its relationship with Egypt as a way of approaching other Arab states, but Egypt's gradual resumption of relations with the other Arab states, culminating in its full rehabilitation after a decade in the wilderness, has meant that Israel has in due course reaped the benefit. Now Israel can exploit to the full Egypt's mediation in the current negotiations with the other Arab states at the post-Madrid talks. There has been a sense in which the evolution of Israel's relationship with Egypt has been another manifestation of the internationalisation of the Israel–Arab quarrel, and its appearance as a state-to-state issue.

Lebanon: 1982

The outcome of the 1973 war was to improve the prospects for peace between Israel and the Arabs, and that opportunity was, perhaps surprisingly, taken not by the Israeli Labour Party but by the right wing in Israel, in power for the first time since the country's independence. However, the right wing in Israel ran more true to form when the hard-line Likud Defence Minister, Ariel Sharon, a hero of the tank battles of 1973, initiated the Israeli incursion into Lebanon of 1982. The aim was ostensibly to secure the safety of the northern Israeli province of Galilee, threatened with attacks across the Lebanese border by Palestinian guerrillas and by Katyusha rockets aimed at Israeli farms and villages. The strategic purpose, however, seems to have been twofold: firstly to drive the Palestinian guerrilla groups from their positions in Lebanon, and secondly to ensure the installation of a government in Beirut favourable to Israel's interests. Essentially, this was a straightforward case of the transformation of the antagonism between the Palestinians and Israel into an inter-state conflict. Without the Palestinian guerrillas in Lebanon, the burden of being Israel's antagonist across that border was willingly shouldered by the Shi'ite Lebanese militias, and the conflict became one between Lebanon and Israel.

After a hard campaign in which five hundred Israeli troops lost their lives, Israel withdrew, leaving behind a token force, and a pro-Israeli

Lebanese militia in a zone of south Lebanon which Israel still refers to as its security zone. The number of Israeli casualties far outnumbered the earlier casualties in Galilee, where protecting the Israeli population had been the operation's stated aim. But Israeli casualties were still minute compared with the Arab dead in the invasion. The bombardment of Beirut by Israel, for two months from June to August 1982, cost an estimated 18,000 dead and 30,000 wounded, almost all non-combatant men, women and children. The Palestinian guerrillas first withdrew from Beirut, and were forced to leave by sea, and the PLO leadership re-established its base at its present site in Tunis. Though the war did drive the Palestinian guerrillas out of Lebanon and ended their state-within-a-state there, the war was also to have the effect of strengthening the power of Syria in the country after Israel's withdrawal. On the other hand, the Israeli policy of side-lining the Palestinians was certainly served, and Lebanon now hopes to settle with Israel over the outstanding issue of the security zone without any Palestinian involvement.

The Gulf War

Finally, the Gulf crisis of 1990 and 1991, though there was little direct Israeli involvement, was also instrumental in helping Israel to present its difficulties with the Arab states as one of international conflict, encouraging the Arabs to settle with it on this basis. The war also helped, in a different way, to bring both the Arab states and the Palestinians to the point where negotiation with Israel began to appear an unavoidable option. A key issue was the identification of the PLO with Iraq's cause. At the opening of the Gulf War, Yasser Arafat expressed his support for Iraq's President Saddam Hussein. He may have done this because of a misapprehension on his part of how determined the United States would prove to be to dislodge Saddam Hussein from Kuwait, or he may even have believed that in a land battle fought with conventional weapons the Iraqis could hold their own. But more compelling for Arafat seems to have been the knowledge that the Palestinians, after years of humiliation which they blamed on the United States as much as on Israel, were delighted to see an Arab leader stand up defiantly against Washington. The PLO leader did not try to go against this wave of sentiment, but instead chose to boost the loyalty to him of the Palestinians, and particularly those of the Occupied Territories, by backing President Saddam Hussein.

Israel was the recipient of much of Saddam Hussein's invective, and also of a small but psychologically damaging number of his Scud missiles. Israel stressed the danger from Iraq, and appeared to discount the PLO, disgraced by its support for the Iraqi leader. Its threatened retaliation against Saddam Hussein was, however, quickly suppressed by the United States, which did not want direct Israeli involvement in the war because of the danger of disturbing the carefully built alliance with the Arabs which Washington had constructed. The United States also feared that Israel might if it became involved make irresponsible use of its stock of non-conventional weapons, since Israel was known to have both a chemical and a nuclear arsenal. Israel's objective was to rid itself of the threat from Saddam Hussein's Iraq, which it had identified as the principal current threat to the country. But an additional spin-off would have been Israel's ability to project itself in the postwar settlement as having acted as an 'ally' of those Arab countries which had sided with the United States. This would be a way of promoting the much desired peace with the Arab states and of stabilising Israel's position. Meanwhile, Yasser Arafat and the PLO would have been subjected to the same process of anathematisation as Saddam Hussein, a process in which, in Israel's scenario, Israel and the moderate Arabs would share.

The Palestinian issue would thus have been marginalised, and almost completely separated from the process of making peace with the Arab states: an outcome much desired by Israel. This was not, however, to be. The main reason for that was the determination of the United States, and in particular of President Bush and his State Department advisers and officials, to make Israel settle with the Palestinians. In spite of the way the Palestinian issue had drifted, as we have seen, away from the heart of the Arab–Israeli conflict as it was perceived by both sides and by the world, the assessment of American analysts was that any attempt to stabilise and regularise Israel's position in the region without regulating the Palestinian issue was doomed to failure. There would be a cancer at the heart of any such settlement which would grow secretly and would in due course burst out again in order to upset any new-found regional balance. The United States was able to bring pressure on Israel because of its new assessment that its Arab allies were of equal, if not greater, importance in the new regional dispensation which the post-Cold War United States had in mind. It was also able to bring pressure on the PLO, because of the low point reached by Yasser Arafat and his leadership in Tunis after the collapse of Saddam Hussein and the public invalidation of their pro-Iraqi policy.

The Israelis had hoped after the Gulf War to find themselves moving closer, under American auspices, to a group of Arab states which had also opposed Saddam Hussein. Instead, somewhat to their surprise, they found themselves obliged to talk to the Palestinians, of whom they had perhaps hoped they had heard the last. After Arafat and the PLO leadership's Gulf War performance, the last thing Israel expected was that Washington would insist on the opening of a dialogue. Of course, the PLO itself was theoretically not involved, but, as we have seen, the supposed independence of the Palestinian delegation in Madrid and Washington was of a purely theoretical nature, and the involvement of the PLO in the talks was quickly recognised. Once the talks had been handed over in Israel to the Labour administration, statesmen like Shimon Peres and Yossi Beilin, as well as Yitzhak Rabin himself, became increasingly convinced of the need to talk to the PLO itself, while Arafat and his associates for their part had since 1988 and before been convinced that negotiation with the Israeli government was the only way forward.

The Gulf War's unexpected effect, therefore, was to bring the Palestinian issue back to the centre of the stage, for three reasons. The first of these was that the United States insisted on resolving the Palestinian question, which President Bush and his successor realised was inescapable to any Middle East peace settlement which was not to be merely cosmetic. The second was that the Israeli Labour leadership appears to have abandoned an Israeli policy which dates back to the 1967 war of attempting to settle with the Arab states and not the Palestinians. And thirdly, the Palestinians accepted realistic and not impossible goals. Some on both the Israeli and the Palestinian sides appear to believe the result has been a sell-out to the enemy. But if peace is the outcome, and is desired by the leadership on both sides, it would be prudent to query the wisdom of those who oppose it.

CHAPTER 10

A CHANGING ISRAEL

A New Political Mood

Political change in Israel has also been of central importance in creating the preconditions for the present serious approach to peace and to a resolution of the Palestinian problem. Israel has had to make a psychological leap to be able to understand that it does not have the power to manufacture a solution to the Palestinian problem on its own. Fifteen years of high-pressure government support under Likud for Jewish settlement in the Occupied Territories, combined with a steady erosion of Palestinian rights, has not cowed the Palestinians. The outbreak of the intifada made it clear that the opposite was the case. One analysis of Likud policy is that it was aimed at bringing about an effective annexation to Israel of the Occupied Territories, and of the West Bank in particular, without ever proclaiming the legal annexation of the conquered land. Though Likud never officially endorsed any policy of "transfer", the removal of the Palestinian inhabitants, putatively to Jordan, it has clearly hoped that the Palestinians would perhaps go away.

Economic depression and the lack of careers and opportunities might eventually have induced the younger inhabitants of the Territories gradually to leave, if anywhere could be found to take them. Likud has never attempted to plan for the effect on Israel of an annexation of the Territories, and the potential creation of either 1.75 million new Arab citizens of the country, or of a class of disenfranchised persons. The indications are that Likud's preferred solution would have been that remaining Palestinians would have held some category of Jordanian citizenship. At their most extreme, in a version favoured by Ariel Sharon, right-wing Israeli plans have gone as far as to favour a Palestinian coup in Jordan which would have created an East Bank Palestinian state to which the West Bank Palestinians could have "returned". None of these wilder solutions have ever come anywhere near being tested, and the reason is that even Israel's far right began to grasp that they would not get the backing of the majority of the Israeli people. Now that the Likud government has fallen, much depends on the success of the peace negotiations begun in 1993. If they produce a solution which satisfies Palestinian aspirations, and begins a return to normality in Israel, Likud will probably not be in a position to return to office: indeed Likud's policies will have wholly lost their relevance to the real world.

These changes have happened because Israel is a democracy. That is a feature of Israel's society of which its citizens are rightly proud. Since the foundation of the Israeli state, the government has been headed by a prime minister who has been able to command a majority in the country's parliament, the 120-member Knesset. The Knesset itself closely mirrors the political make-up of the country, since in broad terms Israeli elections are run on a system of proportional representation, with the whole country as a single constituency. Each party puts up a list for election, and seats are allotted in strict proportion to the number of votes cast for each party. This system means that Israeli politics is very sensitive to shifts of opinion within the country, since the Knesset reflects exactly the proportionality of differing political views.

Those views spread from the Arab members of the Knesset and the pro-peace Meretz party, at the extreme left, through Labour and Likud on the left and right of centre, to the religious parties and the extreme right, represented now by Tsomet and Moledet. At the centre of the spectrum Labour hawks and Likud doves agree and disagree on different issues. Left and right in terms of Israeli politics relate to some extent to the kinds of social and political positions normally associated with such terms. They also have other dimensions. "Left-wing" in Israeli terms has tended to imply at least a less than extreme anti-Arab stance, though a position truly favourable to the Palestinians is rare in any part of Israeli politics except the far left. Meanwhile "right-wing" in Israel implies a "hard-line" approach to the Palestinians, and also a populist appeal. Right-wingers often depict the left as a self-contained and self-serving élite, which does not have the interests of the whole Israeli nation in view.

A Divided Society

These differing political views are in turn closely linked with the divisions of Israeli society. In a sense, Israel is a simple society. Apart from the 900,000 Palestinian Israelis, whom Israel likes to call Israeli Arabs, the vast majority of its citizens are Jews. But in fact the Jewish population is very varied. Many of Israel's original immigrants came from Russia, eastern Europe and Germany, in the days of the expansion of the Yeshuv from the late nineteenth century up to 1948. Since the foundation of Israel, Jews have come from virtually every country in the world, to exercise the "right of return" built in to the Israeli constitution, which means that every Jew has the right to immediate citizenship of the state. That right of return is of great emotional importance to Israelis, but has caused great offence to the Palestinians; who find that a Jew with no previous connection to the historic land of Palestine can become an Israeli, while Palestinians born on Palestinian soil often have no right of entry either to Israel or the Occupied Territories.

The exercise of the right of return, and Israel's active campaign to gather up communities of Jews round the world, have greatly diversified Israel's population. Jews from Europe and from the United States, often the descendants of earlier migrations from eastern Europe, have joined the first waves of immigrants. There is now a large group of recently arrived Russians, as the result of the outflow from the Soviet Union and then from Russia in recent years: the Russians sometimes speak neither Hebrew nor English, and are coming to constitute a separate social community. There is a community of black Ethiopian Jews which is finding social assimilation into Israel extremely difficult. There are Jews who were born in Palestine, and a growing proportion of "sabras", born in Israel. But most important as a source of social division is the distinction between western and oriental Jews: Yemenis, Moroccans, and Jews from virtually every other Arab country, who have come to constitute a class of their own in Israeli society. The oriental, or "sephardic" Jews are better accepted in Israel today, and many have been in the end as socially and economically successful as their western or "ashkenazi" compatriots, but at first they found themselves almost as much outside Israeli society as the Ethiopians do today.

Seven years after Israeli independence this was how the split between the two main communities was seen by an American Jewish educator:

> There is a marked difference between the two groups in technical skill
> and knowledge. The oriental Jews came from countries which were
> backward in regard to technical development, while the Ashkenazim
> came to Palestine with the know-how of western civilisation. The result is
> that the orientals have been relegated to the simpler and more primitive
> occupations, while the Ashkenazim are engaged in occupations calling
> for skilled knowledge.[1]

At the time of the foundation of the state Israeli leaders, and in particular David Ben Gurion, held a low view of the abilities of the sephardic Jews: for example, he called the Jews of Morocco "human beasts" and "a primitive community", and said that "they have no culture"; and he said that in comparison with the ashkenazi people of Israel, the Yemeni Jew was "2000 years away from us and needs to be taught the most basic concepts of civilisation."[2]

From 1948 to 1977, Labour held power in Israel. The original Zionist leaders were closely identified with the Israeli Labour Party, which constituted a closely knit ashkenazi élite. This élite broadly shared European ideas and liberal values, and was strongly conscious of its own worth. This worth did not always appear so self-evident from outside. A sephardic commentator Gideon Giladi puts the point in a study made in 1990:

> The Jews of Israel can be divided into two ethnic groups. The first is the
> Ashkenazi community, made up of the Zionist colonist minority who
> emigrated to Palestine mainly from Eastern Europe, and also from
> Central and Western Europe and America. This community represents
> the summit of the Zionist ruling establishment's hierarchy, the
> overwhelming majority in the Cabinet, Parliament, the top civil service
> and the upper echelons of the trade unions, private and public capital,
> the leadership of the police and secret service, the media etc. . . . The
> second community is that of the . . . Sephardim, representing the
> majority of Israelis.[3]

By the election of 1977 a substantial part of the sephardic

---

1. Abraham Shumsky, *The Clash of Cultures in Israel*, Columbia University, New York 1955.
2. Gideon Giladi, *Discord in Zion*, Scorpion Publishing, London 1990, pp. 209–10.
3. Ibid.

population, together with an ashkenazi leadership from the older immigrant community, had begun to tire of the assumption made by the old Zionist élite that it had the automatic right to rule. The Labour ruling class was visibly confused and demoralised in the aftermath of the semi-defeat of the 1973 war, and its share of the vote fell by 15 per cent; while the right-wing Likud made an advance which was modest but enough to secure victory. An analysis of voting figures demonstrates that Likud's share of the vote was best where there were most sephardic Jews. The Likud's leadership was largely ashkenazi, but even here a historical distinction can be seen between Likud and Labour. While the Labour élite was associated before independence with the Haganah self-defence movement, the men who were to become the Likud leadership, including Menachem Begin and Yitzhak Shamir, were linked with the Irgun Zvai Leumi and other independent terrorist groups, associated first with anti-British activity and then with anti-Arab extremism. Shamir, a leader in the Stern Gang, was at one time wanted as a terrorist by the British. Irgun Zvai Leumi, was mainly responsible for (but continued to deny) the notorious massacre of Palestinians at Deir Yassin in 1948.

The Occupied Territories were in the hands of Likud to dispose of once it was in government. It was easy for Likud to take the decision to hold on to the Territories, to develop them economically for the benefit of Israel by the implantation of Jewish settlers, to use them as a buffer against Jordan to the east, and, in the case of the Golan Heights, against Syria. It became a commonplace of Likud's discourse that the Territories were necessary as space for Israel's expansion, as it absorbed the new Jewish immigrants from Russia and grew as a nation. The possession of the Territories also bought Likud the support of the religious parties and the extreme right wing, both of which for slightly different reasons were determined to keep and hold the whole of what they regarded as the historic Eretz Israel. This determination by Likud to hold on to the Territories was undiminished by the Camp David Accords of 1978, which the Likud leadership tried to implement without offering the Palestinians sovereignty over any land. Other discussions about the possible future of the Palestinians, through to the so-called Shamir Plan of 1989, continued to steer clear of the question of ceding sovereignty. Likud was interested in persuading Jordan to play some part in governing the Palestinians, but that hope was ended when King Hussein abrogated Jordan's responsibility for the West Bank in 1988. However, the basic idea of the Allon Plan as it was conceived by Labour, which involved handing back part of the territory to Jordan, was not in line with Likud's policy.

The Origin of the Problem: Labour's Responsibility

The problem of the Occupied Territories as we have it today has been largely created by the Likud government and by the settler movement in the last fifteen years. But Labour must also take its share of the blame: it was under a Labour government that the West Bank and Gaza were occupied in 1967, and it was the Labour government which took the fateful decision not to hand them back to Jordan and Egypt. In the aftermath of the 1967 war, Israel was dizzy with success. It had entered the war uncertain as to whether it was equipped and able to overcome the Arab forces. It came out of the war bloated with a sense of its own invincibility: Israel's view of itself was well portrayed in an anthology of cartoons published by the newspaper *Maariv* after the end of the war: "It is a country where nobody expects miracles, but everybody takes them for granted."[4] In this mood, Israel saw no reason to hand back conquered territory. Israel's triumphalism was also paradoxically combined with caution, and the government was very unwilling to hand back territory which might still be essential for Israel's security. In due course, Likud decided to bargain away Sinai for peace with Egypt. But as regards the West Bank, the best Labour was prepared to offer was the Allon plan, where a complex map was drawn, in which Israel was to keep a swathe of the West Bank next to the Jordan river for security, as well as a wide circle of territory round Jerusalem, while Jordan would get two segments of the West Bank in the north and south, and a neck of territory including Jericho leading down to the Jordan river.[5] The latest version of this Israeli plan was on the table in 1977 when the election removed Labour from power.

The story of Likud's administration of the Occupied Territories was, from the Arab point of view, one of repression and neglect. The Palestinians were taxed, but received poorer services than their new

4. Ephraim Kishon and Kariel Gardosh, *So Sorry we Won*, English edition, Maariv Library, Tel Aviv 1967.
5. Meron Benvenisti and Shlomo Khayat, "The West Bank and Gaza Atlas", *The Jerusalem Post*, Jerusalem 1988.

Israeli neighbours. They had their elected mayors, but they were subject in most practical matters to an arbitrary and distant Israeli military administration. There were endless disputes over land and water with Israeli settlers. Worst of all, there was an ongoing policy of government sequestration of land, for settlement and for military purposes. All those policies eventually gave rise to the intifada, the Palestinian uprising, about which we hear more in the next chapter. If there was a turning point, it could be said to be the outbreak of the intifada, when Israel could no longer delude itself that it had a complaisant Arab population in the Occupied Territories. Some Israelis had even convinced themselves that the disenfranchised and dispossessed Palestinians of the Occupied Territories had actually come to prefer Israeli administration to that of Jordan.

How Change Came

It was in the first place the intifada which was both the cause and the symptom of the Israeli people's disenchantment with Likud's approach. The growing tension and stress which it engendered, and Israel's awareness of the inexorable deterioration of its image abroad was a major factor leading to the swing against Likud government policies that eventually caused the Likud government's fall from office in 1992. Many Israelis no longer wanted to continue the hostile relationship with the Occupied Territories. The military aspect of Israeli life has begun to alarm the old and depress the young. Many Israelis fear that the experience of military service and the hostile contact between young Israelis and the Palestinians of the Territories is brutalising the young. Opinion polls after the opening of the Madrid talks began consistently to show that Israelis favoured the exchange of land for peace, if that was the only way of ending the apparently eternal confrontation with the Palestinians, and the never ending state of hostility between Israel and the neighbouring Arab states. The idea of a greater Israel, and the permanent settlement of the Territories, began to lose its appeal, except for the far right and the settlers themselves.

Increasingly, commentators began to remark that Israel was weary: of war, of hostility, of hatred. The vote for Labour in the 1992 elections which gave it a working majority was symptomatic of that weariness, since the electorate was convinced that Labour would enter more earnestly into the peace talks. The return of twelve Meretz members, who were explicitly committed to peace with the Palestinians and to the return of Palestinian territory, was an even more striking testimony of the extent to which Israelis had turned against the policies of Likud. Part of Labour's electoral success clearly came from traditional Labour voters who had flirted over the last decade with an alternative which had promised to take a tough line on the Palestinian issue. That was now seen to have been a dead end. Labour may also have attracted voters from Likud's traditional constituency.

Especially when the United States government began to withhold some of the support it had traditionally extended to Israel, the electorate began to see the drawbacks of a policy of promoting a greater Israel and rejecting compromise. It is also worth conjecturing that in the changed circumstances of 1992, Likud's populist appeal to the sephardi population was less effective. Simplistic solutions had perhaps lost their appeal to people who favoured a hard approach to the Palestinian issue, but who had in the event seen Likud's iron fist policy fail to produce the desired result. At the same time, Likud was also losing its support because it was conspicuously failing to control the intifada. For all these reasons the mechanism of Israel's democracy has put representatives of the traditional Labour Party Zionist élite back in power.

Of course, even for Labour a genuinely conciliatory approach to the Palestinian problem is a new phenomenon. It was Labour which fought the war in 1948, and the Labour leadership which planned the strategy to dispossess the Palestinians of much of the historic territory of Palestine. The Labour leader of the 1960s, Mrs Golda Meir, gave currency to the much quoted statement that the Palestinians do not exist. But at least in the 1990s the Labour leadership has been better able to make the necessary psychological and philosophical adjustments in its approach. The two Labour leaders who head the new government differ in their approaches, but they have been able to reach a degree of unanimity. Foreign Minister Shimon Peres is the more subtle politician, who has always seen the value of Arab contacts and who has constantly hoped that the resolution of Israel's problems would be found through a rapprochement with the Palestinians and the Arab states.

On the other hand, Prime Minister Yitzhak Rabin is a hawk; indeed in the context of that confluence of opinions in the centre of the Israeli political spectrum, he has in the past taken up a tougher stand than some in Likud. He served under Yitzhak Shamir as Defence Minister during the Likud-led coalition government, and was probably farther to the right than some of his Likud colleagues on the Palestinian issue. In the past, the pinnacle of his career as a soldier was to bring him to the position of Chief of Staff, and he served in that capacity in the war of 1967. There is a famous photograph of Rabin with Moshe Dayan, then the Minister of Defence, and army commander Uzi Narkiss, striding into the Old City of Jerusalem hours after its capture in 1967, looking every inch the image of warlike Israel.[6] During his first term as Prime Minister, from 1974 to 1977, while Israel was still riding on a wave of unquestioning American support, Rabin was not notably conciliatory towards the Palestinians. But even he has been able to adopt a more flexible attitude in keeping with the times.

By the spring of 1994, it had begun to appear as if a failure of the talks to implement the interim agreement could endanger the electoral popularity on which the Labour government depends. In the immediate aftermath of the signing ceremony in Washington on 13 September 1993, Rabin's backing at home was solid. The new leader of the Likud opposition, Binyamin Netanyahu, opened himself almost to ridicule by his opposition. The country saw a chance for peace and wanted the government to take it. But as the implementation of the agreement began to seem as if it was about to run into the sand, as negotiations between Israel and the PLO failed to agree on the details, support for the opposition began once more to climb. The resurgence of disturbances in the Occupied Territories, after the first wave of euphoria there, also had the effect of bringing a swing back to the right in Israel. The newly emergent violent movements in the Territories, the Hamas fighters of the Izzedin el-Qasim, Hamas's armed wing, the PFLP Red Eagles and even the Fatah Hawks, nominally Arafat's supporters, have brought guns and blood to their fight against Israeli occupation where previously the weapons were stones and ridicule. Violence breeds violence, and some Israelis have obviously returned to their right-wing allegiance. Labour's continuing success depends on the implementation of the interim agreement.

6. Reproduced in Yitzhak Rabin, *The Rabin Memoirs*, Little, Brown, Boston 1979.

CHAPTER 11

THE NEW STYLE PLO

Revolution in the Revolution

The evolution in the Palestinian movement itself is the last and in many ways the most important factor in opening the way for peace. Of course the Palestinian movement and its philosophy have not mutated spontaneously. The change has come in response to the changes in the world of international politics, many of which we have already spoken of. But the fact remains that the face of the PLO has changed, and Palestinian attitudes across the various Palestinian communities have changed. The centre of discussion now is the interim agreement made in Oslo, whether it can be made to stick and whether it should be made to stick. After an initial euphoria, there are naturally questions about whether the agreement is what the Palestinians need, and about whether they have in some sense been cheated. A hard core of militants has pushed ever farther in the direction of rejectionism, and contends that the current talks represent a sell-out of Palestinian rights. These are the group of ten rejectionist organizations based in Damascus and the other radicals such as Abu Nidal and Ahmed Jibril. Other Palestinians have come under the influence of the radical Islamic organisations, Hamas and Islamic Jihad, and believe for different reasons that there should not be a settlement.

There are also more moderate opponents of the agreement Yasser Arafat is trying to negotiate: those who believe that the PLO has settled for too little and could have got more, or who have misgivings about the real intentions of Israel. Many of these are ordinary thoughtful people in the Occupied Territories, who may have greeted the news of the Oslo breakthrough with relief but now have begun to harbour doubts. Nonetheless, the mainstream PLO broadly backs Yasser Arafat in his search for a peace settlement for the Palestinians based on the return of the Occupied Territories to Palestinian rule, under the agreement whose outlines were laid down last September and whose details are now being fleshed out. Round the world, PLO officials are deeply committed to making the agreement work, and in the capitals of Europe and elsewhere PLO representatives are eagerly explaining how they believe the remaining problems can be resolved, and how on the basis of the Oslo agreement Israel and Palestine will ultimately be able to live together.

Palestinian attitudes have not suddenly changed. The idea of two states in the territory of mandatory Palestine goes back a long way, even to the 1970s, but took firm root in the PLO's official thinking in 1988. The PLO has in effect recognised the state of Israel since the momentous 19th session of the Palestine National Council (PNC) meeting held in Algiers from 12 to 15 November 1988, at which the delegates declared Palestine's independence, but also decided to accept UN Resolution 242. Resolution 242 calls for Israel's withdrawal to the pre-1967 frontiers, but also calls for the "respect for the sovereignty ... of every state in the area", so that in the act of accepting it, the PLO had also acknowledged that Israel was there to stay, and implicitly that it was there to be negotiated with. Some historians argue that the implicit recognition of Israel by the PLO goes further back still, since the PLO endorsed the proposal made at the Arab League Summit at Fez on 6 September 1982. This acknowledged the PLO as the sole legitimate representative of the Palestinians, but recognised Israel's sovereign status by calling for "Israel's withdrawal from all Arab territories occupied in 1967, including Arab Jerusalem."[1]

A bid for peace: this was how contemporary analysts interpreted the PNC's deliberations, which were carefully steered by PLO Chairman Yasser Arafat. Godfrey Jansen covered the meeting at the Club des Pins, outside Algiers:

> The PNC has made many concessions to its antagonists. It has, by implication, recognised Israel, forsworn terrorism, and set aside its Charter. Is there any reaction from the other side? From Israel the chances are nil but the PLO now hopes that the world will see which party is ready to make concessions in the cause of peace. That should be some consolation, but not much. The only faint hope is that the new Bush administration may, perhaps, be encouraged to change America's Middle East policy.[2]

1. The text is quoted by Yehuda Lukacs, *The Israeli–Palestinian Conflict: a Documentary Record, 1967–1990*, Cambridge University Press, Cambridge 1992, p. 478.

2. Godfrey Jansen, "Independence and the recognition of Israel", *Middle East International*, 338, 18 November 1988.

That interpretation, from five years ago, now has a prophetic ring. It has taken not merely the departure of President Reagan, with his automatic pro-Israel posture, but also the Gulf War and the fall of Soviet Communism to put the American administration into the frame of mind to seek Middle East peace. But this has been the final outcome, and the preparatory work put in by the PLO in 1988 must be recognised as a necessary piece of groundwork.

The next field for PLO action was international diplomacy. Yasser Arafat accepted an invitation to speak to the General Assembly of the United Nations on 13 December 1988. The Arab nations and other non-Western countries energetically lobbied for the invitation. Sari Nusseibeh, a Palestinian academic of the younger generation from the University of Bir Zeit in the West Bank, has been intimately concerned with Palestinian peace for many years. He wrote:

> On the level of international diplomacy, the scene has now been set for a radical transformation of the status of the PLO and of the national rights of the Palestinian people which it represents . . . With the radical changes agreed in Algiers, the political map has so changed that it is no longer possible to envisage a peace process that will bypass the PLO and the Palestinian people's national rights.[3]

Reagan and his equally pro-Israeli Secretary of State George Shultz did their best to prevent Arafat from taking up the United Nations invitation by refusing him a visa to come to the United States, in violation of America's treaty obligations to the world body, but the United Nations relocated its session to Geneva, at immense expense, in order to hear Arafat's 80-minute discourse.

Arafat's aim was to get the maximum of publicity for the PLO's new standpoint. He must have been keenly aware of the contrast between this occasion and his previous address to the United Nations in 1974, after the failure of the December 1973 Geneva conference, when he outlined a plan for a single secular state in Palestine. What the PLO wanted now, Arafat said, was a comprehensive solution to the Middle East problem, which would include consultation with Israel, in the framework of an international conference based on UN resolutions 242 and 338. Speaking to the representatives of the nations who had invited him to the UN, Arafat said: "I, as Chairman of the Palestine Liberation Organization, hereby once more declare that I condemn

3. Sari Nusseibeh, "Time for Palestinian offensives", *Middle East International*, 339, 2 December 1988.

terrorism in all its forms, and at the same time I salute those sitting before me in this hall who, in the days when they fought to liberate their countries from the yoke of colonialism, were accused of terrorism . . ."[4] Arafat also issued a very explicit invitation to Israel to make peace: "I ask the leaders of Israel to come here under the sponsorship of the United Nations, so that, together, we can forge that peace. I say to them, as I say to you, that our people, who want dignity, freedom and peace for themselves and security for their state, want the same thing for all the states and parties involved in the Arab–Israeli conflict."[5]

Arafat's plea fell on stony ground, but the PLO in due course got from it the opening of a dialogue with the United States. This was carried on by PLO officials and the American ambassador in Tunis, and amounted to American recognition for the Palestinians. Before that was to happen, however, there was a difficult time. The closing days of the Reagan administration were not the moment to raise the issue of PLO participation in Middle East peace. Israel's Likud administration was also implacably opposed to any proposal from the PLO. Israel's then Prime Minister, Yitzhak Shamir, called the PLO leader's UN statement a "monumental deception", and the United States claimed that it was "ambiguous on the key issues". Scandinavian diplomacy was to play a part in getting Washington to recognise that the PLO Chairman had given the necessary assurance of the PLO's peaceful intentions.

American acceptance of the validity of Arafat's declaration came in the end only after a session when Arafat met Swedish diplomats, followed by a press conference at which Arafat repeated the assurance he had given in his UN speech, in a form of words acceptable to Washington. The part played by Sweden's Foreign Minister, Sten Andersson, foreshadowed that of Norway's Johan Joergen Holst in the Oslo negotiations, and it was this that Arafat referred to when he told Holst that he hoped Norway could succeed Sweden as a Scandinavian mediator. Sweden conveyed messages between the PLO and the United States, and according to PLO official, Yasser Abed Rabbo, who became the principal Palestinian interlocutor with America, the Swedes conveyed a message to Arafat to the effect that Washington

4. Liesl Graz, "Arafat's plan for peace", *Middle East International*, 340, 16 December 1988.
5. Ibid.

would open a dialogue in Tunis if the PLO leader would give satisfactory assurances in his UN speech.

That dialogue was to continue until June 1990, when it lapsed because of Arafat's refusal to make a formal apology for a terrorist attack carried out by a small militant Palestinian group. The question of whether the United States would have resumed the dialogue became irrelevant when the Gulf War broke out, and Arafat made the tactical error of supporting Saddam Hussein. That put an end to American contacts with the PLO until the Bush administration decided that the Palestinians would have to come to the Madrid conference, and that the supposedly non-PLO delegation which came to that conference could not, in the real world, be denied access to PLO advisers. The break in PLO diplomacy was however only a break in continuity. We have already looked at the question of why Arafat supported Iraq: the answer may well have been that he had little choice. In spite of that anomalous period, when Arab and Palestinian emotions ran high and decisions were not always the most rational, it can be seen that from 1988 up to the opening of the Madrid conference, Palestinian policy had moved in a straight line from the recognition towards the opening of negotiation.

Origins of the PLO

At the beginning, the PLO had nothing and wanted everything. The Organization's origins were far from the diplomatic purlieus of international negotiation, and a long way away from any thought of seeking a negotiated solution. The Organization came into being in 1964, when President Nasser of Egypt called an Arab summit meeting in Cairo, and asked for support for a Palestinian movement. The Palestine Liberation Organization came into existence at a founding conference in May 1964. On 28 May 1964 the Palestinian Charter was approved: the controversial document whose clause calling for the annihilation of Israel has only just been disowned by Yasser Arafat, as part of the peace-making process in the autumn of 1993. The Organization's first leader was Ahmed Shuqairy. The young Yasser Arafat, after his studies in Cairo and a career as an engineer in Kuwait, was already at the head of Fatah, which had been organizing itself for the guerrilla struggle since 1959 and carried out its first raid in 1965.

The Palestinian guerrillas were drawn from the generation of young men who had lost their homes and the prospect of their lives in Palestine in 1948. Many young Palestinians who had family resources and had been able to benefit from an education, drifted into the Palestinian diaspora, and into professional careers abroad. The Palestinians today have found their way to virtually every country round the world, where they have worked as professionals and in business. Others, less lucky or less talented, nursed their grievances in the refugee camps, and many live today in the camps of Gaza, the West Bank and Jordan. Others again, who stayed in Israel, founded the Israeli Arab community which has survived in the face of social discrimination. Some of these Palestinians put their home country and its fate to the backs of their minds, though few have ever forgotten it. Others, as they grew older, decided to commit themselves to the battle for the liberation of their country.

At first that did not seem so impossible a prospect. The Israelis had won a war to found their state in 1948: in 1957 in Kuwait, when Arafat and his friends first began to talk about the idea of beginning a guerrilla movement and committing themselves to the struggle, that was less than a decade earlier. The catastrophe of 1948 did not seem irreversible, and Israel did not seem as yet to be insuperable. The young guerrillas continued to organize, and then to carry out their first operations. However, it was the build-up to the war of 1967 that brought the young guerrillas the excitement of the prospect of Israel's imminent defeat and opened the prospect of their return to the homeland of Palestine. There was no clear indication which side would win the war which seemed by the spring of 1967 to have become inevitable. Israel was well aware that its survival, at least in its present form, depended on victory. On the other hand the leadership of Nasser gave the Arabs a feeling of confidence. In the event Egypt's defeat caused recrimination, heartache and despair throughout the Arab world, and in Egypt brought the emotional upheaval of Nasser's resignation and return. Meanwhile, the young guerrillas of Fatah and the other Palestinian organizations suffered their own heartache. For a brief period, the recovery of Palestine, two decades after its loss, had seemed possible. Now that hope was farther away than ever.

Jordan was now the Palestinian guerrillas' base, and in the years after 1967 they reacted to the frustration and shame of defeat by redoubling their efforts against Israel. Operating now from across the Jordan river, Fatah made forays into the Occupied Territories, and

Israel itself, planting bombs and carrying out hit-and-run attacks. According to John Wallach the number of attacks leapt to an impressive total by 1969: "That year, intent on wiping out the Jewish nation, Arafat's PLO carried out 2432 attacks on Israel, three times the number of incidents in 1968, and more than 20 times the number carried out in 1967."[6] It was at a Palestine National Council meeting in February 1969 that Arafat, as the head of Fatah, the largest and most effective Palestinian movement, effectively took over the PLO. Egypt, and other Arab governments, still smarting from the defeat of 1967, decided to back Fatah. Only King Hussein, whose control over his own territory was increasingly challenged, viewed Fatah's growing influence with concern, though that concern was also shared by the political leadership in neighbouring Lebanon. For the Israelis, it was at this time that Arafat, known sometimes as Abu Ammar, became identified with the idea of Palestinian terrorism. But the most spectacular Palestinian guerrilla operations were to begin in 1970. These were the work of the smaller factions, men who, as the Palestinian struggle developed, were to show themselves to be more militant than Arafat's Fatah.

World attention was what the guerrillas now sought. The next target of the Palestinian militants was to be the international airlines of the Western nations. The Palestinians knew that seizing civilian jets would attract the attention they needed. They also realised that attacks on planes would focus the attention of the Western world, which could otherwise disregard the Palestinian problem as something happening in a turbulent region which could be ignored. A hijack, however, introduced a new element: anyone, anywhere, could be a victim. They reasoned that the adverse publicity they might get from attacks on innocent and uninvolved civilians would be more than made up for by the publicity for the Palestinian cause. There is every reason to believe that they were right. Before 1970, when the hijackings took place, little was known about the PLO. Afterwards it was globally known, and it became impossible to forget the Palestinians' grievance. Most of the publicity was bad, but the Palestinian issue was now firmly on the global agenda.

On 6 September 1970 guerrillas of George Habash's Popular Front for the Liberation of Palestine (PFLP) seized no less than four civilian

6. John and Jane Wallach, *Arafat*, new edition, Mandarin paperbacks, London 1992, p. 166.

aircraft on the same day. The crew of one of the four planes hijacked, an Israeli El Al flight, succeeded in fighting off the hijackers, but three others, belonging to Pan Am, TWA and Swissair, were taken. The Pan Am plane was blown up in Beirut after its passengers were released, but the others were flown to Jordan, where they sat in the sweltering sun at a deserted airstrip, Dawson's Field, while the world looked on with consternation. Three days later a further plane, this time a British BOAC flight, was hijacked and taken to join the others. More than six hundred passengers were kept on the planes for days as hostages. All were released in a few days, apart from 16 Jews who were held for a further month. In the later 1970s, as hijackings and airport attacks in Europe were taken up by fringe groups, passengers were killed, and the benefits to the Palestinians began to be outweighed by the burden of international antagonism. Other attacks across the world also kept the Palestinians in the public eye. Oil installations were destroyed in the Netherlands, Germany and Italy, and Israelis abroad were attacked.

Black September

King Hussein of Jordan decided in September 1970, while the hijacking crisis at Dawson's Field was under way, to cleanse the Palestinian fighters from Jordan and rid himself of what had become a threat to his own authority. The operation was later dubbed Black September by the Palestinian fighters. Half of Jordan's population was of Palestinian origin, as the result of the two wars, and the Palestinians were beginning too visibly to ask themselves why they should continue to recognise the supremacy of the king. In Israel and elsewhere, the territory across the Jordan river was known with some justice as Fatahland. King Hussein was losing control of his own territory, and he believed the moment had come to fight or quit. He fought, and his army drove the Palestinians out. Syria, which threatened to intervene on the Palestinians' behalf, in fact held back. Egypt's President Nasser died of a heart attack while trying to mediate between King Hussein and the PLO, precipitating mourning and despair across the Arab world, where Nasser had come to be regarded by many as the only hope for the future.

The Palestinians retired from Jordan to regroup in Lebanon, which was to be Arafat's base for the next twelve years, until 1982. There were already Palestinian refugee camps in Lebanon, which were a fruitful recruiting ground for young angry Palestinians. Black September became the title of a new faction of yet more desperate extremists, and the series of Black September operations round the world began. Black September's most spectacular coup was at the Munich Olympic Games of 1972, when on 5 September the Israeli athletic team at the games was taken prisoner in their quarters, and eleven Israeli athletes were ultimately killed. This time the world was appalled, and Arafat's Fatah severed its ties with the extremists. A newspaper photograph of a hooded guerrilla looking over a balcony at the Munich Olympic village summed up everything about the idea of Palestinian guerrillas which the world was learning to fear. Arafat and his associates saw that the time had come to alter their image. As the 1970s went on, Palestinian exploits became more extravagant, and Israel developed its own techniques against terrorism. The high point of this confrontation came at Entebbe, the capital of Uganda, in July 1976, when an Israeli force rescued a plane full of Israeli hostages in a long-range operation of almost incredible organisation and daring.

The PLO began to act more like a government while it was in Lebanon. The Palestine National Council, with representatives from the Occupied Territories and the diaspora as well as the guerrilla groups themselves, had met on a yearly basis since 1964. It began now to function as the PLO's validating body, the parliament, from which it drew its claim to represent the Palestinian people. The other institutions which were already in existence started to operate more regularly. The guerrilla organizations which made up the PLO elected an executive committee of 18, with the duty of approving the Chairman's decisions from day to day. The central council was a larger body, to which executive committee decisions could be referred, which in theory represented the cumbrous PNC, whose four hundred members took some time to assemble. It was also during the 1970s that the PLO's worldwide diplomatic representation took shape, and the many groups and committees looking after the many kinds of refugee welfare and grass roots activity sponsored by the PLO. The bill was paid by Saudi Arabia and the Gulf states, as well as a tax levied on Palestinians lucratively employed in the Gulf. It could be said that it was now that the PLO first developed into a state in exile, a shape it was to take up more fully later in Tunis. Within Lebanon itself, the PLO's activities as a state-within-a-state began to outdo the more primitive organization of Fatahland in Jordan, and Arafat has recently referred to his time in Lebanon as his apprenticeship in national government. According to Raymond Eddé: "The PLO took over the capital to such an extent that we felt like foreigners in our own country."[7]

The Lebanese civil war spelled the beginning of the end for the Palestinians in Lebanon. The complexities of the war which began in Lebanon in 1975 are too great to go into here: it is enough to say that the Palestinians became drawn in as participants. The civil war in Lebanon was in very general terms a struggle over the country's resources, between Lebanon's communities, which could be seen in religious, economic or political terms. In its religious dimension, the war was broadly between the Maronite Christians on the one hand and the poorer Muslims on the other, especially the Shiʿites and the Druzes. In economic terms it was between those social groups in Lebanon which commanded the country's resources and controlled its economy and the country's poor and dispossessed. In its political aspect the war was for the control of the Lebanese government, and an attempt to prise the control of the state out of the hands of the Maronites and their Sunni Muslim friends who were also committed to the status quo. The Palestinians fitted into this jigsaw as a faction which played an important part on the Muslim side of the fight. As we have seen, that came to an end, as did the whole Palestinian political structure in Lebanon, when the Israelis invaded in 1982 in a move which resulted in the Palestinian departure from the country.

In Tunis, where Arafat eventually set up his new headquarters, he had to rethink his strategy. In both Jordan and Lebanon, he had a constituency of Palestinians in the country, both refugees and others who had been making their own way in their new countries. He had resources, and legions of fighting men at his disposal. In Tunis, the government helped him to set up an efficient headquarters for the PLO's organisation and gave him privileged diplomatic status, but there was no local Palestinian community of any size, and his forces were dispersed among different countries. It was in this new situation that the politics of the PLO began to evolve into something like their modern form, and the guerrilla organization that the PLO had indubitably been, began to evolve into the administration of a world-wide Palestinian community which had in its sights in the longer term

7. Ibid., p. 246.

the task of running a Palestinian state. For Arafat, an unexpected benefit of the move to Tunis has been that control of the PLO has passed as never before entirely into his hands.

More power in the Occupied Territories, a goal the PLO soon achieved after moving to Tunis, was what really changed the Organization. In the Jordanian and Lebanese phases of its existence, it was preoccupied with local developments. From the detached vantage point of Tunis, it has concentrated not so much on the Palestinian diaspora in the Middle East and elsewhere, as on developing its constituency closest to home, in the Occupied Territories themselves. Phyllis Bennis writes: "On the ship to their new home-in-exile in Tunis, PLO leaders acknowledged the fact that a strategy relying on centres of the Palestinian diaspora to lead the fight for independence had not achieved its aims. Instead, a new approach galvanised long-standing PLO commitments to support organizing efforts inside occupied Palestine."[8] That paid off in 1991, when such was the extent of Arafat's grip that it would have been entirely impossible to find a Palestinian delegation to go to Madrid which did not owe its allegiance ultimately to the PLO. Fatah, the PFLP, and the Democratic Front for the Liberation of Palestine (DFLP) are the bodies which have real support in the Occupied Territories, and though George Habash's PFLP challenges Fatah's popularity among the young, it is seen within the PLO as a "loyal" opposition to Arafat's Fatah.

The expansion of the PLO's linkage, support, and interests in the Occupied Territories constitute what the Palestinian historian Yezid Sayigh calls a "shift in the centre of gravity of Palestinian politics".[9] Meanwhile the more radical groups, the "disloyal" opposition, based in Damascus and elsewhere, lost their constituency, and their support is now confined virtually to their own membership. That is why Arafat is largely unworried in 1994 by the empty threats of the small groups based in Damascus, although if the PFLP were to throw in its weight wholly against the current negotiations the damage would be considerable. Arafat's Fatah is central to the PLO, and Yezid Sayigh describes the evolution he has seen in Fatah's style and its role: "It is Fatah's success in rebasing itself in the Occupied Territories that has preserved its centrality in the Palestinian national movement as a

8. Phyllis Bennis, *From Stones to Statehood*, Zed Books, London 1990, p. 23.
9. Yezid Sayigh, "The transformation of PLO politics since 1982", *International Affairs*, 65:2, Spring 1989.

whole and reinforced its hold on PLO decision-making. At the core of this process has been a break with its previous emphasis on clandestine military action, to which social and political activity in the Territories was subordinated."[10]

Meanwhile Arafat's policy was to consolidate his own role at the head of both the PLO and Fatah, and to maintain Fatah's grip on the PLO's decision-making process, while continuing to build the organs of the Palestinian state in exile. Throughout this period the PLO was also concerned to boost the standing of its now worldwide network of representative offices, and to get diplomatic status for its representatives wherever possible, as a challenge to Israel's claim to sole legitimacy within the territory of Palestine. Arafat also threw himself personally into the task of projecting the Palestinians' image abroad, and began in earnest the punishing schedule of worldwide diplomatic missions which took him constantly from country to country in his personal jet: a mobility and unpredictability which also improved his security during a period when Israel was intensifying its attacks on PLO personnel and in April 1988 succeeded in killing a senior PLO man, Abu Jihad, in a raid carried out in Tunis itself.

The Intifada

The intifada, the Palestinian uprising in the Occupied Territories, was the one single development which changed the face of Palestinian politics, and challenged the Israeli hold over the Occupied Territories. Perhaps more than any other event it opened the way for the Madrid conference of 1991. The word "intifada" means throwing off the yoke, or an upheaval: and this was what began to happen in the Occupied Territories in December 1987, when suddenly after twenty years of relatively trouble-free occupation the people of the Occupied Territories themselves began to rebel against the Israeli occupiers. By this time, the Israeli presence was everywhere in the Occupied Territories. Israeli troops patrolled the streets, and Israeli intelligence monitored the people's activities. The Israeli military administration administered the law, and the people had to deal with Israelis at every level of day-to-day existence.

10. Ibid.

Israeli settlements had meanwhile spread throughout the West Bank, and there were even 3000 settlers in the Gaza Strip. There had been endless disputes about land and water, and almost wherever the eye turned, new Israeli flats and houses were to be seen on the hilltops, while new roads cutting through the West Bank took the settlers from place to place. The number of settlers in the West Bank was approaching 100,000, while there were a further 120,000 in areas the Israelis regarded as sovereign territory round Jerusalem. Those figures have risen today to 120,000 settlers in the West Bank and 140,000 round Jerusalem. The mounting discontent of the Palestinians in 1987 and how it turned to anger is described by two Israeli journalists, Ze'ev Schiff and Ehud Ya'ari:

> Most of all they were bristling with fury over the crude discrimination practiced against them and the crass arrogance that demeaned them further with every passing day. They seethed over Israel's presumptuousness, which had led it, in the words of one of the fundamentalist groups in Gaza, to 'assault both the land and the people': the land in a series of expropriation actions and the building of settlements by 'force and coercion, skulduggery and seduction'; the people by 'inhuman behaviour' towards defenceless individuals, the arrest and abuse of thousands, the collection of ruinous taxes, even the barring of kin from attending their relatives' funerals.[11]

The intifada began on 8 December 1987, according to common lore. Four Palestinians were killed by an Israeli truck at a checkpoint in Gaza, probably by accident, perhaps deliberately. The incident sparked a wave of violent but unarmed reprisals across the Occupied Territories which took the Israeli authorities by surprise. The intifada had a spontaneous quality, because of the sporadic and improvised nature of the anti-Israeli action: stone-throwing, tire-burning, slogan painting. But there had been efforts to plan resistance, and there was organization, almost from the first. According to one representative from the popular committees: "The intifada was spontaneous at first. But after about one month our earlier organizing efforts took root, and gained control of the political motion of the intifada. That is what allowed the uprising to continue."[12] Soon the Palestinian activists were able to form the Unified Leadership of the Uprising, a body of Palestinians who have operated clandestinely to coordinate the

11. Ze'ev Schiff and Ehud Ya'ari, *Intifada,* Simon and Schuster, New York 1989, p. 99.
12. Phyllis Bennis, op. cit., p. 22.

intifada's activities. But the members of the intifada's leadership were in intimate contact with the PLO, whose local organization in the Occupied Territories now came into its own. An activist from a committee in Ramallah had this to say in the intifada's earlier days: "We have to say that the Unified Leadership, in whose name the Calls have been issued, is the voice of the PLO in the West Bank and Gaza, in all the occupied land. Really we are not disconnected from the PLO, we are one people, inside and outside the territories. We have one aim, and the PLO is our representative."[13]

The link between the PLO and the intifada was close from the beginning: that seems clear. Arafat's declaration of Palestinian statehood, announced by the PNC meeting in November 1988, as well as the UN speech and international diplomacy of December 1988, linked closely with developments in the Occupied Territories on the home front. In the public arena, Arafat and the PLO were pressing for international recognition of Palestinian statehood and for negotiations with Israel. Meanwhile in the streets of the West Bank and Gaza, the Palestinian youth was making its demand for freedom known by pelting Israeli soldiers with stones. Since 1987 images of the intifada have become part of the stock-in-trade of television news broadcasts round the world. The image of the hooded Palestinian guerrilla with the gun which implanted itself in the Western imagination at the time of the Munich Olympics was replaced with another image. This time it was that of the boy with the kefiyyeh and the slingshot, hurling a stone towards an Israeli patrol: irresistibly suggestive of David and Goliath. The inevitable implication was that here was a defenceless people trying to defend themselves against the oppression of a superior power. That change of image suited the new peacemaking PLO very well.

Sacrifices were demanded from the people of the Occupied Territories in the cause of the intifada. In its first year, over 400 Palestinians died in various ways as the result of it. Of these, almost 300 were shot by Israeli troops. By the opening of the Madrid conference, a thousand Palestinians had died, including 450 children and young people, who throw the stones and bear the brunt of Israeli retaliation. That total mounted by the end of 1993 to over 1500, of whom more than a thousand have been shot. Many Israelis have also lost their lives, but they are numbered in hundreds rather than

13. Ibid.

thousands. The families of intifada victims have suffered greatly, and their economic hardships have increased. In April 1993, Israel closed off the Gaza Strip and prevented Gazans from seeking work in Israel. That has now been relaxed, but of the 40,000 Gazans who worked in Israel before, only half have returned. Young men are still barred. Schools have been closed for half the time, and the universities in the Occupied Territories have been closed for long periods. Many young men have been imprisoned for long periods, on suspicion or as the result of convictions. The release of prisoners was meant to be an early consequence of the 13 September 1993 agreement. Twelve thousand Palestinian prisoners were held in Israeli prisons for intifada-related offences. At the end of 1993, however, only some hundreds had been released.

Israel's mood, however, has been affected by the intifada, in a way that has put pressure on Israeli politicians. That is the effect it was designed to have. National service and service in the reserves meant that few in Israel were unaware of the situation in the Occupied Territories which was conveyed to them by a family member. Some came to hate the Arabs, others to fear them, and others to sympathise with them. Most simply wished that the problem of the Occupied Territories could be resolved so that the intifada could be ended and Israeli troops would no longer be involved. Images from the intifada found their way into popular journalism and music and into the mythology of everyday life in Israel. Israelis were also well aware of the unfavourable image of Israel that was being projected to the world through the news media. The sense of alarm some Israelis already felt about the intifada was heightened and spread after the first of a series of killings of Israelis took place inside Israel proper. A security clampdown and the closure of the Territories only went some way to calm what could have become panic.

For the first four years, until 1991, the intifada broadly maintained its positive image. More recently, attacks by Palestinians on fellow Palestinians who are alleged to have collaborated with Israel have marred the intifada's record. Today the increasing violence and the use of guns by young men belonging to groups such as the so-called Fatah Hawks in Gaza, or the Red Eagles of the PFLP, is turning the intifada into something more like a conventional armed uprising. The armed faction of Hamas is also a factor of growing importance. The virulence of the new intifada based on firepower rather than stones grew in the closing months of 1993 as frustration mounted at the failure to implement the interim peace agreement. Violence has also come from the armed wing of Hamas, the militant Palestinian movement, which is opposed both to Israel and to the PLO and wants a Palestinian state in Israel.

Hamas: A Challenge for the PLO

Control has been the PLO's aim in the Occupied Territories, but there has been an element which has eluded Arafat's grasp. This is Hamas, whose name means "zeal". Hamas has grown in importance during the intifada years, and has vied with the PLO and the Unified Leadership of the Uprising in calling strikes and issuing anti-Israeli proclamations. Hamas is intrinsically rejectionist, since its members believe that Palestine is historically a Muslim state and must therefore, in theory at least, return as a whole to Islamic rule. It is impossible for Hamas to contemplate the explicit acceptance of a permanent compromise with Israel, in which Israel will continue to occupy part of Palestine's historical territory. However, some Hamas factions have indicated that they will participate in Palestinian politics in Gaza and Jericho when the interim accord has been implemented. That idea was given a boost in November 1993 when Sheikh Ahmed Yasin, the Hamas leader who is serving a 15-year sentence in an Israeli jail, added his weight to the move for Hamas to take part in the elections. Hamas had been talking to the Damascus-based radical groups about a strategic alliance, but Sheikh Yasin's apparently more moderate stance may have changed its position.

The most vehemently rejectionist Hamas spokesmen are those in Amman who claim to speak for the Palestinian Hamas movement from a base in exile. Hamas activists within the Occupied Territories have always been more conciliatory, and Sheikh Yasin's stand has made that more likely. Hamas has also said it does not intend to get involved in clashes between Palestinian factions. However, it has reserved its right to continue to mount attacks on Israel and Israelis, irrespective of any truce which might be agreed or observed by Israel and the PLO. Hamas is the one force in Gaza and the West Bank which is genuinely beyond Arafat's control. It could even be conjectured that part of its attraction as a vehicle for protest by the young men who join it is its autonomy. It is outside the sphere of the

PLO, which otherwise seems sometimes in the Occupied Territories to be all-embracing, and provides a medium for independent protest. Hamas provides a framework for the angry young of Gaza, and its Islamic philosophy answers their questions. In the midst of an uncertain life, Hamas is a pillar of certainty.

Cynics say that it was the anti-Israeli violence of Hamas which made the Israelis want to withdraw from Gaza, and that Arafat and the PLO benefited from the work which Hamas had done. Certainly on 13 September, Arafat stole Hamas's thunder. From a low point immediately after the agreement, when the people of Gaza and the West Bank seemed for the most part to be delighted by the news from Washington, Hamas support has crept back. The PLO may have to find a way of coping with Hamas if it is to keep control of the Occupied Territories. On the other hand, a Hamas victory in any post-autonomy elections would in any case give Israel grave misgivings about proceeding with the implementation of the agreement.

Prospects

Will the PLO eventually be able to push the interim agreement to a full conclusion? Will the provisions laid down for Gaza and Jericho lay the foundation for an independent Palestinian entity, even for a Palestinian state? Much will depend on how Yasser Arafat can manipulate various factors: the negotiations with Israel, the dissent which exists within the PLO, the antagonism of the rejectionist front and its appeal to the people, and finally the siren call of Hamas. Arafat has himself over the years attracted the soubriquet of "the great survivor", but for perhaps the first time he will have to survive a democratic verdict. Arafat is said to be secretive and authoritarian. He holds all decisions in his own hands, puts his own men in positions of power, and keeps information to himself: hardly the profile of a democratic leader, and yet democracy is what will be needed in Palestine if the new state is to come into being with international support. Arafat's image, with his uniform, is still that of the guerrilla rather than the politician. His style is dictatorial and his life still appears solitary, in spite of his recent marriage. Arafat will need to manipulate both the politics of Palestine and those of Israel, if he is to emerge as President of a state. The outcome remains to be seen.

The Palestinian people of Gaza and Jericho will be the first to cast their votes, and Arafat himself has predicted a ballot for peace. Ultimately the question of whether the peace agreement will stick and the future of the Middle East will lie in the approval of the whole Palestinian people. In addition to the conservatively estimated 750,000 in Gaza, and the million in the West Bank, and the 900,000 Palestinians of Israel proper, two million or more live in Jordan. The world's overall population of Palestinian descent is around six million. All these people will in the end be able to make their views known one way or another about the future of Palestine. But the change from rejectionism to compromise may well prove to be a wise one. It has for a long time been inconceivable that the Palestinian movement could get more than the return of the Occupied Territories. That, with limitations, is now on offer. It is difficult to see how the rejectionists can justify the continuation of a futile struggle for more. In the end, idealism must be tempered by realism. The people of Gaza will say whether they want to continue the struggle for more, or not.

IV Shining Prospects

CHAPTER 12

"THE FUTURE: HOPES AND FEARS"

A False Start

Anxiety and doubt, confusion and uncertainty: these characterised the mood of the weeks and months which succeeded the signing of the interim agreement. Talks designed to finalise the agreement soon ran into trouble. By February 1994, however, there seemed to be a breakthrough which had put the process of negotiation back on the rails, when PLO Chairman Yasser Arafat and Israel's Foreign Minister Shimon Peres signed an agreement in Cairo settling some of the questions which had bedevilled the talks. Nonetheless the snags had shaken the initial confidence of both sides that the road to peace would now be short and direct. More problems remained to be ironed out, and it seemed there might be more trouble ahead. Prime Minister Yitzhak Rabin said that the dates for the various stages of the procedure, which had rashly been given with some precision in the original document, were not sacrosanct and that both sides would need longer than anticipated to reach a satisfactory position.

The handshake on the White House lawn had seemed to signify the end of a long era of doubt and uncertainty in the Middle East. The agreement contains a precise timetable. Israeli troops would begin to withdraw from Gaza and Jericho on 13 December 1993, and by 13 April 1994 the Israeli withdrawal would be complete. Then by 12 July at the latest, the redeployment of the Israeli forces in the whole of the Occupied Territories should be completed, ready for the elections for the Palestinian Council, to be held not later than 13 July. Looking into the longer term, a transitional period for the Occupied Territories was set to end five years after the Israeli withdrawal from Jericho and Gaza, and three years into the transitional period negotiations were to begin to settle the final status of the Territories.[1]

1. See the text of the agreement in the Appendix.

What was it that went so quickly wrong? The disappointing lack of progress in the talks between PLO teams and Israel in Taba, el-Arish, Cairo and elsewhere seemed a surprising anticlimax after the optimism of Washington. Teams of Palestinian and Israeli negotiators were at first reported to be romping ahead with the negotiation of the detailed procedures that would be necessary to put the agreement into practice. A much reproduced photograph of the two chief negotiators at Taba summed up the mood. Against the background of a calm sunset, Nabil Shaath for the PLO and Amnon Shahak for Israel sat at an outside table at the conference hotel, conversing earnestly face to face, glasses of orange juice at hand. At last, it seemed, pretence was being put aside, and the Israelis and Palestinians were fielding negotiators of real authority to settle once and for all their disagreements.

Nabil Shaath had been the PLO spokesman attached to the Washington talks, and was known to be close to PLO Chairman Arafat. Amnon Shahak is the Israeli Deputy Chief of Staff. Here were delegates with responsibility to make binding agreements, as distinct from the Washington negotiators, who, on both sides were obliged constantly to refer back. The problem was that the document signed in Washington combined excessive vagueness with too much precision. The interim agreement proved harder than had been anticipated to develop from the status of a declaration of principles into a working agreement. On the other hand, the precision of the dates built into the agreement created the impression of deadlines which were being missed, generating the feeling that the agreement itself was coming apart. The proposed deadline of 13 December 1993 for the beginning of military withdrawal came and went without action, which caused great disappointment on both sides. Meanwhile both the Israeli people and the Palestinians, in the Occupied Territories and elsewhere, began to wonder if the declaration of principles would in fact come into force.

The actual issues on which it had been impossible to reach agreement concerned mainly security. The Palestinians were not content with the way the Israelis proposed to put into practice the agreement's call for withdrawal from the Gaza Strip and Jericho, describing it as a redeployment rather than a withdrawal. The declaration of principles certainly specified withdrawal from Gaza and Jericho, reserving the word redeployment for the proposed Israeli troop movements in the Occupied Territories as a whole, to be completed in theory by 12 July. The Palestinian negotiators complained that what Israel proposed for Gaza and Jericho was in practice redeployment rather than withdrawal. For example, resting on the provision that Israel would continue to ensure the security of Israelis in the Territories, troops in Gaza were going to continue to control almost half of the Strip's area, in order to protect the three thousand Israeli settlers there. In addition, the whole question of the control of the crossing points between Gaza and Egypt, as well as Jericho and Jordan, had remained unresolved. Wrangling over what form of joint control would be acceptable to both sides had bogged the talks down. Finally, the area of Jericho to be released to Palestinian control in the first stage of the implementation of the agreement had not been decided. Given that the agreement was soon to be extended to the whole of the Occupied Territories, this might not seem to have been important, but the Palestinians wanted to make sure that they also had some say in the control of a crossing point between Jericho and Jordan.

The best efforts of the negotiating teams were insufficient to get round these problems until the meetings between Yasser Arafat and Shimon Peres got the talks restarted. Though by mid-February the two sides were once again apparently engaged in fruitful discussions, one casualty of the early delays was the precise timetable which had originally been agreed. In addition, it had become evident that in spite of the upgrading of the negotiating teams to the level of men like Nabil Shaath and Amnon Shahak, progress was not going to be made except by reference to the level of policy-makers. In other words, only the Chairman of the PLO on the one hand, and the Foreign Minister or Prime Minister of Israel on the other, would have the necessary authority to agree to the concessions and re-interpretations that might be needed to keep the talks moving along. Both sides, it would also appear, have been hampered by the constant re-emergence of internal disagreements close to the decision-making centres. Rabin and Peres have always been rivals, and while they are willing to work together there has sometimes been little love lost between them. Rabin is also said to distrust Yossi Beilin, Peres's deputy and a prime mover of the present talks. In Tunis, Arafat needs constantly to carry his senior lieutenants such as Abu Mazen with him, and to persuade them of the wisdom of concessions he may need to make.

In February 1994, after several days of intense negotiation in Cairo, conclusions had been reached which answered some of Israel's outstanding security worries, while satisfying Palestinian aspirations to control their own territory. The Palestinians agreed that Israel would have the right to veto the entry of any individual into the Palestinian areas, though there will be a Palestinian presence at the checkpoint between Jericho and Jordan. Israel will run the crossing point with Egypt. The Palestinians will also have some access to the Dead Sea. On internal security, there will be joint Israeli–Palestinian patrols, but they will be led by the Israelis in Gaza and by the Palestinians only in Jericho. However, the right of hot pursuit of Palestinian subjects into Palestinian areas by Israeli forces will be limited. In Gaza, the area in which Israeli troops can be deployed will be limited, though there will be an Israeli base near each of the three areas of settlement, and the Israelis will also patrol the main roads.

What remains to be settled includes the size of the Jericho region to be handed over in the initial move. In the longer run, the transfer of authority in 13 of the 38 fields of administration run by the Israeli military remains to be discussed, including electricity, land zoning, broadcasting rights and, crucially, water allocation. The details of a trade agreement also need to be decided, and some aspects of the deployment of the proposed Palestinian police force. Finally, the Israelis still have to agree a schedule for the release of the remaining Palestinian prisoners in Israeli jails for intifada-related offences.

Palestinian Doubts

On the Palestinian side, real misgivings have come to the surface about the wisdom of the declaration of principles and the possibility of negotiating it into a foundation for genuine Palestinian independence. We are not talking here about extremist opponents of the agreement: those for whom nothing but the unattainable whole of historical Palestine would be an acceptable goal. The sheer unrealism of that position draws the observer inexorably to the conclusion that for such extremists, the struggle is preferable to any solution. That may be because they cannot easily abandon the goal to which they have dedicated their lives. In a sense, that can only be seen as admirable if misguided. On the other hand it may also be that without the struggle, men who are accustomed to power may lose the base on which it depends: this is a less sympathetic position. But the misgivings of which we speak are not of this kind. They are voiced by moderate and realistic Palestinians, in many cases PLO supporters or sympathisers, who feel that the agreement negotiated in Oslo and signed in Washington will in the event deprive the Palestinians of the freedom they seek. Such doubters believe that Israel has driven a hard bargain, and that the Palestinians' birthright may be irrevocably lost if negotiation goes ahead.

Once again, the most eloquent of the Palestinian doubters has been Edward Said, the distinguished American academic who resigned his seat on the Palestine National Council last year. In an article published as the Cairo negotiations between Arafat and Peres ended, he criticised the Palestinians' lack of attention to detail, which has led, he says, to their being once more outsmarted by the Israelis:

> The PLO accepted the declaration of principles on the grounds that Palestinian autonomy would somehow lead to independence if enough rhetorical statements about an independent Palestine were made. When it came to negotiating the details, we had neither the plans nor the facts. They had the plans, the territory, the maps, the settlements, the roads; we have the wish for autonomy and Israeli withdrawal, with few details and little power to change anything very much. What is needed is a discipline of detail.[2]

Said believes that the Palestinians have given away virtually everything in exchange for very little, and he makes accusations both against the Palestinian leadership and against Israel. Arafat and his aides, Said says, "have very little to offer": they should be thanked for their past achievements and asked to resign. Against Israel he levels the accusation that it is "doing all it can to make the likelihood of a truly independent Palestine more and more remote".

A criticism of a different sort is proposed by Raja Shehadeh, a Palestinian lawyer who works with the Palestinian human rights organization, al-Haq, who advised the Palestinian negotiators in Washington in 1992. Shehadeh believes the Palestinians were well aware of the detailed implications of the agreement they signed, but that the Palestinian negotiators in Oslo and after were too anxious to dash to a conclusion. He comments:

2. Edward Said, "Declaration of Independence", *New Statesman*, 11 February 1994.

Since the signing of the Oslo Accords on 13 September, I have wondered how it happened that the Palestinian side acceded to so many of the Israeli positions which before the secret talks in Oslo it had forcefully rejected. . . . It cannot be said that the Palestinian side was not privy to detailed information on the proposals submitted by the Israeli side. . . . We were able to provide the leadership in Tunis with clear information about Israeli proposals as well as with full briefings on the legal and administrative changes Israel had carried out in the territories to prepare for self-rule by Palestinians over their own population but excluding the land and the Israeli settlers. Yet none of this seems to have been taken into consideration in arriving at the Oslo Accords.[3]

More damningly still, Shehadeh points out that the wording of the Oslo declaration implies that a Palestinian entity will derive its legitimacy ultimately from its recognition by Israel and not from its own existence.

Notably, however, neither of these critics offers an alternative approach, except perhaps to suggest that the Palestinians should have been more wary of the implications of the agreements they were signing, and should have refrained from going ahead without a clearer idea of their objectives and without better guarantees. However, the Palestinians who favour pressing ahead would argue that that would have been a recipe for replicating at Oslo the stalemate which had dogged the talks in Washington. In the end, the Palestinian leadership desperately wanted an agreement of some kind because it feared that if it continued to stonewall, American pressure on the Israelis to continue with meaningful negotiations could be relaxed. The PLO backed the Oslo agreement because it wanted to move away from the static confrontation where the Washington talks had come to rest. Any agreement which gave the PLO a foothold in Palestine was better than none: this was Arafat's judgement.

Israeli Concern

On the Israeli side, the misgivings have taken different forms. Again there are the extremists on the far right, whose opposition to the

3. Raja Shehadeh, "Flaws in the Oslo Accords – an insider's view", *Middle East International*, 467, 21 January 1994.

agreement is predictable, and the religious settlers who claim they will conduct a last-ditch stand against any Israeli withdrawal. The Likud leader Binyamin Netanyahu is also vehemently and predictably against the present agreement, because of the danger he sees to Israel's security. According to Netanyahu, Jordan is already a Palestinian state and should be the Palestinians' national home. The entity to which the Palestinians themselves aspire and which is also advocated by the Arab states would be, in Netanyahu's philosophy, "a Palestinian state bordering Tel Aviv that would obviously jeopardise Israel's existence."[4] Netanyahu favours the classic right-wing Israeli solution of negotiation with the Arab states over the Palestinians' heads; in the book he wrote after the Madrid conference, *A Place among the Nations*, he voices quite explicitly the old Zionist concern about Israel's right to existence.

The kind of opposition which will perhaps have the most telling effect on Rabin's determination to pursue the post-Oslo negotiations does not wholly come from his diametric political opponents. It emerges from politicians nearer to his own standpoint, for example from among the hawkish wing of the Israeli Labour Party. Those doubts are underlined by the mounting violence in the Territories which continued as the negotiations between Israeli ministers and the PLO continued in early 1994. That violence ominously now seemed to involve young armed men who were, theoretically at least, adherents of the PLO itself as well as of other movements. In a single week in February 1994 there were no fewer than 15 Palestinian deaths: five killed by Israeli troops and ten in inter-Palestinian fighting. A few days later an Israeli secret policeman was killed and two others injured in Ramallah.[5]

One right-wing Labour Knesset member, Ra'anan Cohen, says Labour has been "hijacked by history and the doves". He goes on to say: "There is a mood of creeping conciliation, and the country as a whole seems to have gone crazy." Another right-wing Labour Knesset member, who has been trying to organize opposition to the deal, says:

> the government should be demanding more of the PLO. He would have insisted on Arafat putting a halt to violence in the territories before coming in with his police force; on more unequivocal denunciation of

---

4. Binyamin Netanyahu, *A Place among the Nations: Israel and the World*, Bantam 1993, p. 332.

5. Since the massacre at Hebron on 25 February, these figures have dramatically worsened. See the Prologue.

continuing acts of terror; on abrogation of the Palestinians' National Covenant in those forums in which Arafat does have a majority; and on Palestinian moves aimed at having the Arab economic boycott of Israel lifted.[6]

There is also another kind of doubt: namely the question of whether Israel will be able to resolve the contradictions involved in reconciling a withdrawal from the Occupied Territories with its commitment to ensure the security of Israeli settlers remaining there. The wording of the agreement is vague precisely because of the difficulty of envisaging a solution, argues Joseph Alpher, the director of the Jaffee Centre, Israel's leading defence think-tank. "How do we deal with the fact that previous governments established some 100 settlements in the Arab-populated heartland of the West Bank with the express strategic purpose of preventing a territorial-political solution of the sort negotiated at Oslo?" This will require in the end a major national debate in Israel, Alpher argues, which cannot be avoided by Yitzhak Rabin's government:

> The debate will be between those for whom the Land of Israel is the highest priority of Zionism, taking precedence over such values as democracy, a Jewish state, and reducing war risks; and those for whom the values embodied in a democratic Jewish state, with enhanced possibilities of peace with its neighbours warrant concessions regarding the Land of Israel. This is a legitimate debate, and hardly a new one in Zionist history. It should be out in the open, not glossed over by political slogans. It should be the issue of the next elections.[7]

It remains to be seen whether Prime Minister Rabin will choose to bring that debate out into the open. There are some indications that he hopes that the settlers themselves may bring the problem down to a more manageable scale by moving out of the Occupied Territories as the Palestinians take over the responsibilities which will become theirs in the second phase of the implementation of the agreement. There was some indication by the spring of 1994 that this may be about to happen. In the last resort, Rabin's remaining problem may be the settlers of the extreme right and of the religious movements,

6. Leslie Susser, "The dissidents", *The Jerusalem Report*, 27 January 1994.
7. Joseph Alpher, "Leaving Gaza is the easy part", *Jerusalem Post, International Edition*, 5 February 1994.

encouraged to stay by right-wing politicians like Ariel Sharon, who speaks of the right of the Jews to live where they choose.

The Practicalities

In spite of mounting doubts on each side in early 1994 the planners on the ground went on thinking about what structures would need to be put in place for the new Palestinian entity to function. Much had been said about political structures, security and control in the agreement itself and in the discussions in the early days after it was revealed. But economics was at the root of the new Palestine's needs. The new Palestinian state needed cash: the Palestinians were looking to the international community to invest in a peace proposal that everyone round the world had applauded. In addition to cash, they also needed effective planning, and hard thinking about how the new entity would function.

First, there was the question of the wide disparities in the relative prosperity of the adjacent economic zones, and the kind of relationship between them that would be practical and desirable. The difference in GDP between Israel and the Occupied Territories was large: Israel's per capita GDP in 1994 was around ten times that of the Occupied Territories, much of which was in any case dependent on the remittances of workers earning their living every day across the Green Line in Israel proper. Israel's GDP per head is approximately 11,000 dollars a year, putting it roughly in the same economic bracket as Greece or Portugal, while the GDP per head in the Occupied Territories is 1350 dollars. A quarter of the income in the Occupied Territories has historically come from workers earning wages inside Israel. GDP in Gaza is more like 1100 dollars per head, and much of what does not come from Israel originates with UNRWA, the United Nations Relief and Works Agency, which has looked after Palestinian refugees since 1948. In the West Bank, where there is more indigenous economic activity, income does not depend on wage earners bringing money back from Israel and is around 1550 dollars per head.

A primary question was: how much would the new entity depend on Israel, and how close would their links be. In the short term, it was hard to see how the economic tie between Israel and the Occupied Territories could be broken without adversely affecting the economy of the Occupied Territories. The Palestinian entity will need the wages its workers bring back from Israel and will also need Israeli markets for its agricultural produce and for the goods that Palestinian industry plans to produce. If Israel can absorb the competition from the Palestinians, the new Palestinian economy could be a source of cheap goods and services for Israel, and this could bring the Palestinians the hard currency they need. Senior Palestinian economists argue that Israel needs a free trade area with the new Palestine, so that goods can freely cross the frontier. On the other hand, others argue against a free trade area as the new Palestine's industries may need protection from Israeli competition. Israel's economy is eight times the economies of Jordan and the Palestinian entity combined, and many Palestinians fear that Palestine will simply become an economic satellite of Israel within a free trade area. A full customs union, which some Israeli economists want, would make the situation worse, and Palestine could become even more subservient if it became part of a shekel zone. A Western economist made this comment: "Dependence on Israel has done nothing to lessen the gulf of Arab fear and misunderstanding. A repeated refrain, in conversation with Jordanian and Palestinian policy-makers and business people, is that Israel will exercise imperial powers in the region by virtue of its industrial prowess rather than its military might."[8]

Jordan will also be important. The currency of the Palestinian area looks likely now to be the Jordanian dinar, and Jordan will back the Palestinians' banking system. But another factor in the equation will be the Palestinian relationship with the Jordanian economy. Though per capita GDP in the Occupied Territories is low, it is higher than that of Jordan, which runs at under 1000 dollars per head. Jordan has a high percentage of Palestinians in its population: of over four million inhabitants about half are of Palestinian origin. There are refugee camps in Jordan housing very poor fugitives from both the 1948 conflict (and their descendants) and the 1967 war. Jordan's population of Palestinians has also been swollen by the outflow from Kuwait and elsewhere in the Gulf during the Gulf War, when Arafat's pro-Saddam Hussein stance made the Palestinians *personae non gratae* in their former host countries. Some of these people may have access to the new Palestine, and could flood in if there was work. Jordan's own economic position has been precarious since the Gulf War, when

8. Christopher Huhne, "Israel holds key to Palestinian state's prosperity", *The Independent*, 6 October 1993.

it lost both its trade with Iraq and its good relations with the Gulf, since King Hussein's neutrality and refusal to side with the West was interpreted by Saudi Arabia and Kuwait as pro-Iraqi. Palestine's relations with Jordan will need to be carefully managed.

Ambition is the Palestinians' own keynote: as far as they are concerned the sky is the limit for their new economy. The Gaza Strip is at present one of the most densely populated and ill-favoured areas in the world. It entirely lacks natural resources, and boasts an abundance of unemployed people. PLO economists say it can be turned into a new Hong Kong or Singapore. Using a potentially skilled and highly trainable workforce in conjunction with potentially good communications, the area could become a centre of industry, trade, commerce and finance. Plans for the West Bank are equally ambitious. All this will cost money, and an early draft of the plan Palestinian economists are working on calls for 11 billion dollars over a six-year period. That looks likely to be more than will be forthcoming, but the World Bank had promised almost five billion dollars, phased over ten years at 475 million dollars a year. The European Community is also going to put in another half billion dollars, with substantial sums coming from Japan and other countries. Saudi Arabia has so far promised only a relatively small contribution, but Yasser Arafat has recently made his first visit to the Saudi capital since before the Gulf War and relations may improve. Rich Palestinians round the world will also make their own investments.

Disappointment could follow too much optimism. The World Bank will want an open and free-trading economy to follow its own recommended model, which could mean that the Palestinians will find themselves limited in what they can spend on social improvement and subsidies for the poorest consumers, just as governments are similarly confined elsewhere in the Middle East. But the World Bank's projections suggest that the Palestinian economy could grow by three per cent a year. The more far-reaching of the Palestinians' ambitions may have to be curtailed. A separate Palestinian airport and airline may not attract foreign finance, for example. Another plan, seemingly more down to earth, for an international port in Gaza, may stumble on the conviction of aid donors that the Palestinians would be better off using the Israeli port at Ashdad. The Palestinians will first need to spend money on basic infrastructure projects which have been neglected during the Israeli occupation, leaving prestige projects until later.

Water

Water is in short supply in the Middle East, and water use will have to be very high on the Palestinians' agenda of subjects to be discussed with the Israelis. Control over water has not so far been explicitly decided, but it will be crucial. Military security has been a frequently cited reason why Israelis of all political persuasions have from time to time thought the retention of the West Bank was necessary for Israel. The right of Jews to live in Eretz Israel has for some Israelis been another motivation. But underlying these arguments is Israel's desire to control some of the water resources of the immediate region. In 1989 Rafael Eitan, the leader of the extreme-right Tsomet party and then Agriculture Minister in the Likud-led coalition government, said that Israel could never leave the West Bank because of its water reserves. It is hard to say whether water needs have been a determining factor in Israeli policy, or whether they have served as an excuse for conservative politicians to preach retention of the West Bank. It is certainly true that, in contrast to the hard-line political view, some Israeli water experts believe that Israel can afford to let the Palestinians greatly increase their usage of water in the West Bank because their present consumption is so low.

Israel's two main water sources are the Sea of Galilee and the northern reach of the Jordan river, from which it takes a third of its water, and from two main underground aquifers from which over 60 per cent of Israel's water comes. The underground sources are so heavily used that experts believe it would take ten years of above-average rainfall to restore them from the low levels to which they fell during the drought of the late 1980s. Up to a point, the river water will continue to be adequate if it is not overused. On the other hand, by international standards both Israel and the Occupied Territories are short of water. But if Israel does not control the West Bank militarily, some of what it regards as its vital sources of water will be in Arab hands, and this must almost inevitably lead to trouble. A Jordanian water expert, Professor Elias Salameh, believes that, "some time between 1995 and 2005 there is a high probability that Israel, Jordan and the West Bank will face such progressively worsening water shortages that there will be conflict."[9]

9. Quoted by Fred Pearce, "Rivers of blood, waters of hope", *The Guardian*, 6 December 1991.

At the moment, Israel siphons water out of the Sea of Galilee, into a system which it calls the Israeli National Water Carrier, cutting off much of the supply to the Jordan river. Jordan is negotiating to build a dam on the river Yarmuk, in its own territory, which feeds the Jordan river below the Sea of Galilee. This would replace a dam destroyed by Israel in the 1967 war. The effect of this project would be further to diminish the resources available to the West Bank from the Jordan, which are already very restricted. Water in the West Bank comes therefore mainly from underground aquifers, which are connected to one of Israel's two main underground sources. This is one reason why Israel has during the quarter century of occupation severely limited Palestinian water usage, so that per head the Palestinians of the West Bank use only half what is used in Jordan. On the other hand, the Israeli settlers do not go short of water. Settlers in the West Bank, who total 260,000 including the Jerusalem settlements, get as much water as the West Bank's million Arab inhabitants, and Israelis have lush lawns and swimming pools while their Arab neighbours have even had restrictions imposed on their usage of wells.

Opinions about the reality of the shortage of water vary widely. Whether the availability of water in Israel and the Occupied Territories is going to lead to an immediate crisis or not, it is something that the two sides will need to negotiate about with the greatest care. As long ago as April 1993, Abu Ala asked at the multilateral talks about water at Geneva for an international commission to investigate the allocation of water. He said that water rights were "at the basis of any kind of cooperation between the parties," and added, "that is why we say this is the first step that must be accepted."[10] While some Israeli experts may believe the situation is not critical, others take the opposite view: "Israel fears that if a new Palestinian state comes into existence on the West Bank it might pursue a policy of deep, heavy pumping: not just to use the water but to deprive Israel. Says one water expert, "Anybody, in my opinion, who would give away their water resources is simply mad, sick in the head."[11]

10. Quoted by Robert Evans, "Middle East water talks deadlocked", *The Independent*, 30 April 1993.

11. Priit J. Vesilind, "Water, the Middle East's critical resource", *National Geographic Magazine*, May 1993, p. 63.

Political Structures

Survival for the new Palestinian entity will depend in the last resort on economics and geography: on food and water. But much will also hang on the kind of political structures the new proto-state sets up. We heard at the beginning of this book that Yasser Arafat has said he favours democracy. Others have their doubts about whether that will happen. There are a number of possible scenarios, but of these there are four main variants, which arise from the question whether in the longer term the Palestinians will have a democratically elected government or not, and the parallel question of whether or not Yasser Arafat will continue to lead the PLO in peacetime as he has in the years of the PLO's struggle. Arafat may be elected to head a new government, or it is possible that he will be edged out by his opponents, those who doubt that he is capable of adapting to democracy after years in which he has exercised autocratic control. The former PLO executive council member, Shafiq al-Hout, who resigned his post on 22 August 1993, before the current agreement was signed, thinks that Arafat's days are numbered: "I wouldn't expect anything more than very short-term support for Arafat. The Palestinians in the diaspora feel ignored and betrayed. If this is the maximum that Arafat could get after all the years of the intifada, what will he get, now that he's in the hands of the Israelis, on the really important things like sovereignty?"[12]

Doubt is expressed by other critics about whether the new Palestinian entity will opt for full democracy in the Occupied Territories. Soon after 13 September 1993 some influential Palestinians began to try to make sure that Yasser Arafat does not exercise what they believe will be his preferred procedure: simply to put all decision-making power into the hands of trusted associates.

> Personalities in the Occupied Territories say they fear that Palestinians from the exterior will be parachuted in. Paradoxically, members of the PLO leadership fear that the 'old man' is willing to sacrifice them for the sake of the agreement made with Israel. Four figures from the diaspora, who have recently demanded the democratisation of Palestinian institutions, have formed a monitoring committee with that aim in view, after demanding in a petition the setting up of what they called

12. Shafiq al-Hout, interviewed by Alexander Cockburn, *New Statesman*, 1 October 1993.

a constitution guaranteeing a democratic authority and observance of human rights in the Occupied Territories.[13]

The former spokeswoman for the negotiating team at the Washington talks, Hanan Ashrawi, has also stepped down from an active part in the current negotiations in order to head a human rights monitoring group which will closely observe the activities of any new Palestinian authority in the Occupied Territories.

In the medium term, the Palestinians will also need to find their own way round the demand for an Islamic state which will come from some of the people of the Occupied Territories. Support for Hamas and the other Islamic movements is hard to gauge exactly, but it is certainly not less than a quarter and may be more than half the population. One poll carried out in the Occupied Territories by the Norwegians suggested that only a quarter of the people were in favour of open democracy, while over half wanted an Islamic political system.[14] Hamas supporters may take part in elections for the Palestinian Council, but may wish thereafter to remodel Palestinian institutions in their own interests. The support for Islamic politics came from women as well as men, a phenomenon which seems to contradict some observers' supposition that after taking an important part in the intifada women will want more social freedom in the new Palestinian entity. In spite of the efforts which may come from leading female personalities like Hanan Ashrawi and Yasser Arafat's wife, Suha Tawil, it may be that women on the ground needed Islam to give them the strength to face the Israeli army and saw in Islam a liberating force.

Legitimacy within and credibility without: these will be the dividend the Palestinians will get from democracy. A democratic system will undercut the criticism certain to come from Israeli right-wingers if the Palestinian authority takes an autocratic route. It will also attract the approval and therefore the all-important support of the United States and the European Union. There are many in Palestine who fear that a system where power is exercised by Arafat and his aides from Tunis, under the veneer perhaps of democratic validation, could arouse scepticism about the new entity's credentials to statehood. There are too many doubters in the wings, waiting to point at neighbouring states, and especially at Syria, and to say that the Palestinians have

13. Mouna Naim, "Les méthodes contestées de Yasser Arafat", *Le Monde*, 28 November 1993.

14. Quoted in *The Economist*, 18 September 1993, p. 24.

constructed for themselves a government on a pattern predictable in the region. In spite of the existence of democratic institutions in Lebanon, and the degree of genuine consultative democracy reintroduced in Jordan, there are many in the West and elsewhere who believe the Palestinians will be hard put to avoid autocracy.

The Syrian Dimension

Syria's future will certainly affect the new Palestinian state. The foreign state with which the Palestinians cannot fail to be most involved is Jordan, but Syria is also a near neighbour and has been intimately connected with the Palestinian movement. The Syrian track at the bilateral talks in Washington was hailed as the likely avenue of a possible breakthrough as long ago as 1992, and Israel's hopes of getting a peace treaty with Syria resurfaced in 1993. Much will depend on whether Israel can reconcile the concessions Syria wants in the Golan Heights with its own perceived security needs. On 16 January 1994, at their meeting in Geneva, President Assad seemed to have given assurances to President Clinton that Syria would negotiate seriously with Israel. Syria's stated position on Golan remains that all the territory must be returned, but negotiations with Israel may be going on behind the scenes. Certainly the Israeli settlers in the Golan are beginning to conjecture that their own future is uncertain. Yossi Beilin has said that in the longer run if they wish to continue to live there, they must do so under Syrian rule.

When the Syrian track first sprang into the limelight, the Palestinian negotiators in Washington were angry that Damascus appeared to be considering going ahead with a separate peace agreement with Israel, while leaving the Palestinians' grievances unanswered. The Palestinians felt that this would be playing into Israel's hands and offering Israel precisely the solution negotiated over their heads that Israel has always wanted. In September 1993, the boot was suddenly seen to be on the other foot: President Assad of Syria was angry that the Palestinians had negotiated the interim agreement in Oslo behind his back, as he saw it, and without taking Syrian interests into account. Now Syria seems very likely to make its own peace agreement with Israel in the medium-term future if not sooner, when a formula can be found to reconcile Israel's demand for security with Syria's claim to its former territory. With Syria firmly aboard the peace bandwagon, the Palestinians will have less to fear from the radical dissident groups based in Damascus, which Syria currently supports, and relations between a new Palestinian authority and Damascus can be more open and straightforward.

The Newly Minted State

The seeds of statehood will have been firmly planted in Palestine after the new entity has taken its first steps. That is the belief of many thinking Palestinians, who are now confident that what has been agreed will come to pass according to plan, though perhaps along a more protracted timetable than was originally envisaged. The Palestinians will not only elect their own government, but they will also have control over territory, an important aspect of sovereignty. They will also have some rights to the employment of coercive power. The establishment of a strong Palestinian police force is firmly laid down in the declaration of principles, and the legitimate exercise of force is widely regarded as a further prerequisite of sovereignty. Israel for the moment holds back from any acknowledgement that there will be a Palestinian sovereignty. At the Cairo talks on 9 February 1994, a Palestinian official said that the clash between Israeli and PLO bargaining positions was that Israel refused to admit that any sovereignty had been granted to the Palestinians: "It is all about sovereignty. They are trying to remind us that the Palestinian self-rule area is not an independent state, that it is only an interim stage."[15] Nevertheless in areas where Israeli authority will be limited by law, and where no other sovereignty runs, it will be hard to resist the suggestion that Palestinian sovereignty has come into existence.

It is impossible today to see what the future will hold. Certainly Jordan is now once again interested in links with the new Palestine, though again the issue of sovereignty is all-important. In 1988, King Hussein relinquished his responsibilities for the West Bank, and he will not reassume them. He will however be more open to the idea of a sovereign confederation involving Palestine and Jordan. Israel's

15. Christopher Walker, "Peace talks boost as Israel and PLO sign border pact", *The Guardian*, 10 February 1994.

present government is quite openly interested in the idea of a long-term regional cooperation in which it could become involved with both Palestine and Jordan, and that is an idea which finds favour with outside powers which can help the region, especially the European Union. The new Palestinian entity will want to develop its links with other Palestinian communities, namely the Palestinians inside Israel itself, who are Israeli citizens, and the Palestinians of the diaspora. The question of the refugees of 1967 and 1948 will need to be looked at closely, and there will need to be discussion of what level of right of return will be available.

"Palestine is once again on the map": this was the word of PLO Chairman Yasser Arafat on 9 February 1994[16] in Cairo. Israel may continue to deny this, but as the implications of the deal with the Palestinians are digested, its truth will be hard to deny. The Israeli settlements in the Occupied Territories were Likud's way of creating facts on the ground. Facts on the ground have now been created by the Palestinians, thanks to the Oslo negotiators and to the backing they had from Arafat himself. Israel's Labour government made a major choice when it came into office. It opted to pursue Israel's goal of security and peace of mind through real negotiation with the Palestinians and through compromise. The philosophy of occupation and continuing force, developed over 15 years by Likud, has been put on one side, as an aberration in the history of Israel. The Zionists took Arab territory in the first place, and the Arab resentment has been deep and strong. But the clock cannot be turned back. Israel is saying that it wants to hold what has become its own, and not exercise domination over others. The Palestinians have said they will live at peace with Israel. There has been a change, and the future will be different.

16. Charles Richards, "Cairo deal brings little joy in Gaza", *The Independent*, 11 February 1994.

APPENDIX 1

THE OSLO DECLARATION OF PRINCIPLES
Final draft 19 August 1993

**DECLARATION OF PRINCIPLES ON INTERIM SELF-GOVERNMENT
ARRANGEMENTS**

N.B.: *In the preamble, the words Palestine Liberation Organization were substituted for
"Palestinian team" before the document was signed. PLO was also substituted for
"Palestinian" in other parts of the document.*

The Government of the State of Israel and the Palestinian team (in the
Jordanian–Palestinian delegation to the Middle East Peace Conference) (the
"Palestinian Delegation"), representing the Palestinian people, agree that it is
time to put an end to decades of confrontation and conflict, recognize their
mutual legitimate and political rights, and strive to live in peaceful coexistence
and mutual dignity and security and achieve a just, lasting and comprehensive
peace settlement and historic reconciliation through the agreed political process.
Accordingly, the two sides agree to the following principles:

Article I *Aim of the negotiations*
The aim of the Israeli–Palestinian negotiations within the current Middle East
peace process is, among other things, to establish a Palestinian Interim Self-
Government Authority, the elected Council, (the "Council") for the Palestinian
people in the West Bank and the Gaza Strip, for a transitional period not
exceeding five years, leading to a permanent settlement based on Security Council
Resolutions 242 and 338.
It is understood that the interim arrangements are an integral part of the overall
peace process and that final status negotiations will lead to the implementation of
Security Council Resolutions 242 and 338.

Article II *Framework for the interim period*
The agreed framework for the interim period is set forth in the Declaration of
Principles.

Article III *Elections*
1. In order that the Palestinian people in the West Bank and Gaza Strip may
    govern themselves according to democratic principles, direct, free and
    general political elections will be held for the Council under agreed supervi-
    sion and international observation, while the Palestinian police will ensure
    public order.
2. An agreement will be concluded on the exact mode and conditions of the
    elections in accordance with the protocol attached as Annex I, with the goal
    of holding the elections not later than nine months after the entry into force
    of this Declaration of Principles.

3. These elections will constitute a significant interim preparatory step toward the realization of the legitimate rights of the Palestinian people and their just requirements.

Article IV

Jurisdiction of the Council will cover West Bank and Gaza Strip territory, except for issues that will be negotiated in the permanent status negotiations. The two sides view the West Bank and the Gaza Strip as a single territorial unit, whose integrity will be preserved during the interim period.

Article V *Transitional period and permanent status negotiations*

1. The five-year transitional period will begin upon the withdrawal from the Gaza Strip and Jericho area.
2. Permanent status negotiations will commence as soon as possible, but not later than the beginning of the third year of the interim period, between the Government of Israel and the Palestinian people representatives.
3. It is understood that these negotiations shall cover remaining issues, including: Jerusalem, refugees, settlements, security arrangements, borders, relations and cooperation with other neighbors, and other issues of common interest.
4. The two parties agree that the outcome of the permanent status negotiations should not be prejudiced or preempted by agreements reached for the interim period.

Article VI *Preparatory transfer of powers and responsibilities*

1. Upon the entry into force of this Declaration of Principles and the withdrawal from the Gaza Strip and Jericho area, a transfer of authority from the Israeli military government and its Civil Administration to the authorized Palestinians for this task, as detailed herein, will commence. This transfer of authority will be of preparatory nature until the inauguration of the Council.
2. Immediately after the entry into force of this Declaration of Principles and the withdrawal from the Gaza Strip and Jericho area, with the view to promoting economic development in the West Bank and Gaza Strip, authority will be transferred to the Palestinians in the following spheres: education and culture, health, social welfare, direct taxation, and tourism. The Palestinian side will commence in building the Palestinian police force, as agreed upon. Pending the inauguration of the Council, the two parties may negotiate the transfer of additional powers and responsibilities, as agreed upon.

Article VII *Interim agreement*

1. The Israeli and Palestinian delegations will negotiate an agreement on the interim period (the "Interim Agreement").
2. The Interim Agreement shall specify, among other things, the structure of the Council, the number of its members, and the transfer of powers and responsibilities from the Israeli military government and its Civil Administration to the Council. The Interim Agreement shall also specify the Council's executive authority, legislative authority in accordance with Article IX below, and the independent Palestinian judicial organs.

3. The Interim Agreement shall include arrangements, to be implemented upon the inauguration of the Council, for the assumption by the Council of all of the powers and responsibilities transferred previously in accordance with Article VI above.
4. In order to enable the Council to promote economic growth, upon its inauguration, the Council will establish, among other things, a Palestinian Electricity Authority, a Gaza Sea Port Authority, a Palestinian Development Bank, a Palestinian Export Promotion Board, a Palestinian Environmental Authority, a Palestinian Land Authority and a Palestinian Water Administration Authority, and any other authorities agreed upon, in accordance with the Interim Agreement that will specify their powers and responsibilities.
5. After the inauguration of the Council, the Civil Administration will be dissolved, and the Israeli military government will be withdrawn.

Article VIII   *Public order and security*
In order to guarantee public order and internal security for the Palestinians of the West Bank and the Gaza Strip, the Council will establish a strong police force, while Israel will continue to carry the responsibility for defending against external threats, as well as the responsibility for overall security of the Israelis to protect their internal security and public order.

Article IX   *Laws and military orders*
1. The Council will be empowered to legislate, in accordance with the Interim Agreement, within all authorities transferred to it.
2. Both parties will review jointly laws and military orders presently in force in remaining spheres.

Article X   *Joint Israeli–Palestinian liaison committee*
In order to provide for a smooth implementation of this Declaration of Principles and any subsequent agreements pertaining to the interim period, upon the entry into force of this Declaration of Principles, a Joint Israeli–Palestinian Liaison Committee will be established in order to deal with issues requiring coordination, other issues of common interest, and disputes.

Article XI   *Israeli–Palestinian cooperation in economic fields*
Recognizing the mutual benefit of cooperation in promoting the development of the West Bank, the Gaza Strip and Israel, upon the entry into force of this Declaration of Principles, an Israeli–Palestinian Economic Cooperation Committee will be established in order to develop and implement in a cooperative manner the programs identified in the protocols attached as Annex III and Annex IV.

Article XII   *Liaison and cooperation with Jordan and Egypt*
The two parties will invite the Governments of Jordan and Egypt to participate in establishing further liaison and cooperation arrangements between the Government of Israel and the Palestinian representatives, on one hand, and the Governments of Jordan and Egypt, on the other hand, to promote cooperation between them. These arrangements will include the constitution of a Continuing

Committee that will decide by agreement on the modalities of the admission of persons displaced from the West Bank and Gaza Strip in 1967, together with necessary measures to prevent disruption and disorder. Other matters of common concern will be dealt with by this Committee.

Article XIII *Redeployment of Israeli forces*
1. After the entry into force of this Declaration of Principles, and not later than the eve of elections for the Council, a redeployment of Israeli military forces in the West Bank and the Gaza Strip will take place, in addition to withdrawal of Israeli forces carried out in accordance with Article XIV.
2. In redeploying its military forces, Israel will be guided by the principle that its military forces should be redeployed outside the populated areas.
3. Further redeployments to specified locations will be gradually implemented commensurate with the assumption of responsibility for public order and internal security by the Palestinian police force pursuant to Article VIII above.

Article XIV *Israeli withdrawal from the Gaza Strip and Jericho area*
Israel will withdraw from the Gaza Strip and Jericho area, as detailed in the protocol attached as Annex II.

Article XV *Resolution of disputes*
1. Disputes arising out of the application or interpretation of this Declaration of Principles, or any subsequent agreements pertaining to the interim period, shall be resolved by negotiations through the Joint Liaison Committee to be established pursuant to Article X above.
2. Disputes which cannot be settled by negotiations may be resolved by a mechanism of conciliation to be agreed upon by the parties.
3. The parties may agree to submit to arbitration disputes relating to the interim period, which cannot be settled through conciliation. To this end, upon the agreement of both parties, the parties will establish an Arbitration Committee.

Article XVI *Israeli–Palestinian cooperation concerning regional programs*
Both parties view the multilateral working groups as an appropriate instrument for promoting a "Marshall Plan," the regional programs and other programs, including special programs for the West Bank and Gaza Strip, as indicated in the protocol attached as Annex IV.

Article XVII *Miscellaneous provisions*
1. This Declaration of Principles will enter into force one month after its signing.
2. All protocols annexed to this Declaration of Principles and Agreed Minutes pertaining thereto shall be regarded as an integral part hereof.

Done at Washington, D.C. this day of —
For the Government of Israel —
For the Palestinian Delegation —
Witnessed by
The United States of America —
The Russian Federation —

Annex I *Protocol on the Mode and Conditions of Elections*
1. Palestinians of Jerusalem who live there will have the right to participate in the election process, according to an agreement between the two sides.
2. In addition, the election agreement should cover, among other things, the following issues:
    a. the system of elections;
    b. the mode of the agreed supervision and international observation and their personal composition; and
    c. rules and regulations regarding election campaign, including agreed arrangements for the organizing of mass media, and the possibility of licensing a broadcasting and TV station.
3. The future status of displaced Palestinians who were registered on 4th June 1967 will not be prejudiced because they are unable to participate in the election process due to practical reasons.

Annex II *Protocol on Withdrawal of Israeli Forces from the Gaza Strip and Jericho Area*
1. The two sides will conclude and sign within two months from the date of entry into force of this Declaration of Principles, an agreement on the withdrawal of Israeli military forces from the Gaza Strip and Jericho area. This agreement will include comprehensive arrangements to apply in the Gaza Strip and the Jericho area subsequent to the Israeli withdrawal.
2. Israel will implement an accelerated and scheduled withdrawal of Israeli military forces from the Gaza Strip and Jericho area, beginning immediately with the signing of the agreement on the Gaza Strip and Jericho area and to be completed within a period not exceeding four months after the signing of this agreement.
3. The above agreement will include, among other things:
    a. Arrangements for a smooth and peaceful transfer of authority from the Israeli military government and its Civil Administration to the Palestinian representatives.
    b. Structure, powers and responsibilities of the Palestinian authority in these areas, except: external security, settlements, Israelis, foreign relations, and other subjects mutually agreed upon.
    c. Arrangements for assumption of internal security and public order by the Palestinian police force consisting of police officers recruited locally and from abroad (holding Jordanian passports and Palestinian documents issued by Egypt). Those who will participate in the Palestinian police force coming from abroad should be trained as police and police officers.
    d. A temporary international or foreign presence, as agreed upon.
    e. Establishment of a joint Palestinian–Israeli coordination and cooperation committee for mutual security purposes.
    f. An economic development and stabilization program, including the establishment of an Emergency Fund, to encourage foreign investment, and financial and economic support. Both sides will coordinate and cooperate jointly and unilaterally with regional and international parties to support these aims.
    g. Arrangements for a safe passage for persons and transportation between the Gaza Strip and Jericho area.

4. The above agreement will include arrangements for coordination between both parties regarding passages:
   a. Gaza–Egypt; and
   b. Jericho–Jordan.
5. The offices responsible for carrying out the powers and responsibilities of the Palestinian authority under this Annex II and Article VI of the Declaration of Principles will be located in the Gaza Strip and in the Jericho area pending the inauguration of the Council.
6. Other than these agreed arrangements, the status of the Gaza Strip and Jericho area will continue to be an integral part of the West Bank and Gaza Strip, and will not be changed in the interim period.

PROTOCOL ON ISRAELI–PALESTINIAN COOPERATION IN ECONOMIC AND DEVELOPMENT PROGRAMS

The two sides agree to establish an Israeli–Palestinian Continuing Committee for Economic Cooperation, focusing, among other things, on the following:

1. Cooperation in the field of water, including a Water Development Program prepared by experts from both sides, which will also specify the mode of cooperation in the management of water resources in the West Bank and Gaza Strip, and will include proposals for studies and plans on water rights of each party, as well as on the equitable utilization of joint water resources for implementation in and beyond the interim period.
2. Cooperation in the field of electricity, including an Electricity Development Program, which will also specify the mode of cooperation for the production, maintenance, purchase and sale of electricity resources.
3. Cooperation in the field of energy, including an Energy Development Program, which will provide for the exploitation of oil and gas for industrial purposes, particularly in the Gaza Strip and in the Negev, and will encourage further joint exploitation of other energy resources. This Program may also provide for the construction of a Petrochemical industrial complex in the Gaza Strip and the construction of oil and gas pipelines.
4. Cooperation in the field of finance, including a Financial Development and Action Program for the encouragement of international investment in the West Bank and the Gaza Strip, and in Israel, as well as the establishment of a Palestinian Development Bank.
5. Cooperation in the fields of transport and communications, including a Program, which will define guidelines for the establishment of a Gaza Sea Port Area, and will provide for the establishing of transport and communications lines to and from the West Bank and the Gaza Strip to Israel and to other countries. In addition, this Program will provide for carrying out the necessary construction of roads, railways, communications lines, etc.
6. Cooperation in the field of trade, including studies, and Trade Promotion Programs, which will encourage local, regional and inter-regional trade, as well as a feasibility study of creating free trade zones in the Gaza Strip and in Israel, mutual access to these zones, and cooperation in other areas related to trade and commerce.
7. Cooperation in the field of industry, including Industrial Development

Programs, which will provide for the establishment of joint Israeli–Palestinian Research and Development Centers, will promote Palestinian–Israeli joint ventures, and provide guidelines for cooperation in the textile, food, pharmaceutical, electronics, diamonds, computer and science-based industries.

8. A program for cooperation in, and regulation of, labor relations and cooperation in social welfare issues.

9. A Human Resources Development and Cooperation Plan, providing for joint Israeli–Palestinian workshops and seminars, and for the establishment of joint vocational training centers, research institutes and data banks.

10. An Environmental Protection Plan, providing for joint and/or coordinated measures in this sphere.

11. A program for developing coordination and cooperation in the field of communication and media.

12. Any other programs of mutual interest.

PROTOCOL ON ISRAELI–PALESTINIAN COOPERATION CONCERNING REGIONAL DEVELOPMENT PROGRAMS

1. The two sides will cooperate in the context of the multilateral peace efforts in promoting a Development Program for the region, including the West Bank and the Gaza Strip, to be initiated by the G-7. The parties will request the G-7 to seek the participation in this program of other interested states, such as members of the Organization for Economic Cooperation and Development, regional Arab states and institutions, as well as members of the private sector.

2. The Development Program will consist of two elements:

   a) an Economic Development Program for the West Bank and the Gaza Strip:

   b) a Regional Economic Development Program.

A. *The Economic Development Program for the West Bank and the Gaza Strip* will consist of the following elements:

   (1) A Social Rehabilitation Program, including a Housing and Construction Program.

   (2) A Small and Medium Business Development Plan.

   (3) An Infrastructure Development Program (water, electricity, transportation and communications, etc.).

   (4) A Human Resources Plan.

   (5) Other programs.

B. *The Regional Economic Development Program* may consist of the following elements:

   (1) The establishment of a Middle East Development Fund, as a first step, and a Middle East Development Bank, as a second step.

   (2) The development of a joint Israeli–Palestinian–Jordanian Plan for coordinated exploitation of the Dead Sea area.

   (3) The Mediterranean Sea (Gaza) – Dead Sea Canal.

   (4) Regional Desalinization and other water development projects.

   (5) A regional plan for agricultural development, including a coordinated regional effort for the prevention of desertification.

   (6) Interconnection of electricity grids.

(7) Regional cooperation for the transfer, distribution and industrial exploitation of gas, oil and other energy resources.

(8) A Regional Tourism, Transportation and Telecommunications Development Plan.

(9) Regional cooperation in other spheres.

3. The two sides will encourage the multilateral working groups, and will coordinate towards its success. The two parties will encourage international activities, as well as pre-feasibility and feasibility studies, within the various multilateral working groups.

AGREED MINUTES TO THE DECLARATION OF PRINCIPLES ON INTERIM SELF-GOVERNMENT ARRANGEMENTS

A. General Understandings and Agreements

Any powers and responsibilities transferred to the Palestinians pursuant to the Declaration of Principles prior to the inauguration of the Council will be subject to the same principles pertaining to Article IV, as set out in these Agreed Minutes below.

B. Specific Understandings and Agreements

Article IV

It is understood that:

1. Jurisdiction of the Council will cover West Bank and Gaza Strip territory, except for issues that will be negotiated in the permanent status negotiations: Jerusalem, settlements, military locations and Israelis.

2. The Council's jurisdiction will apply with regard to the agreed powers, responsibilities, spheres and authorities transferred to it.

Article VI(2)

It is agreed that the transfer of authority will be as follows:

(1) The Palestinian side will inform the Israeli side of the names of the authorized Palestinians who will assume the powers, authorities and responsibilities that will be transferred to the Palestinians according to the Declaration of Principles in the following fields: education and culture, health, social welfare, direct taxation, tourism, and any other authorities agreed upon.

(2) It is understood that the rights and obligations of these offices will not be affected.

(3) Each of the spheres described above will continue to enjoy existing budgetary allocations in accordance with arrangements to be mutually agreed upon. These arrangements also will provide for the necessary adjustments required in order to take into account the taxes collected by the direct taxation office.

(4) Upon the execution of the Declaration of Principles, the Israeli and Palestinian delegations will immediately commence negotiations on a detailed plan for the transfer of authority on the above offices in accordance with the above understandings.

Article VII(2)
The Interim Agreement will also include arrangements for coordination and cooperation.

Article VII(5)
The withdrawal of the military government will not prevent Israel from exercising the powers and responsibilities not transferred to the Council.

Article VIII
It is understood that the Interim Agreement will include arrangements for cooperation and coordination between the two parties in this regard. It is also agreed that the transfer of powers and responsibilities to the Palestinian police will be accomplished in a phased manner, as agreed in the Interim Agreement.

Article X
It is agreed that, upon the entry into force of the Declaration of Principles, the Israeli and Palestinian delegations will exchange the names of the individuals designated by them as members of the Joint Israeli–Palestinian Liaison Committee.
It is further agreed that each side will have an equal number of members in the Joint Committee. The Joint Committee will reach decisions by agreement. The Joint Committee may add other technicians and experts, as necessary. The Joint Committee will decide on the frequency and place or places of its meetings.

Annex II
It is understood that, subsequent to the Israeli withdrawal, Israel will continue to be responsible for external security, and for internal security and public order of settlements and Israelis. Israeli military forces and civilians may continue to use roads freely within the Gaza Strip and the Jericho area.

Article XVI
Israeli–Palestinian Cooperation Concerning Regional Programs
Both parties view the multilateral working groups as an appropriate instrument for promoting a "Marshall Plan," the regional programs and other programs, including special programs for the West Bank and Gaza Strip, as indicated in the protocol attached as Annex IV.

Article XVII
Miscellaneous Provisions
1. This Declaration of Principles will enter into force one month after its signing.
2. All protocols annexed to this Declaration of Principles and Agreed Minutes pertaining thereto shall be regarded as an integral part hereof.

   Done at Washington, D.C. this — day of —, 1993
   For the Government of Israel —
   For the Palestinian Delegation —
   Witnessed by:

APPENDIX 2

THE LETTERS OF RECOGNITION
10 September 1993

FROM ARAFAT TO RABIN

Mr Prime Minister,

The signing of the Declaration of Principles marks a new era in the history of the Middle East. In firm conviction thereof, I would like to confirm the following PLO commitments:

The PLO recognises the right of the State of Israel to exist in peace and security. The PLO accepts United Nations Security Council Resolutions 242 and 338.

The PLO commits itself to the Middle East peace process, and to a peaceful resolution of the conflict between the two sides and declares that all outstanding issues relating to permanent status will be resolved through negotiations.

The PLO considers that the signing of the Declaration of Principles constitutes a historic event, inaugurating a new epoch of peaceful coexistence, free from violence and all other acts which endanger peace and stability.

Accordingly, the PLO renounces the use of terrorism and other acts of violence and will assume responsibility over all PLO elements and personnel in order to assure their compliance, prevent violations and discipline violators.

In view of the promise of a new era and the signing of the Declaration of Principles and based on Palestinian acceptance of Security Council Resolutions 242 and 338, the PLO affirms that those articles of the Palestinian Covenant which deny Israel's right to exist, and the provisions of the Covenant which are inconsistent with the commitments of this letter, are now inoperative and no longer valid.

Consequently, the PLO undertakes to submit to the Palestinian National Council for formal approval the necessary changes in regard to the Palestinian Covenant.

Sincerely,

Yasser Arafat,

Chairman, The Palestine Liberation Organization

FROM RABIN TO ARAFAT

Mr Chairman,

In response to your letter of September 9, 1993, I wish to confirm to you that, in light of the PLO commitments included in your letter, the Government of Israel has decided to recognise the PLO as the representative of the Palestinian people and commence negotiations with the PLO within the Middle East peace process.

Yitzhak Rabin
Prime Minister of Israel

FROM ARAFAT TO THE NORWEGIAN FOREIGN MINISTER JOHAN JÖRGEN HOLST

Dear Minister Holst,

I would like to confirm to you that, upon the signing of the Declaration of Principles, I will include the following positions in my public statements:

In light of the new era marked by the signing of the Declaration of Principles, the PLO encourages and calls upon the Palestinian people in the West Bank and Gaza Strip to take part in the steps leading to the normalisation of life, rejecting violence and terrorism, contributing to peace and stability and participating actively in shaping reconstruction, economic development and cooperation.

Sincerely,
Yasser Arafat, Chairman
The Palestine Liberation Organization

APPENDIX 3

THE WASHINGTON SPEECHES
13 September 1993

RABIN'S SPEECH

The following is a partial text of Yitzhak Rabin's speech:

This signing of the Israeli–Palestinian declaration of principles here today, it's not so easy, neither for myself as a soldier in Israel's war, nor for the people of Israel, nor for the Jewish people in the diaspora who are watching us now with great hope mixed with apprehension.

It is certainly not easy for the families of the victims of the wars, violence, terror, whose pain will never heal; for the many thousands who defended our lives in their own and have even sacrificed their lives for our own. For them, this ceremony has come too late.

Today, on the eve of an opportunity . . . for peace, and perhaps end of violence and wars, we remember each and every one of them with everlasting love.

We have come from Jerusalem, the ancient and eternal capital of the Jewish people. We have come from an anguished land. We have come from a people, a home, a family that has not known a single year, not a single month, in which mothers have not wept for their sons.

We have come to try and put an end to the hostilities so that our children, our children's children, will no longer experience the painful cost of war, violence and terror. Let me say to you, the Palestinians, we are destined to live together on the same soil in the same land.

We, the soldiers who have returned from battles stained with blood; we who have seen our relatives and friends killed before our eyes; we who have attended their funerals and cannot look into the eyes of their parents; we who have come from a land where parents bury their children; we who have fought against you, the Palestinians, we say to you today in a loud and a clear voice enough of blood and tears.

Enough! We have no desire for revenge, we have – we harbour no hatred towards you. We, like you, are people – people who want to build a home, to plant a tree, to love, live side by side with you in dignity, in affinity, as human beings, as free men. We wish to open a new chapter in the sad book of our lives together. Today here in Washington we will begin a new wakening in the relations between peoples, between parents tired of war, between children who will not know war.

Our inner strength, our higher moral values have been derived for thousands of years from the Book of the Books, in one of which, Koheleth [Ecclesiastes], we read: "To every thing there is a season and a time to every purpose under heaven.

"A time to be born and a time to die, a time to kill and a time to heal, a time to weep and a time to laugh, a time to love and a time to hate, a time of war and a time of peace." Ladies and gentlemen, the time for peace has come.

In the Jewish tradition, it is customary to conclude our prayers with the word "amen" . . . with your permission, men of peace, I shall conclude with words taken from the prayer recited by Jews daily, and I would ask you to join me in saying "amen". Amen.

ARAFAT'S SPEECH

The following is a partial text of Yasser Arafat's speech:

In the name of God, the most merciful, the passionate, I would like to express our tremendous appreciation to President Clinton and to his administration for sponsoring this historic event which the entire world has been waiting for. Mr President, I am taking this opportunity to assure you and to assure the great American people that we share your values for freedom, justice and human rights – values for which my people have been striving.

My people are hoping that this agreement which we are signing today marks the beginning of the end of a chapter of pain and suffering which has lasted throughout this century.

My people are hoping that this agreement which we are signing today will usher in an age of peace, coexistence and equal rights. We are relying on your role, Mr President, and on the role of all the countries which believe that without peace in the Middle East, peace in the world will not be complete.

Enforcing the agreement and moving toward the final settlement, after two years, to implement all aspects of UN Resolutions 242 and 338 in all of their aspects, and resolve all the issues of Jerusalem, the settlements, the refugees and the boundaries will be a Palestinian and an Israeli responsibility.

It is also the responsibility of the international community to help the parties overcome the tremendous difficulties which are still standing in the way of reaching a final and comprehensive settlement.

Now as we stand on the threshold of this new historic era, let me address the people of Israel and their leaders, and let me assure them that the difficult decision we reached together was one that required great and exceptional courage.

We will need more courage and determination to continue the course of building coexistence and peace between us. This is possible, and it will happen with mutual determination and with the effort that will be made with all parties on all the tracks to establish the foundations of a just and comprehensive peace.

Our people do not consider that exercising the right to self-determination could violate the rights of their neighbours or that it might infringe on their security.

Rather, putting an end to their feelings of being wronged and of having suffered an historic injustice is the strongest guarantee to achieve coexistence and openness between our two peoples and for future generations.

Our two peoples are awaiting today this historic hope, and they want to give peace a real chance. Such a shift will give us an opportunity to embark upon the process of economic, social and cultural growth and development, and we hope that international participation in that process will be extensive as it can be. This shift will also provide an opportunity for all forms of cooperation on a broad scale and in all fields.

APPENDIX 4

THE MADRID PEACE CONFERENCE: OPENING SPEECHES
31 October 1991

EXTRACTS FROM YITZHAK SHAMIR'S SPEECH

We come to this process with an open heart, sincere intentions and great expectations. We are committed to negotiating without interruption until an agreement is reached. There will be problems, obstacles, crises and conflicting claims. But it is better to talk than to shed blood.

Wars have not solved anything in our region. They have only caused misery, suffering, bereavement and hatred.

We know our partners to the negotiations will make territorial demands on Israel. But, as an examination of the conflict's long history makes clear, its nature is not territorial. It raged well before Israel acquired Judea, Samaria, Gaza and the Golan in a defensive war. There was no hint of recognition of Israel before the war in 1967, when the territories in question were not under Israeli control.

We are a nation of four million. The Arab nations from the Atlantic to the Gulf number 170 million. We control only 28,000 square kilometers. The Arabs possess a land mass of 14 million square kilometers. The issue is not territory but our existence.

It will be regrettable if the talks focus primarily and exclusively on territory. It is the quickest way to an impasse. What we need, first and foremost, is the building of confidence, the removal of the danger of confrontation and the development of relations in as many spheres as possible.

The issues are complex, and the negotiations will be lengthy and difficult. We submit that the best venue for the talks is in our region, in close proximity to the decision-makers, not in a foreign land. We invite our partners to this process to come to Israel for the first round of talks. On our part, we are ready to go to Jordan, to Lebanon and to Syria for the same purpose.

I am sure that there is no Arab mother who wants her son to die in battle – just as there is no Jewish mother who wants her son to die in war. I believe every mother wants her children to learn the art of living, not the science of war.

Today, the gulf separating the two sides is still too wide; the Arab hostility to Israel too deep; the lack of trust too immense, to permit a dramatic, quick solution. But, we must start on the long road to reconciliation with this first step in the peace process.

We believe the blessing of peace can turn the Middle East into a paradise; a centre of cultural, scientific, medical and technological creativity.

We can foresee a period of great economic progress that would put an end to misery, hunger and illiteracy. It could put the Middle East – the cradle of civilisation – on the road to a new era.

EXTRACTS FROM HAIDER ABDELSHAFI'S SPEECH

We, the people of Palestine, stand before you in the fullness of our pain, our pride, and our anticipation, for we have long harboured a yearning for peace and a dream of justice and freedom. For too long the Palestinian people have gone unheeded, silenced and denied – our identity negated by political expediency, our rightful struggle against injustice maligned, and our present existence subsumed by the past tragedy of another people.

We have been denied the right publicly to acknowledge our loyalty to our leadership and system of government, but allegiance and loyalty cannot be censored or severed.

Jerusalem, the city of peace, has been barred from a peace conference and deprived of its calling. Palestinian Jerusalem, the capital of our homeland and future state, defines Palestinian existence – past, present and future – but itself has been denied a voice and an identity.

We come to you from a tortured land and a proud, though captive, people, having been asked to negotiate with our occupiers, but leaving behind the children of the *intifada*, and a people under occupation and under curfew, who enjoined us not to surrender or forget.

As we speak, thousands of our brothers and sisters are languishing in Israeli prisons and detention camps, most detained without evidence, charge or trial, many cruelly mistreated and tortured in interrogation, guilty only of seeking freedom or daring to defy the occupation. We speak in their name and we say: set them free.

As we speak, the tens of thousands who have been wounded or permanently disabled are in pain: let peace heal their wounds.

As we speak, the eyes of thousands of Palestinian refugees, deportees, and displaced persons since 1967, are haunting us, for exile is a cruel fate: bring them home. They have the right to return.

As we speak, the silence of demolished homes echoes through the halls and in our minds: we must rebuild our homes in our free state.

The settlements must stop now. Peace cannot be waged while Palestinian land is confiscated in myriad ways and the status of the occupied territories is being decided each day by Israeli bulldozers and barbed wire.

This is not simply a position; it is an irrefutable reality. Territory for peace is a travesty when territory for illegal settlement is official Israeli policy and practice.

We wish directly to address the Israelis with whom we have had a prolonged exchange of pain: let us share hope instead. We are willing to live side by side on the land and the promise of the future.

APPENDIX 5

CAMP DAVID AGREEMENTS: PROVISIONS OF THE CAMP DAVID ACCORDS ON THE WEST BANK AND GAZA
17 September 1978

1. Egypt, Israel, Jordan and the representatives of the Palestinian people should participate in negotiations on the resolution of the Palestinian problem in all its aspects to achieve that objective, negotiations relating to the West Bank and Gaza should proceed in three stages.

(A) Egypt and Israel agree that, in order to ensure a peaceful and orderly transfer of authority, and taking into account the security concerns of all the parties, there should be transitional arrangements for the West Bank and Gaza for a period not exceeding five years. In order to provide full autonomy to the inhabitants, under these arrangements the Israeli military government and its civilian administration will be withdrawn as soon as a self-governing authority has been freely elected by the inhabitants of these areas to replace the existing military government.

To negotiate the details of transitional arrangement, the Government of Jordan will be invited to join the negotiations on the basis of this framework. These new arrangements should give due consideration to both the principles of self-government by the inhabitants of these territories and to the legitimate security concerns of the parties involved.

(B) Egypt, Israel and Jordan will agree on the modalities for establishing the elected self-governing authority in the West Bank and Gaza. The delegations of Egypt and Jordan may include Palestinians from the West Bank and Gaza or other Palestinians as mutually agreed. The parties will negotiate an agreement which will define the powers and responsibilities of the self-governing authority to be exercised in the West Bank and Gaza. A withdrawal of Israeli armed forces will take place and there will be a redeployment of the remaining Israeli forces into specified security locations.

The negotiations shall be based on all the provisions and principles of UN Security Council Resolution 242. The negotiations will resolve, among other matters, the location of the boundaries and the nature of the security arrangements. The solution from the negotiations must also recognize the legitimate rights of the Palestinian people and their just requirements. In this way, the Palestinians will participate in the determination of their own future through:

(i) The negotiations among Egypt, Israel, Jordan and the representatives of the inhabitants of the West Bank and Gaza to agree on the final status of the West Bank and Gaza and other outstanding issues by the end of the transitional period.

(ii) Submitting their agreement to a vote by the elected representatives of the inhabitants of the West Bank and Gaza.

(iii) Providing for the elected representatives of the inhabitants of the West Bank and Gaza to decide how they shall govern themselves consistent with the provisions of their agreement.

(iv) Participating as stated above in the work of the committee negotiating the peace treaty between Israel and Jordan.

The agreement will also include arrangements for assuring internal and external security and public order. A strong local police force will be established, which may include Jordanian citizens. In addition, Israeli and Jordanian forces will participate in joint patrols and in the manning of control posts to assure the security of the borders.

(C) When the self-governing authority (administrative council) in the West Bank and Gaza is established and inaugurated, the transitional period of five years will begin. As soon as possible, but not later than the third year after the beginning of the transitional period, negotiations will take place to determine the final status of the West Bank and Gaza and its relationship with its neighbours, and to conclude a peace treaty between Israel and Jordan by the end of the transitional period. These negotiations will be conducted among Egypt, Israel, Jordan and the elected representatives of the inhabitants of the West Bank and Gaza.

Two separate but related committees will be convened; one committee, consisting of representatives of the four parties which will negotiate and agree on the final status of the West Bank and Gaza, and its relationship with its neighbours, and the second committee, consisting of representatives of Israel and representatives of Jordan to be joined by the elected representatives of the inhabitants of the West Bank and Gaza, to negotiate the peace treaty between Israel and Jordan, taking into account the agreement reached on the final status of the West Bank and Gaza.

2. All necessary measures will be taken and provisions made to assure the security of Israel and its neighbours during the transitional period and beyond. To assist in providing such security, a strong local police force will be constituted by the self-governing authority. It will be composed of inhabitants of the West Bank and Gaza. The police will maintain continuing liaison on internal security matters with the designated Israeli, Jordanian and Egyptian officers.

3. During the transitional period, the representatives of Egypt, Israel, Jordan and the self-governing authority will constitute a continuing committee to decide by agreement on the modalities of admission of persons displaced from the West Bank and Gaza in 1967, together with necessary measures to prevent disruption

and disorder. Other matters of common concern may also be dealt with by this committee.

4. Egypt and Israel will work with each other and with other interested parties to establish agreed procedures for a prompt, just and permanent implementation of the resolution of the refugee problem.

APPENDIX 6

UNITED NATIONS SECURITY COUNCIL RESOLUTIONS 242 AND 338

TEXT OF UN SECURITY COUNCIL RESOLUTION 242
22 November 1967

The Security Council,

Expressing its continued concern with the grave situation in the Middle East,

Emphasizing the inadmissibility of the acquisition of territory by war and the need to work for a just and lasting peace in which every State in the area can live in security,

Emphasizing further that all Member States in their acceptance of the Charter of the United Nations have undertaken a commitment to act in accordance with Article 2 of the Charter

1. *Affirms* that the fulfilment of Charter principles requires the establishment of a just and lasting peace in the Middle East which should include the application of both the following principles:

(i) Withdrawal of Israel's armed forces from territories occupied in the recent conflict;

(ii) Termination of all claims or states of belligerency and respect for the acknowledgement of the sovereignty, territorial integrity and political independence of every State in the area and their right to live in peace within secure and recognized boundaries free from threats or acts of force;

2. *Affirms further* the necessity

(a) For guaranteeing freedom of navigation through international waterways in the area;

(b) For achieving a just settlement of the refugee problem;

(c) For guaranteeing the territorial inviolability and political independence of every State in the area, through measures including the establishment of demilitarized zones;

3. *Requests* the Secretary-General to designate a Special Representative to proceed to the Middle East to establish and maintain contacts with the States concerned in order to promote agreement and assist efforts to achieve a peaceful and accepted settlement in accordance with the provisions and principles in this resolution;

4. *Requests* the Secretary-General to report to the Security Council on the progress of the efforts of the Special Representative as soon as possible.

UN SECURITY COUNCIL RESOLUTION 338
22 October 1973

UN Resolutions between 1967 and October 1973 reaffirmed Security Council Resolution 242 (see above). In an attempt to end the fourth Middle East war, which had broken out between the Arabs and Israel on 6 October 1973, the UN Security Council passed the following Resolution:

  The Security Council,

  1. *Calls upon* all parties to the present fighting to cease all firing and terminate all military activity immediately, not later than 12 hours after the moment of the adoption of the decision, in the positions they now occupy;

  2. *Calls upon* the parties concerned to start immediately after the ceasefire the implementation of Security Council Resolution 242 (1967) in all of its parts;

  3. *Decides that,* immediately and concurrently with the ceasefire negotiations start between the parties concerned under appropriate auspices aimed at establishing a just and durable peace in the Middle East.

INDEX